Political Economy, Linguistics and Culture

European Heritage in Economics and the Social Sciences

Edited by: Jürgen G. Backhaus
University of Erfurt

Frank H. Stephen
University of Strathclyde

Volume 1

Joseph Alois Schumpeter
Jürgen G. Backhaus

Volume 2

The Soul of the German Historical School:
Methodological Essays on Schmoller, Weber, and Schumpeter
Yuichi Shionoya

Volume 3

Friedrich Nietzsche (1844–1900): Economy and Society
Jürgen G. Backhaus and Wolfgang Drechsler

Volume 4

From Walras to Pareto
Jürgen G. Backhaus and J. A. Hans Maks

Volume 5

Political Economy, Linguistics and Culture: Crossing Bridges
Jürgen G. Backhaus

Political Economy, Linguistics and Culture
and Culture
Crossing Bridges

edited by

Jürgen G. Backhaus
University of Erfurt, Germany

 Springer

Editor
Jürgen G. Backhaus
University of Erfurt, Germany
63 Nordhäuser Str.
Erfurt 99089
e-mail: juergen.backhaus@uni-erfurt.de

ISBN: 978-0387-73371-5   e-ISBN: 978-0-387-73372-2

Library of Congress Control Number: 2007934756

Printed on acid-free paper

9 8 7 6 5 4 3 2 1

springer.com

Contents

PART III

List of Contributors

Jürgen G. Backhaus
Faculty of Law, Economics and Social Sciences, University of Erfurt, Erfurt, Thuringia, Germany

Mark E. Blum
Department of History, University of Louisville, Louisville, KY, USA

Jim F. Couch
Department of Economics and Finance, University of North Alabama, Florence, AL, USA

Brett A. King
Department of Economics and Finance, University of North Alabama, Florence, AL, USA

Peter R. Senn
1121 Hinman Avenue Evanston, IL, USA

William F. Shughart II
Department of Economics, School of Business Administration, University of Mississippi, Oxford, MS, USA

William H. Wells
Department of Economics and Finance; Department of Finance and Quantitative Analysis, University of North Alabama, Florence, AL, USA

Peter M. Williams
Department of Economics and Finance, University of North Alabama, Florence, AL, USA

Robert J. Williams
Department of Management, University of North Alabama, Florence, AL, USA

Leland B. Yeager
Department of Economics, Auburn University, Auburn, AL, USA

Introduction

During the late nineteenth and throughout the twentieth century, the social sciences in general and economics in particular have undergone an enormous progress. This has led to something of an embarrassment of riches. While certain topics have been fully researched to the point where the marginal benefit from further research is approaching zero, others have remained largely underresearched or are being ignored altogether. It is this discrepancy which prompted the research paradigm of "Crossing Bridges." This volume documents the efforts of ten authors who have joined forces in addressing this problem of underresearched topics.

Why could this situation occur? Five reasons come to mind. First, each social science has a history. In fact, the history of economic thought is much broader than the history of economic analysis, as Schumpeter had observed with the choice of the title of his classic.[1] Due to path dependence, research topics have been developed and continued as research ideas and topics for books and scholarly papers. What had not been in the focus of earlier scholars may not readily enter the discourse of academics today. There is hence a barrier to entry as far as topic choice is concerned. Language plays a big role. Until about 1937, the primary language of the social sciences and economics in particular was German. Then, it switched to English. But the different language communities, due to the growth of the discipline, continued to maintain their own research paradigms. This is why in Japan the history of economic thought, so I am told, is taught in terms of German history of economic thought, British history of economic thought, French history of economic thought, and so on. Indeed, the choice of topics in the Spanish academic community as compared to the German academic community or the Italian academic community is starkly different. Hence, language is another dividing and differentiating factor, another entry barrier. In particular, most academic economists today, whose lingua franca is English, have no access to the heritage of their discipline that is locked into the German script.

The nineteenth century also saw in Europe the formation of national identities which defined research programs to an extent. Due to previously mentioned reasons, therefore, there tended to emerge further differences in national research programs. The University of Macerata has emphasized these aspects of economic theory and national identity[2] and in particular different appointment practices stimulate different research strategies by young academic scholars. This is, in particular, the case when universities have to follow particular guidelines that standardize their behaviour in a national area, be this because they are all state institutions or because they have to be accredited by a single or several similarly operating accrediting bodies.

The purpose of doing research may also play a role. The purpose can be, as in the case of basic research, simple scholarly curiosity, the best of motivations. But the purpose can also be defined externally. Think of the star wars economic research program funded during the Reagan years. The program was only a very small part of total money spent, but it changed the research landscape. This is true for other programs as well and actually has had the intended effect of those who sponsored the programs.

Finally, the science of state has now developed into a lot of different and differently operating disciplines with their own language, media of publications and research paradigms, to wit economics, business economics, management, marketing, transportation, personnel, finance, sociology, public administration, statistics, econometrics, and various others. Communication is not always a strong point between these disciplines. That is why some universities, such as Cornell, have excelled in developing interdisciplinary programs such as their western societies program.

The essays collected in this volume have been grouped in several parts.

The first paper (by Leland Yeager) makes the reasonable and often overlooked point that if there were a lingua franca based on the major natural (not constructed) languages, communication and the protection and tradition of the international heritage of knowledge would be much facilitated. This essay bridges the gap between economics and linguistics. Peter Senn, the author of important studies exploring the influence of particular scholars, an influence that is more likely to be ignored the bigger it is, since insights and methods are then taken for granted, poses the question of what "influence" actually means in the history of, for example, economic thought. This paper actually presents us a multiriver bridge across the social sciences including the philosophy of sciences. The third essay by Jürgen Backhaus provides a bridge between art and economics in terms of discussing a painting by Courbet, *L'Origine du Monde*, which has been widely discussed in the literature, although it has only recently become available to the public. This is a paradox in itself. Next to the picture, there is a literature proposing a particular point of view on social policy. Gustave Courbet, an artist, achieved such an impact by painting a picture to be hidden from public view.

The second set of papers, all by Mark Blum, tries to bridge in various ways the divide between cultural history and the social sciences. The first paper offers an interesting take on the so-called "Methodenstreit" between first Schmoller and Menger, the Weber brothers, and an undisclosed adversary. The underlying cultural premises were different, he argues. The following two papers continue this line in terms of documenting the changing metaparadigms.

The third set of papers is in the public choice tradition conceived by its originator, Gordon Tullock, as a multidisciplinary exercise in itself. These papers, all coauthored by Jim Couch, provide first, and in particular, a link to history, discussing the peculiar implementation of the New Deal totally overlooked in contemporary macroeconomic teaching, second, another link to ecology by pointing out that the enforcement and implementation of environmental policy have little to do with their stated purpose, and third, a link to population studies by providing a similar exercise: an analysis of the implementation of immigration policies.

The series of these meetings is to be continued, and the reader finds a call for papers at the end of this book.

Erfurt, May 2007 Jürgen G. Backhaus

NOTES

1. Joseph Alois Schumpeter, *History of Economic Analysis*, New York, Oxford University Press, 1954.

2. See my paper: "Historical and Philosophical Theories of Money: Schmoller and Simmel Reconsidered," in: Vitantonio Gioia and Heinz D. Kurz (eds.), *Science, Institutional and Economical Development: The Contribution of the „German" Economy and the Reception in Italy (1860–1930)* (Gli Italiani e la Scuola Storica Tedesca dell'Economia), Milano, Giuffrè, 2000, pp. 77–106.

PART I

1. A Language Bridge between Peoples and Disciplines

Leland B. Yeager

Department of Economics

Abstract   Interlingua is a means of communication among speakers of different native languages. If widely adopted for this purpose, it would have obvious economic advantages.

Keywords: Hayek, Ferguson, Interlingua, linguistics

JEL Codes: A19, B20, Z19

1.   INTRODUCTION

I'll describe Interlingua, which is a means of communication among speakers of different native languages. If widely adopted for this purpose, it would have obvious economic advantages.

Furthermore, Interlingua offers an approach to and insights into linguistics, which, –along with economics, can plausibly claim to be a prototypical social science. Both disciplines investigate how people cooperate with one another and coordinate their activities. Both investigate instruments of communication (for markets, money, and prices do convey information, as well as incentives). It is no coincidence that several eminent economists, including Adam Smith (1985) and Ludwig von Mises (1983, esp. pp. 9–30), have written knowledgeably on language. F. A. Hayek has drawn several parallels between the two disciplines. Economic institutions and language alike, along with ethics and the common law, illustrate what Hayek, following Adam Ferguson, called "results of human action but not of human design" (1967, Chapter 6); both illustrate spontaneously evolved phenomena that are highly useful yet may be

Correspondence to: Leland B. Yeager, Auburn University, Auburn, Alabama 36849-5242 open to deliberate improvement. Language is material for cultural anthropology. Language affinities provide clues to homelands, migrations, technologies, and other features and events before history became written. Vernon Smith (1992) finds the emergence of speech and later of writing critically important to the acceleration of cultural and economic development that began roughly thirty thousand years ago.

Language illustrates the sense in which the individual is a product of his society. The example is relevant to questions of a suitable blend of individualism and communitarianism in the shaping of institutions and policies.

All the words and meaning and structure of a language existing at a given time were contributed by individuals, mostly members of earlier generations. Each person grew up "into" an already functioning language, which helped shape his thoughts, reasoning, values, and activities. Words convey moral appraisals. Each individual and perhaps each generation has been influenced more by language than he or it has influenced language. Yet it is the creation of individuals, past and present. (Cf. Henry Hazlitt, 1964, p. 167). Recognizing the individual as a social product in no way denies that happiness and misery, success and frustration, are experienced by individuals; there is no such thing as collective happiness distinct from and transcending the happiness of individuals. Recognizing how society shapes its members in no way imposes collectivist or communitarian rather than individualist thinking and policies.

Like economics and other sciences, linguistics seeks uniformities amidst diversities; it propounds hypotheses; it develops laws. Sir William Jones, a British judge in India, published in 1786 his discoveries of systematic resemblances among Sanskrit, Latin, and Greek. He conjectured about a common ancestor of these languages and other language families and about processes of linguistic change. Subsequently, Grimm's law described a whole series of sound changes that occurred as the Indo-European ancestor language evolved into Greek, Latin, and the Germanic languages and made those languages diverge from one another in systematic ways. Laws of the High German sound shift codify several systematic deviations between English and other Germanic languages on the one hand and modern standard German on the other. The individual Romance languages have diverged from their Latin ancestor in ways characteristic of each language. Their divergences exhibit systematic patterns and lawlike regularities.

Linguistics, like economics, employs methodological individualism: both try to trace their laws to the circumstances and actions of individuals. Linguistics seeks to explain changes in language by their physiological and psychological convenience for the individual speaker in the environment confronting him. This environment includes the sounds and other features of his language itself and various natural, technological, cultural, and political circumstances. The linguist André Martinet devotes sections of one of his books (1972, Chapter 6) to the economics (or economy) of language and the costs of accomplishing its functions.

2.   INTERLINGUA

What does all this have to do with Interlingua? For one thing, as a so-called artificial language (incorrectly so called, as I'll explain), Interlingua provides a convenient entry to the issue of constructivism, which is a charge leveled by F. A. Hayek against attempts to deliberately shape institutions and practices that he thought better left to the processes of spontaneous evolution and natural selection. The charge of constructivism is valid, in my opinion, only if construed quite narrowly; that is a topic best left to discussion at the conference. Anyway, the charge does not properly apply to the founders and adherents of Interlingua.

By the very way that it was extracted from its source languages, Interlingua incorporates the already existing vocabulary of science and technology. It has aptly been called "modern Latin". As such it illustrates Grimm's law at work between itself and the Germanic and other language families. As such it is an as-if ancestor of its modern "descendants" or "dialects"– Italian, Spanish, Portuguese, French, Rumanian, Catalan, and the minor Romance languages. These deviate from each other in systematic ways that Interlingua helps to illuminate. English is closely related to it as well, since, although basically a Germanic language, English has borrowed heavily from Greek, Latin, and French and other Romance languages. By bringing these similarities to the fore, Interlingua is a great aid for learning foreign languages beyond itself.

The vocabulary of Interlingua is already familiar to the hundreds of millions of speakers of Spanish and the other Romance languages and to a lesser but still large extent to speakers of English. Another great advantage is its grammar, which has been stripped of the complexities that any of its source languages gets along without. It thus lacks grammatical gender and the complicated declensions and conjugations and irregular verbs that plague an adult studying a foreign language. Another factor tending to relieve the inhibitions of a learner speaking or writing Interlingua is that it lacks any native speakers on whom an imperfect accent or other slips might especially grate.

The definitive Interlingua dictionary and grammar were published in 1951 by the research team of professional linguists of the International Auxiliary Language Association (IALA, 1951; Gode and Blair, 1951). IALA had been founded in 1924, and for its first decade or so it sought a widely acceptable choice among or compromise among the already existing projects of international language. As this effort proved fruitless, the IALA researchers gradually turned toward creating a language of their own.

But "creating" is the wrong word. The researchers came to realize that what they sought already existed in latent form in the main Western languages: their task was to identify or extract this language by standardizing its vocabulary and activating it with a simple yet natural grammar.

IALA was funded partly by foundations but mainly by Mrs. Alice Vanderbilt Morris. Her death in 1950 left enough money to publish the dictionary and grammar but not enough for an adequate publicity campaign. A trust fund established by Mrs. Morris's daughter, Alice Sturges, turned out to have had its purposes specified with inadequate precision; still, it funded Interlingua activity on a modest scale in the United States until recently. Most Interlingua activity has been volunteer activity, in Switzerland in the 1950s and notably, in recent decades, in Scandinavia, the Netherlands, and Brazil. Interest seems to be growing in the recently liberated countries of Eastern Europe. Union Mundial pro Interlingua embraces many national Interlingua societies as its "sections". UMI's website, www.interlingua.com, gives information about the language and about magazines and books printed in it and provides links to many other Internet sites dealing with Interlingua in one way or another.

3.   ALTERNATIVES AND OBJECTIONS

Any mention of an international auxiliary language prompts a question about Esperanto. I regret that rather diversionary question, but it does routinely arise; so I'll face it. I mean not to knock Esperanto or its author, whom I rather admire, but just to describe the project. First published in 1887 by Dr. Ludwig Zamenhof, a Warsaw oculist, Esperanto is the product of a single man.

Dr. Zamenhof plucked word roots rather arbitrarily from the many European languages that he happened to know, distorted them according to his own scheme, and activated them with an ingenious and simple yet bizarre grammar of his own invention. Esperanto, unlike Interlingua, cannot be understood by someone who has not studied it. To demonstrate the contrast, an appendix to this paper translates an Esperanto passage into Interlingua (another example, a passage from an Esperanto textbook translated into Interlingua, appears in my 1993, p. 135).

Another common question is: Why not English? It seems to be prevailing in any case. Partly for admittedly personal reasons, which include my affection for my native language, I find it charming that each nationality have a language distinctively its own that it does *not* share with all mankind. Language is a bearer of culture; and although I value our Anglo-American culture on the whole, I would hate to see it crush cultural diversity on a worldwide scale.

A related answer develops the case for *neutrality*: Unlike English, Interlingua does not favor a particular nationality and put native speakers of other languages at a relative disadvantage, even influencing what particular persons are chosen to take part in international negotiations and conferences. Unlike English, Interlingua is easy to learn and to speak and write passably well.

Still another objection asks whether Interlingua is not too parochial. (If this objection is justified, it applies *a fortiori* to English). Interlingua admittedly standardizes the Romance languages and English and their Greek-Latin heritage. Shouldn't an international language give adequate representation to the peoples of Asia and Africa? One answer is that the vocabulary standardized in Interlingua is an international fact: many unrelated languages across the globe borrow from that vocabulary. (My paper of 1993 provides examples from Indonesian. The appendix below shows a few examples from Czech and Rumanian translations of Paul Heyne's economics textbook). Besides words borrowed in their quasi-Interlingua form, the phenomenon of loan-translations or calques further supports the claim of objective internationality (Yeager 1991a provides examples from German and Russian and even Hungarian, a non-Indo-European language).

A second answer to the charge of parochialism is that a language giving supposedly due representation to miscellaneous languages all across the globe would necessarily require rather arbitrary choices of words and even of grammatical features. It would be an arbitrary construct lacking a coherent character and intelligible to no one without arduous study. The internationality of the Greek-Latin-RomanceEnglish vocabulary remains an objective fact to be ignored only at heavy cost. For speakers of Asian and African languages, Interlingua provides an excellent introduction to this international vocabulary. (Yeager 1991b faces the charges of parochialism in more detail).

4. NETWORK EFFECTS AND WHY THEY ARE NOT DECISIVE

Another set of doubts about Interlingua concerns network effects. (Here we see another overlap with economic theory). Why should anyone bother to learn Interlingua until a great many other people have learned it first? With whom would the isolated student use it?

The answer has several parts. The services of Interlingua do *not* presuppose a large population of fellow users. (Here is another contrast with Esperanto). As many experiences by me and other Interlinguists testify, one can successfully communicate in speech and writing with native speakers of Romance languages who may never even have heard of Interlingua. Using Interlingua with such people may sometimes be a welcome gesture of avoiding Anglo-American parochialism.

Interlingua is of great value in studying linguistics. Systematic departures in the Romance languages from the Latin ancestor and thus from its Interlingua counterpart occur in large numbers. The consonant group -*ct*- simplifies itself in a characteristic way in each of the individual Romance languages. The order of the words that follow is Interlingua, Italian, French, Spanish, Portuguese, Rumanian, Catalan, and English or an English cognate: *nocte, notte, nuit, noche, noite, noapte, nit, nocturnal*; *lacte, latte, lait, leche, leite, lapte, llet, lactic.* An initial consonant + *l*, to mention another example of systematically related changes, undergoes characteristic simplifications in Italian, Spanish, and Portuguese: *plen, pieno, plein, lleno, cheio, plin, ple, plenty*; *flamma, fiamma, flamme, llama, chama, flacără, flama, flame.* (Yeager 1991a presents many more such examples).

Finally, Interlingua is a key to understanding word derivations and to vocabulary-building in English. The appendix provides examples. Paradoxically, or not so paradoxically, it is also an aid to avoiding an excessively Latinate style in writing English.

5.   CONCLUSION

I can testify from personal experience that while Interlingua is *much* easier to learn than any national language, it functions as a complete language. I have read it and written in it since publication of its basic documents in 1951 (and even before, since I was acquainted with a few members of IALA's research team and their preliminary versions of the language). I attended the biennial conferences of Union Mundial pro Interlingua in Europe from 1985 through 1997. At these conferences the participants live together for one week, speaking only (or almost only) Interlingua–in formal sessions (sometimes including heated spontaneous debates), in social sessions, in casual conversations, and on tourist excursions. It is reassuring to observe even relatively new recruits quickly developing conversational ability in the language.

Interlingua is indeed a bridge between peoples and disciplines. Any similar project–a simple language for international communication rooted in linguistic reality–would necessarily diverge from Interlingua in details too minor to impede understanding between speakers of the two. Interlingua is an objective reality, and effort spent on it will yield ample returns.

REFERENCES

Gode, A., and Blair, H. E. (1951). *Interlingua: A Grammar of the International Language.* New York: Ungar.

Hayek, F.A. (1967). "The Results of Human Action but not of Human Design." In *Studies in Philosophy, Politics, and Economics.* Chicago: University of Chicago Press, Chapter 6.

Hazlitt, H. (1964). *The Foundations of Morality.* Princeton, NJ: Van Nostrand.

Heyne, P. (1991). *Ekonomický Styl Myšlení.* Translated from his *The Economic Way of Thinking* by a team headed by Ji_í Schwartz. Prague: Vysoká Škola Ekonomická.

Heyne, P. (1991). *Modul Economic de Gîndire.* Translated from his *The Economic Way of Thinking* by Nicolae Nistorescu and Martin Frâncu. Bucharest: Editura Didactică _i Pedagogică.

International Auxiliary Language Association (1951). *Interlingua-English: A Dictionary of the International Language.* Prepared by the research staff under the direction of Dr. Alexander Gode. New York: Ungar.

Martinet, A. (1972). *Elementos de Lingüística General*, 2nd ed. Translated from French by Julio Calonge Ruiz. Madrid: Editorial Gredos.

von Mises, L. (1983). *Nation, State, and Economy.* Translated from the German of 1919 by Leland B. Yeager. New York: New York University Press.

Smith, A. (1985). "Considerations Concerning the First Formation of Languages." Originally 1761 and 1790. In *Lectures on Rhetoric and Belles Lettres.* Indianapolis: Liberty Classics, 203–226.

Smith, V. L. (1992). "Economic Principles in the Emergence of Humankind." **Economic Inquiry** 30 (January): 1-3. [Another version appears as "The Economics of the Emergence of Humankind," *Liberty* 5 (May 1992): 43–48, 51.]

Yeager, L. B. (1991a). "Le linguistica como reclamo pro Interlingua." In Ingvar Stenström and Leland B. Yeager (eds.), *Interlinguistica e Interlingua.* Beekbergen, Netherlands: Servicio de Libros UMI, 46–57.

Yeager, L. B. (1991b). "Artificialitate, ethnocentrismo, e le linguas oriental: le caso de Interlingua." In Ingvar Stenström and Leland B. Yeager (eds.). *Interlinguistica e Interlingua.* Beekbergen, Netherlands: Servicio de Libros UMI, 58–72.

Yeager, L.B. (1993). "Interlingua for Communication and Linguistic Science." In *Language in Contemporary Society.* Proceedings of a conference of October 1992. New York: American Society of Geolinguistics, 135–144.

APPENDIX

Specimen of Esperanto with translation into Interlingua

Contribution to the Internet newsgroup soc.culture.esperanto from anra@esperanto.nu, 2 July 1999, with a brief response from "Antonio."

Marko Rauhamaa, "Lingvokverelo en EU"

Mi ĵus legis, ke Germanujo bojkotos kunvenon de EU-industriministroj en Oulu, Suomujo, ĉar Suomujo decidis ne uzi la germanan lingvon kiel neoficialan laborlingvon en la kunveno.

Germanujo minacas bojkoti ankaŭ plurajn aliajn laborkunvenojn. Mi aplaŭdas la decidon de la suoma registaro, ĉar ĝi emfazas – kvankam ne solvas – la lingvan problemon de EU kaj la efektivan diskriminacion kontraŭ la tn malgrandaj lingvoj.
- - - - -

Mi 100%-e subtenas vin. Jam delonge EU spertas lingvan problemon.

Onidire mi iam audis pri iniciato de EU parlamentanino, Êu Ema Bonino (Radikala partio), kiu iniciatis pri Esperanto kiel laborlingvo de EU. Bedaurine [Beda*breveu*rinde], mi ne posedas fontojn por konfirmi tion. – Antonio
[Interlingua version:]

Marko Rauhamaa, "Disputa super linguas in le EU"

Io ha justo legite que Germania va boycottar le reunion del ministros de industria del UE in Oulu, Finlandia, proque Finlandia decideva non emplear le lingua german como lingua non official de labor in le reunion.

Germania menacia anque boycottar plure altere sessiones de labor.

Io applaude le decision del governamento finnese proque illo accentua–ben que non solve–le problema linguistic del UE e le discrimination effective contra le si-nominate parve [micre] linguas.
- - -

Io appoia vos 100%. Jam desde longe le UE ha experientia del problema linguistic. Io aliquando ha audite un rumor del initiativa del parlamentaria del UE, Emma Bonino (Partito Radical), qui habera proponite le esperanto como lingua de labor in le UE. Regrettabilemente, io non possede fontes pro confirmar isto. –Antonio

THE INTERNATIONAL VOCABULARY
IN EASTERN EUROPE

Czech, although a Slavic language, includes many Latin- and Greek-derived words. Here are several found in the Czech translation of Paul Heyne's *The Economic Way of Thinking*: ekonomicka teorie, politicka ekonomie, technologicka efektivnost, substituty, cenová elasticita {as in Russian, cena = price}, administrativeni cena, metody cenove diskriminace, implicitni cenovy deflator, informace, spekulanti, spekulaci, konkurence, problem monopolu, antimonopolni politika v kapitalistickych ekonomikach, inflace, recese, desta-bilizujici faktory, stabilizace, centralni banka, bankovni rezervy, and many others.

Rumanian, the only national language in Eastern Europe that is a Romance language, provides many examples of its being a "dialect" of Interlingua. Here is a sentence from Heyne's book in Rumanian translation (p. 383) and translated into Interlingua:

El [J. M. Keynes] a avut o carieră str_lucitoare ăi diversificatăca investitor, editor, profesor, scriitor, funcţionar guvernamental şi arhitect al sistemelor pentru reconstruirea finanţelor internaţionale.

Ille ha habite un carriera brillante e diversificate como investitor, editor, professor, scriptor, functionario governamental e architecto de systemas pro le reconstruction del financias international.

Like English, Rumanian exhibits a curious duality. In English, many identical or related concepts are expressed both by native (Germanic) roots and by Greek-Latin-French roots ("kingly" and "regal," for example). In Rumanian, similarly, many Slavic (or Turkish or other) roots occur in parallel with Romance roots. Here are a few examples, with the Interlingua in brackets: ban = moneta [moneta]; vreme = timp [tempore]; prieten = amic [amico]; folosi, întrebuinţa = utiliza [utilisar]; slab = debil [debile]; nevoie = necesitate [necessitate]; slobozenie = libertate [libertate]. Because of these parallelisms in the Rumanian vocabulary, monolingual Rumanian speakers should find Interlingua more understandable than the mere appearance of a Rumanian text might suggest.

THE INTERNATIONAL VOCABULARY IN ENGLISH

Basically, in its words most often used, English is a Germanic language. Most words in the dictionary, however, are borrowings or coinages from Classical Greek, Latin, and languages descended from Latin. Interlingua can well serve as a tool for clinching one's grasp of this vast international component of English. Here are some examples of the many thousands of English words that, in effect, derive from Interlingua words (at the left, underlined).

grege 'flock', 'herd', 'crowd': gregarious, segregate, integrate, aggregate, congregate, egregious;
rader 'scrape': razor, radula, erase, abrade, abrasive;
roder 'gnaw': erode, corrode, rodent;
tener 'hold': tenable, retain, detain, abstain, pertain, tenant;
vader 'go': evade, invade, pervasive, wade, waddle;
carne 'meat' or 'flesh': carnal, carnivorous, carnival, incarnation, carnage, carnation;
seder 'sit' and sede 'seat': see (as in Holy See), session, president, obsession, sedentary, sessile, sediment, residence, residue, assiduous, siege;
premer 'press': print, imprint, pressure, impress, oppress, depress, repress, suppress;

moner 'warn', 'advise', 'remind': admonish, monitor, monitory, premonition, monument, demonstrate, summon;

grave 'weighty': gravity, gravid, aggravate, gravamen, grieve, grief, grievous;

sequer 'follow': second, sequel, sequence, consequent, persecute, prosecute, pursue, obsequious;

funder 'melt', 'pour': foundry, fuse, fusion, confuse, confound, diffuse, effusive, profusion, transfusion, funnel;

ducer 'lead' or 'draw': duke, conduct, conducive, ductile, educate, deduce, abduct, duct, aqueduct;

precio 'price': price, prize, precious, appreciate, depreciate, appraise;

flar 'blow': inflate, deflate, flatulent, afflatus;

pender 'hang': depend, append, pendulum, propensity, appendix, impending, independent, suspenders;

cader 'fall': cadence, case, accident, incident, decadent, casual, casualty, casuistry;

venir 'come': venue, Advent, circumvent, event, prevent, supervene, convene, revenue, eventually;

mitter 'put', 'send': mission, missionary, emissary, Mass, emit, remit, transmit, submit, promise, missile, message, committee;

scriber 'write': scribe, scribble, describe, inscribe, subscribe, circumscribe, prescribe, nondescript, manuscript, scripture, conscription, postscript;

leger 'gather', 'choose': select, collect, college, diligent, predilection, elect, elective, eligible, elite, intelligent;

leger 'read': lecture, lectern, lesson, legend, legible;

creder 'believe': creed, credible, credulous, credit, creditor, credential, discredit, miscreant;

batter 'beat', 'strike': batter, battery, battle, combat, debate, rebate, abattoir;

precar 'pray': precatory, precarious, imprecation, deprecate;

traher 'pull', 'drag': traction, tractor, extract, tract, tractable, contract, treaty, subtract, retraction, trail, trailer;

imperar 'govern', 'command': empire, emperor, imperial, imperative;

ponderar 'ponder', 'weigh': ponder, imponderable, ponderous, ponderosa, preponderate.

Many English words contain two Interlingua roots; for example:

aqua and ducer in aqueduct;

plen 'full' and poter 'be able' in plenipotentiary;

omne 'all' and poter in omnipotent;

melle 'honey' and fluer 'flow' in mellifluous;

carne 'meat' and vorar 'devour' in carnivorous;

ben 'well' and voler 'wish' in benevolent;
pisce 'fish' and coler 'cultivate' (or cultura 'culture') in pisciculture;
mano 'hand' and scriber 'write' in manuscript;
ex 'out of', 'from' and onere 'burden' in exonerate.

Examples occur in the lists above of how Interlingua roots often join with prepositions like ab, ad, con, ex, circum, super, trans, and others. Other examples are abstract, adhere, conference, execute, circumspect, superficial, transitory, and so on. Knowing Interlingua makes dead metaphors come alive. Interlingua pectore 'chest' indicates the literal meaning of "expectorate", to get out of one's chest. Pugno 'fist' brings to mind a pugnacious man, brandishing his fist; "impugn" originally meant to attack by raising one's fist against. An "ebullient" personality is one that enthusiastically bubbles outward (from bullir 'boil'). "Current" (from currer) means literally "running".

2. The Theory and Measurement of Influence in the History of Economic Thought

Peter R. Senn[1]

Abstract   Despite the fact that the study of influence is the central task of the historian of economic thought, there is no generally accepted theory of influence either in the social sciences or in the history of economic thought. Foundational methodological issues such as influence on what and by what means and tracing and measuring influence are the subjects of this paper. The paper is both a commentary on the present understanding of influence in the history of economic thought and a prolegomenon to a more general theory of influence in the history of economic thought. It focuses on how the ideas that make up the corpus of economics are transmitted from one economist to the other. The conclusion is that no general theory of influence for the history of economic thought is possible at the present time. A general theory may never be possible because different scholars will probably continue to interpret the term "influence" differently.

Keywords: General theory of influence in the history of economic thought, influence, economic theory

JEL Codes: A000, B410

> Would you tell me, please, which way I ought to go from here?'
> That depends a good deal on where you want to get to,' said the Cat.
> I don't much care where–' said Alice.
> Then it doesn't matter which way you go,' said the Cat.
> –so long as I get somewhere,' Alice added as an explanation.
> Oh, you're sure to do that,' said the Cat, 'if you only walk long enough.'
>
>   Alice's Adventures in Wonderland, 71–72

Correspondence to: Peter R. Senn, 1121 Hinman Avenue Evanston, Illinois 60202

1.   INTRODUCTION

The study of the development of ideas is the central task of the historian of economic thought. This study requires following the path of the expression of ideas in time – the ideas one person had – and how later people accepted, modified, or rejected those ideas. Understanding influence is a significant part of the study of the history of ideas, of which the history of economic thought is a part.

It is now generally accepted that there is no "systematic study of *influence* in the economics profession" [original italics] (Leeson, 1997, p. 637). Leeson could have gone further. There is no generally accepted theory of influence in either the history of ideas or the history of economic thought. This is despite the fact that economists have written about it for centuries and the study of it is the stock in trade of historians of economic thought.

There are many reasons for this situation. Historians of economic thought define influence in different ways. Questions about what is influenced – ideas, economic techniques, policy – and by what means arise. There are often many problems in trying to trace influence. There has been virtually no progress in measuring influence. Another set of issues revolves about what a theory of influence might be. The net result is that strong and convincing measures of influence are sometimes very difficult to establish despite the fact that there are some obvious cases.

This paper is both a commentary on the present understanding of influence in the history of economic thought and a prolegomenon to a more general theory of influence in the history of economic thought. It focuses on how the ideas that make up the corpus of economics are transmitted from one economist to the other. One of the aims is to construct a bridge between the history of economic thought and the larger epistemological context in which it is embedded.

2.   HOW INFLUENCE IS DEFINED IN SOME OF THE SOCIAL SCIENCES

The concept of influence, like the related concepts with which it is associated – power, inspiration, and authority – has been used in very different ways in economics as well as in the other social sciences. It was not until after the Second World War that serious attention was paid to its meanings in the social sciences.

The *Encyclopaedia of the Social Sciences* has no entry in the index nor is there an article on the subject. The entry in the *International Encyclopedia of the Social Sciences* reads as follows: "*See* Authority; Diffusion, *article on* Interpersonal Influence; Interest Groups; Lobbying; Persuasion; Power; Propaganda;

Public Relations; Suggestion" (Sills, 1968, Vol. 7, p. 301). The *Dictionary of the History of Ideas: Studies of Selected Pivotal Ideas* edited by Philip P. Wiener has no entry in the index nor is there an article on the subject.

There is a useful article, "Influence," by Henry W. Ehrman in the *Dictionary* edited by Julius Gould and William L. Kolb. It emphasizes the way the term is used in political science, psychology, and sociology.

Influence can be thought of as: (1) a *property* of a person, or position; (2) a *relationship* between two people, the one influencing and the other influenced; (3) a *cause* which results in changes in the person influenced; (4) a *process* involving at least two people; (5) a *result* of the exertion of influence and many variations and combinations of these logical forms.

Writing about the development of the concept "influence" in political science, in 1955, J. G. March noted that the formalization of the concept has proceeded in "an *ad hoc* fashion, with little communication either between the 'theorists' and the 'empiricists' or between the several practitioners within each class of that dichotomy" (p. 450). The same situation holds in the history of economics to this day.

Without a theory of influence, it is unlikely that attempts to measure what is difficult to define will get very far.

March felt that, in political science, statements about influence "can just as easily be formulated in terms of causality" (p. 437). According to Ehrman, "Psychologists, including social psychologists, generally do not go beyond describing influence as causal relation" (p. 332). For sociologists, "Influence is a term used by sociologists to refer to the role of intimate, interpersonal relations in the communication of information, influence and innovation" (Katz, 1968, Vol. 4, p. 178).

None of the common usages of the term *influence* in the other social sciences adequately captures its meaning for the history of economic thought. Arnold C. Harberger (b. 1924), a leader of the "Chicago School," was asked, "Who do you point to as those you studied under who influenced you?" He replied, "I am the most blessed economist that I know. Really. I can't exaggerate the amount of luck that I had in my economic education. My three most influential classroom teachers (in alphabetical order) were Milton Friedman, Jacob Marschak and T. W. Schultz" (Levy, 1999).

Harberger is referring specifically to the communication of economic ideas. He does not mean that his teachers exercised power over, or coerced, his thoughts. He does not mean that they caused what was in his later publications. Among the things he means by influence is that his teachers had a role in shaping his ways of thinking about economics.

It is clear that much attention must be given to the variety of meanings influence has in the history of economic thought.

The term *influence* is often a significant issue in arguments in economics, because, while many of the term's denotations and connotations are the same, they often refer to different meanings. There is no agreement on one meaning. Usually the meaning of the term must come from the context in which it is used.

3.   WHAT IS A THEORY OF INFLUENCE IN THE HISTORY OF ECONOMIC THOUGHT?

3.1.   What is a theory?

The foundation of any systematic study of influence ought to be a theory. It is appropriate therefore to consider the important characteristics of a theory for the study of influence in the history of economic thought. This is especially necessary because the term *theory*, like *influence*, is used to mean many different things in the history of economic thought.

Theory always refers to ideas. The history of economic thought is also about ideas. It is easy to understand why there are so many different viewpoints. Any discussion of theory in the history of economic thought refers to ideas about ideas.

Theories can be about many different kinds of ideas. In the history of economic thought they include different value judgments, dissimilar ideas about conceptions of history, explanations, goals, policy, principles, and many other things. To ask for a general theory that covers all these things is asking too much at this time.

The sense in which the term *theory* is used here is that of a general statement that either explains or connects a group of other more specific statements.

A reasonable goal for a theory of influence in the history of economic thought is that it has explanatory power and has at least seven other specific qualities or properties:

(1) It must be a statement from which other statements can be deduced or inferred.
(2) The statement must employ clear and unambiguous concepts.
(3) The main concepts of the theory must be either objective and empirical or operationally defined.
(4) The propositions deduced or inferred from a statement should be applicable to some well-specified thing, process, state, person, or event.
(5) The theory must be testable.
(6) The theory should be logical.
(7) The theory ought to be about important and meaningful subjects.

A highly desirable characteristic would also be that the elements of the theory would be quantifiable.

Most theories about influence in the history of economic thought have some explanatory features. Some theories, mostly implicit, meet some of the criteria. None meet all of the seven essential criteria set forth above and therefore cannot qualify as general theories.

3.2.   What is influence?

There are other important reasons that there is no general theory of influence in the history of economic thought. Perhaps the most important of these reasons is that there is no agreement about the definition of the term *influence*. The term has a fascinating etymology and has been used in a variety of ways throughout the history of economic thought. Although the term *influence* is rich in connotation, there is no agreement on what it means.

An important reason that there is no general theory of influence is the great variety of both the things that exert influence and the things that are influenced. Often the things that exert influence are logically different from the things that are influenced. A transformation issue is involved. How can one thing, say an event like the First World War, have influenced the development of economic theory? The connections must be carefully specified. The old, but highly respected and still useful, eleventh edition of the *Encyclopedia Britannica* has a very short entry about influence.

INFLUENCE (late Lat. *influentia*, from *influere*, to flow in), a word whose principal modern meaning is that of power, control or action affecting others, exercised either covertly or without visible means or direct physical agency. It is one of those numerous terms of astrology (*q.v.*) which have established themselves in current language. From the stars was supposed to flow an eternal stream which affected the course of events on the earth and the fortunes and characters of man. For the law as "undue influence" see CONTRACT (Vol. XIV, p. 552).

The standard dictionaries point out that the term *influence* can be either a noun or a transitive verb. In the literature of economics it is used both ways. Most commonly it is used as a noun.

The synonyms of *influence* when used as a noun show several different meanings. Such synonyms as effect, power, or potency refer to the power or capacity to produce a desired result. Such synonyms as force, impact, or impression refer to the effect exerted by one person or thing on another person or thing. Such synonyms as authority, prestige, or weight refer to the power to produce an effect by direct or indirect means.

The synonyms of *influence* when used as a verb also show several different meanings. Such synonyms as inspire, dispose, incline, predispose, and sway refer to or indicate an impact in a certain way. From the beginning of modern economics, writers on economic subjects have used the term *influence* both as a noun and as a verb.

John Locke (1632–1704), Adam Smith (1723–1790), Gustav von Schmoller (1838–1917), and Irving Fisher (1867–1947) often used the term as a noun. Locke wrote,"Expences in Arms beyond Sea have had little Influence on our Riches or Poverty" (1691, Letter). Smith wrote, "Those theories have had a considerable influence, not only upon the opinions of men of learning, but upon the public conduct of princes and sovereign states" (1937, p. lix).

Schmoller wrote, in translation, "But the question is, if such effects of nature, not subject to our influence, which we call fortune or chance, are indeed the essential causes of the distribution of incomes and wealth" (1893–4, "The Idea of Justice in Political Economy"). Fisher wrote, "The earliest example which we find of the influence of the economists on the lexicographers is in 1826" (1904, "Precedents for Defining Capital").

This stress on the fact that influence can be used as a noun emphasizes that if there is to be a general theory about influence, some consensus must exist on what the term means.

The other important grammatical issue revolves about its employment as a transitive verb. Transitive verbs require direct objects. These objects can cover almost any subject. David Hume (1711–1776), Anne-Robert-Jacques Turgot (1727–1781), John Kells Ingram (1823–1907), and William James Ashley (Sir, 1860–1927) used the term as a transitive verb.

Hume wrote, "The one considers man chiefly as born for action; and as influenced in his measures by taste and sentiment; pursuing one object, and avoiding another, according to the value which these objects seem to possess, and according to the light in which they present themselves" (1748, p. 585).

Turgot wrote, "To explain how these two metals are become the representative pledges of every species of riches; how they influence the commercial markets, and how they enter into the composition of fortunes, it is necessary to go back again and return to our first principles" (1766, Section 30).

Ingram wrote, "We need concern ourselves only with those modes of thinking which have prevailed largely and seriously influenced practice in the past, or in which we can discover the roots of the present and the future" (1967, p. 2).

Ashley wrote, "They were also pretty sure to be drawn on to express their opinions on trade in general; and, in doing so, they were likely enough to be influenced by the traditional views of their political associates" (1897, "The Tory Origin of Free Trade Policy").

As the examples above illustrate, there are many different direct objects for the term *influence* in economics. It is always important to distinguish between the ideas that are transmitted, the person who is influencing (the influencer), and the person influenced.

3.3.   Motive

The way *influence* is used in economics has some interesting aspects. In its original meaning, the source from which influence flowed was broadcast. It had no necessary end.

In economics this is most often not the case. The term is often used in the sense of power, which, when exercised, has definite aims. I know of no exception to the hopes of economists that their publications will influence or change the thinking of others. One example must suffice. Hume in his comments about economists (the eighteenth-century term for physiocrats) in a letter to Andre Morellet (1727–1819) is scathing. "But I hope that in your work you will thunder them, and crush them, and pound them, and reduce them to dust and ashes!" (1769, pp. 215–216).

3.4.   Influence in the history of economic thought defined

Both economists and historians of economic thought have used the term *influence* in every major language; for example, German: *beeinflussen, Einfluß*; French: *influencer, influence, effet*; Spanish: *influir en, influenciar, influencia;* and Italian: *influire su, influenzare, effetto, influenza*. In each of the languages the meanings of the different terms vary somewhat, as in the English language.

In its current and past usage the term *influence* seems to embrace almost any change agent in almost any context. No general theory can be built on a concept without boundaries. Any boundaries or definitions are arbitrary. For economists and the history of economic thought all the meanings refer to the power exerted by a person, thing, or event over the minds or behavior of others. A general theory of influence for the history of economic thought requires a more precise and narrow meaning.

The following definition is proposed, "Influence in the history of economic thought refers to those ideas of earlier people which later people use or refer to in their publications. In the history of economic thought, influence exists when one person's published idea is referred to in the publication of another person."

This definition does not imply that events, circumstances, and the like do not influence ideas. The point is that meaningful discussions of influence require precise specification of the meaning given to the term *influence*.

Important components of the history of economic thought are controversies. Influence exists even when an idea is refuted as in the case, for example, of

Eugen von Böhm-Bawerk (Ritter, 1851–1914) who sharply criticized the ideas of Karl Marx (1818–1883). But the case is never simple. One can always go back further. Schumpeter said of Böhm-Bawerk that he "was so completely the enthusiastic disciple of Menger that it is hardly necessary to look for other influences" (1954, p. 846).

3.5.   The literature of economics contains the evidence of influence

For economists and the history of economic thought the evidence for who is influenced must be in the printed record, the literature of economics. While it is probably true that most influences go unrecorded, the printed record is essential for both the development of a scientific discipline and comprehensible history.

The printed record, and here is included what is on the Internet, is the medium that contains the ideas, theories, practice, and techniques of both economics and the history of economic thought. It is what contains the only indisputable evidence of influence.

4.   INFLUENCE ON WHAT AND BY WHAT MEANS?

4.1.   What a useful theory should include

To be useful, a general theory of influence for the history of economic thought ought to include who exercised the influence, who is influenced, the means by which the influence is exerted, and the extent of the influence.

An important distinction is that between the source of an influence and its result in the economic literature. Such a source might be an event, a thing, or a person.

The Great Depression and the two World Wars are examples of events that changed the course of economic thinking. The steam engine, railroad, and computer are examples of things that changed the course of economic thinking. Smith and John Maynard Keynes (1883–1946) are examples of people who changed the course of economic thinking.

A general theory of influence in economics might someday include how events or things might have changed the course of economic thinking. A general theory of influence in the history of economic thought must focus on what appears in the literature of economics.

In this paper, the more modest goal of a general theory of influence in the history of economic thought distinguishes the tracing of ideas from person to person from the external factors that might have stimulated the development of the ideas.

4.2.   Many paths of influence

There are many ways that ideas pass from one person to another to end in the printed record–the substance of economics and the history of economic thought. Both hearsay and oral traditions play a role in the development of economics. It is only after hearsay and oral traditions are written about and published that they become indisputable evidence of influence.

4.3.   Students

One path of influence in economics is by way of one's students. Two of the many students of Wilhelm Georg Friedrich Roscher (1817–1894) who became famous were the Italian Luigi Cossa (1831–1896) and the Austrian Carl Menger (1840–1921). Both were strongly influenced by him, as shown in their writings.

An important reason Roscher was more influential in the United States than in England was because far more Americans studied in Germany than in England. This alone explains much of the difference between Roscher's influence in the United States and his influence in England. Another example of influence by way of students is Joseph Alois Schumpeter (1883–1950). More of his students earned Ph.D. degrees than the students of any other professor of his time.

4.4.   Textbooks

Influence can come from a textbook. John Stuart Mill (1806–1873), Alfred Marshall (1842–1924), Charles Gide (1847–1932), Charles Rist (1874–1955), Schmoller, Eugen von Philippovich (1858–1917), and Paul Anthony Samuelson (b. 1915) are examples. All of them published textbooks that were studied by professors and young economics scholars for many years.

4.5.   Ideas

Ideas that are widely accepted or debated, be they correct or not, like those of Karl Marx (1818–1883) or Keynes, are another path of influence. Influence can also come from the solution of problems like those of identifying and estimating simultaneous equation models. It can come from establishing a new set of methods like the use of mathematics of which Antoine Augustin Cournot (1801–1877) is an example.

4.6.   Economic journals

Ever since the late 1800s publication in economic journals has been the most common way for most economists to share their ideas. This has made referees and journal editors important gatekeepers to the world of influence in economics. Three examples of editors as gatekeepers are George Joseph Stigler (1911–1992) who edited the *Journal of Political Economy* for 19 years, Schmoller, the founder and longtime editor of Schmoller's *Jahrbuch, Jahrbuch für Gesetzgebung, Verwaltung und Volkswirtschaft im Deutschen Reich* (Journal of Legislation, Administration and Economics in Germany), and Keynes, longtime editor of the *Economic Journal*–England's foremost economics publication.

4.7.   Histories of thought

Histories of economics have had much influence in how economics is taught and understood. Four examples from languages important in the development of economics can make the point. Histories of lasting importance and influence were published by the Italian Cossa; the Frenchmen Gide and Rist; the Germans Roscher and Pribram, writing in English; and the Austrian Schumpeter, writing in English.

4.8.   "Schools" and organizers

Influence is associated with the establishment of a "school" with followers and disciples as, for example, the Institutionalists or Austrians. It can also come from organizers, those who publish an author's collected works, or organize conferences, seminars, and meetings of economists. Modern-day examples are Warren J. Samuels (b. 1933) and Jürgen G. Backhaus (b. 1950).

4.9.   Associations of economists

Organizations of economists and their publications can be influential. An outstanding example of this was the *Verein für Socialpolitik* (Association for Social Policy), the leading organization of German-speaking economists founded in 1873. Their activities focused on opposing laissez-faire in social policy and the revolutionary social ideas of emerging socialism. By 1936 when it was disbanded it had published 190 volumes of Reports.

4.10.   Policy

Works that change policy can be influential. An example is William Henry Beveridge (Baron, 1879–1963) whose book was important in the post-World War Two establishment of the English welfare state. It is possible that policies can be influenced by works that are not published until long after the influence was exerted. For an example see *Menger's Lectures to Crown Prince Rudolph*.

To be widely influential, the policies must be of widespread relevance, like those of taxes, property ownership, or social welfare. Usually the country for which the policy recommendations apply must have possible applications in other countries. Publications that change policy can be called influential, both when a literature develops around them and when laws are passed that reflect ideas of the author.

4.11.   Indirect paths

Indirect paths are sometimes of importance in establishing influence. Robert Dorfman (b. 1916) is quite specific about when and how the German Historical School came to the attention of the Americans. "The [historical] 'method' first came prominently before the American public in 1875, not through reading of original German treatises, but rather because of what was said about it in the popular journals" (1949, Vol. 3, p. 88). He goes on to develop this point and mentions a specific editorial that singled out Roscher for praise.

Dorfman cites another widely read, translated eulogy "by the eminent Belgian economist, political scientist, and historian Emile de Laveleye [1822–1892 PRS]." Laveleye was a protectionist and a bimetallist. He "stressed that this great new school led by Roscher opposed the optimism, selfishness, cosmopolitanism, and belief in natural laws of the old English classical economics" (1949, Vol. 3, p. 89).

Dorfman's description of the process by which the historical school entered American colleges is interesting. "It is clear that the historical school was not at first taken seriously in this country. Economists, learned and popular, were interested in concrete issues, and labels were generally thrown about for persuasive purposes rather than for exact definition. But as the rising interest in the wider scope of the historical school did allow for broader and more liberal economic thought, the colleges began to understand and value it" (1949, Vol. 3, p. 92).

Adding new knowledge, recasting, reorganizing, and reinterpreting what is known in new ways have been important ways of becoming influential. So is defining a concept or clarifying existing usage. All of these and more besides are how and why people can be important and influential in the history of economic thought.

The domain of what a general theory might include is so large that the construction of a useful general theory will be very difficult.

5.   TRACING INFLUENCE

Tracing the paths of influence for many of the theories and techniques in the history of economic thought is sometimes easy and sometimes difficult. The central criterion is that an idea, the theory or technique, must be of importance in the development of economics and economic thought. The decision about what is important is often, although not always, subject to debate. Once the question of importance is settled, another set of problems revolve around tracing how that influence came about.

Tracing the paths of influence of an idea on an individual must be distinguished from the diffusion of an idea. *Diffusion*, a broader term than *influence*, is used to mean the spread of an idea. It designates the processes that result in the adoption of an idea by many people. Studies of influence should specify the difference between the diffusion of an idea and its transmission. Studies of transmission limit the subject to the tracing of an idea from one person to another. Studies of diffusion focus on tracing how an idea came to be embraced by many people. Although transmission and diffusion are different processes, they are related. If an idea is transmitted to enough people so that it is generally accepted, it can be said to be diffused.

5.1.   Two examples, Malthus (diffusion) and Robbins (person to person)

Tracing the diffusion of the theory of population by Thomas Robert Malthus (1766–1834) poses relatively few difficulties. The importance of his theory is generally accepted. There are innumerable later references to him and his theories. The main problem for the researcher in tracing his influence on mainstream economics is to sharply define the influential idea and when and where the result of the influence is to be found.

Tracing a path of influence from one person to another is often more difficult. An example is that of Lionel Robbins (Baron, 1898–1984). In his autobiography he says, "I was strongly influenced by Cassel in his *Theory Of Social*

Economy – I did not then realize how much of this was derived from Walras – and by Irving Fisher and F. A. Fetter, especially in their work on capital and interest" (1971, p. 105). Despite the fact that he states some sources of influences on him, questions remain. How important were Robbins' publications on the subjects that influenced him? Did his publications reflect these influences? How?

Many things condition the movement of an idea from one person to another. Among these are time, place, historical context, events, and language.

5.2.   The importance of time

Influence is time bound. In order to trace it, the time frame in which it occurred is essential. By the time frame is meant both the time during which the influence occurred and the time of the assessment of the influence. Time periods must be specified. The need for periodization in studies of influence stems from the fact that things and people do change. It is both necessary and convenient to have some idea about when major changes occurred. The history of economic thought was not a seamless, smooth development.

The time lags between the publication of an idea and publications reflecting its influence have been little studied. They could be of some importance.

No matter how influence is evaluated, its importance is conditioned by time. Perhaps the truest measure of lasting influence occurs when a person's contribution passes into everyday usage without attribution, as, for example, with marginal utility and many mathematical techniques.

Even when this happens, if enough time passes, the relative importance of an influential contribution is less, because the total body of knowledge increases. Any single contribution becomes a smaller proportion of the total body of knowledge as it takes its place along with other contributions. For example, the metaphysical and normative economic ideas of Saint Thomas Aquinas (1225?-1274) dominated the medieval era. Today they are still of importance but relatively less now than then.

In the short run, influence is sometimes related to the stature of the person in the academic community, the manner of the exposition of the author, the quality of his disciples, and, perhaps, even fads and fashions. In the long run, it is the quality of the publication that counts. In the long run, influence in the history of economic thought is always manifested in published material.

5.3.   The importance of place

Place also conditions importance and influence. If the subject of a person's work is closely confined to a small area, that contribution is less important than if it were applicable to a larger space. Similarly, what we might call range conditions importance and influence. By range, in this context, we mean the number and kinds of problems to which an idea might be applied.

5.4.   The importance of historical context

Historical context is sometimes significant in its effect on influence. An important reason for the difference in the influence of Roscher in the United States and England lies in the distinctive ways economics developed and was taught in those countries. Development in both was distinct from that of Germany, France, Italy, and Austria, which all followed separate paths in the late 1800s and early 1900s.

5.5.   The importance of events

Events can be important in determining influence. Exactly what their effects were must be carefully specified. The decline of the importance of the German language in economics had much to do with the two world wars. The policies of Adolf Hitler's (1889–1945) regime that drove many outstanding German economists into exile ended their prospects in Germany. Most of them learned and published in the language of their newly adopted countries.

Stigler has a penetrating essay on the influence of events on economic theory. He recognizes that "sane economic theories have always had at least a possible connection with the world in which they were written" (1965, p. 17) and "major economic problems sometimes become matters of paramount interest to economists" (pp. 17 and 18). His conclusion, however, is that no detailed reconciliation of economic theories with their environments is even remotely tenable (p. 17).

The complexities of events, combined with those of the economist's personality, background, and social situation, plus the time and place, are so entangled that the prospects for a systematic understanding of them, much less of a general theory, are, for the present, remote.

5.6.   The problem of reciprocal influence

Tracing influence is very difficult in the case where authors worked closely together. An example is found in the relationship of Mill and his wife Harriet. Mill began the dedication of *On Liberty* "To the beloved and deplored memory of her who was the inspirer, and in part the author of all that is best in my writings ...." Scholars have argued since 1859 about the extent to which the statement is true.

5.7.   The importance of the language

Influence in the history of economic thought is related to the importance of the language in which the work was written at the time of its publication. Latin was for many centuries the most important scientific and literary language. French was for more than a century the language of diplomacy. If we assume that modern economics began about 1800, the first important languages for economics were English and French.

By about the middle of the 1800s, German established itself as one of the three leading languages in economics along with English and French. The importance of German began to decline after the First World War until, about the 1960s, it was no longer required in most important Ph.D. programs in the United States, France, and England. The importance of French declined, starting about the middle of the 1800s.

By about the middle of the 1900s, the hegemony of English was established. English, in the early twentieth-first century, is the *lingua franca* of the social science and economic world. It is the most widely spoken and read language. Most scientific journals and books are published in it. Now it has also become the language of the Internet. Today, no one can hope any works will be influential unless they are written or translated into English.

Language is an important barrier to lasting international fame for those not publishing in English.

Whether a translator should be judged to share the influence of the author translated is a debatable issue. For example, to what extent is the influence of Marie Ésprit Léon Walras (1834–1910) due to his translator, William Jaffé?

6.   MEASURING INFLUENCE

6.1.   What is the measurement of influence in the history of economic thought?

The measurement of influence in the history of economic thought refers to the attempt to quantify, according to some standard, the extent to which a person publishes references to what another, earlier individual published. Measurement includes, not only the assigning of numbers to things, but also the detection of inequality and equality, relationships, continuity, variation, and other properties that might lead to mathematical expressions. Although its achievement may be far in the future, the goal of the measurement of influence is highly desirable.

The term *metrology* refers to either the science that deals with measurement or a system of measurement. I do not recall ever seeing the term in works on the history of economic thought. Knowledge from the science of metrology must, sooner or later, be used in the history of economic thought. An example of where it might be useful is found in the idea of repeatability. In engineering, this refers to the quantity that characterizes the ability of an instrument to return the same value from repeated measurements of the same thing under identical measuring conditions. Applying this to the history of economic thought might mean that the same method of measurement ought to give the same results. A quantity which characterizes the differences in the results from the use of the same methods would be useful in the analysis of the reasons for the differences.

Another concept from metrology that might have uses in the history of economic thought is that of "rangebility." It states the limits within which a quantity is measured by describing the lower and upper range values. Applying this to the history of economic thought might mean more precise descriptions of the limits to which generalizations apply.

6.2.   Why try to measure?

There are several reasons why measurement will be a useful part of a general theory of influence, if and when it comes. With measurement will come more detailed and precise methods for tracing and evaluating the causes, paths, extent, and results of influence. It will show an advanced level of theoretical understanding. It will allow empirical verification. Measurement will also allow accurate and repeatable assessments. Results in mathematical form will be more easily testable. Some measurement will lead to the testing of results by means of falsification.

Measurement will also increase the credibility and utility of research in the history of economic thought. It should also raise standards in the field because the differences between the way research is conducted and the way it is reported will have to be more precise than they are now.

Measurement may even encourage the reporting of one kind of negative results. Negative results are results contrary to a researcher's expectations or to received theory. Although the publication of results contrary to prevailing theory is common, the reporting of negative results that are contrary to a researcher's expectations is almost unheard of among historians of economic thought. Some of these results might be very informative. Negative results ought to be reported even when researchers decide not to pursue them.

6.3. Present status

There are many attempts to measure influence in the field of economics, as a glance at any issue of *American Economic Review* or other leading economic publications will show. Two examples of specific fields are experimental economics and law and economics. It is clear that carefully controlled economic experiments allow the drawing of some kinds of inferences with considerably more confidence than from other, nonexperimental, data.

The main methods of scholarship in the field of law and economics are quantitative and empirical.

An important methodological requirement is that results should be testable by means of falsification. Predictions should be verifiable on the basis of empirical evidence.

Some studies of influence in economics cover important issues related to influence in the history of economic thought. An example of one of these is the 2000 article by Bruno S. Frey, "Does Economics have an Effect? Towards an Economics of Economics." The thrust of the paper is "that economics should endeavor to meet the challenges posed by social problems" (p. 19). Frey argues that it does not.

His paper is of interest because he recognizes that the aggregate production function for economic knowledge lacks a well-specified theory. To develop such a theory, it is "necessary to shift attention to the micro-basis of this relationship, i.e. to look at the process by which ideas are transformed into factors in the production function" (p. 7).

The way Frey does this is by examining the influence of economic ideas along with the sources of economic ideas and their diffusion. He has valuable discussions of the market for economic ideas and the types of ideas transferred. He has a very useful section on "The Influence of Economists as Persons" (p. 11). The paper is well documented. As part of the documentation, Frey has what is probably the most complete list of the political positions of economists in an appendix.

It has been suggested that sociograms, diagrams, and graphs showing interpersonal relationships will be useful ways to trace influence and diffusion in economic thought. Works like this and that of Frey will have to be taken into consideration as progress is made in measuring influence in the history of economic thought. For an introduction to the uses in other fields, see http://www.google.com/search?num=50&hl=en&safe=active&q=sociograms&btnG=Google+Search.

There are other attempts to measure influence in the history of economic thought. The measures are usually indirect and rely on situations where data are easily found. Influence must almost always be inferred by reasoning from a product such as citations or doctoral degrees.

An example of a statistical citation analysis is the study by Stigler and Claire Friedman. They accept that the number of citations of books and articles are "an acceptable statistical measure of influence or attitude, and we believe that this measure deserves deeper and more critical examination than it has so far received" (p. 221).

The most numerous and prominent of statistical studies of influence are those of the research activities of university economics departments. As Jerry G. Thursby put it, "There is a cottage industry that ranks economics departments on research quality/output" (2000, p. 383). In an extensive survey of that industry, Thursby says, "Opinions matter a great deal. One might even infer a purpose of counting output as an attempt to influence opinions" (p. 386).

The inference is that the larger is some combinatorial measure of the quality of research and the number of Ph.Ds turned out by the university, the more influential the university is in the world of economics.

6.4.   Necessary assumptions

Measurement in the history of economic thought requires the hypothesis that the phenomena of economic thought, as they apply to large collections of individuals, are capable of being measured. If influence is always an entirely individual phenomenon, there can be little hope for a general theory.

A second assumption necessary for a general theory is that some structural relationships exist for the phenomena of economic thought. In other words, the phenomena are not indeterminate and random. If influence is to be measured, there must be some kind of underlying pattern to it.

Given these assumptions, for the history of economic thought there are many theoretical issues that must be discussed before much progress toward measurement, much less a general theory of influence, is possible. Some of these issues are briefly commented upon.

6.5.   What might be the units of data?

In order to measure influence directly, a measurand is necessary. A measurand is the parameter being quantified.

Some kinds of units are required to make the data that show influence amenable to analysis. There are many possible measureands and, therefore, units.

There are many possible things capable of exercising influence. It is unlikely that a direct measure of the idea that carries the influence is possible at this time. It is also unlikely that a direct measure of the extent of the influence of one individual on another is possible at this time.

There are indirect ways to measure and infer influence. Among these are the number of references in books and journals and other testimony. The number of times an author is mentioned in relevant books, as, for example, histories of economics, will allow ordinal measurement of some things. If one author is mentioned significantly more often than another in an approving way, it is reasonable to infer greater influence. Caution is required when using books for this purpose. Indexes are no reliable measure. Most indexes are not very good. Misspellings are not uncommon.

Journal citations are another way to infer influence. The idea is that the more often an author is cited in the relevant journals, the more influential he or she is. This method relies on the selection of the journals, the accuracy of the citation counts, and the time covered for the reliability of its results.

Other testimony is often useful in attempts to measure influence.

Dedications, such as that by Philip Charles Newman, "To Wesley Clair Mitchell," show influence. Autobiographies, as in the case of Robbins above, show influence. Memoirs show influence. Stigler writes of himself and his fellow students the University of Chicago, "Chicago had a strong influence on us" (1988, p. 26). Except for simple counts, testimony of this kind seems unquantifiable at the present time.

The questions of what data to collect, what data to report, and how to present them remain more questions of art than clearly defined practice. All researchers need to take care not to let their prior expectations play too great a role in determining which parts of the data to take seriously.

A related issue is that often the methods of data selection are unreported. The more important the methods of data selection are in determining what data are presented, the more important it is that the methods used to collect the data be spelled out.

Very little attention has been paid to the theory of what to measure in order to show influence in the history of economic thought.

6.6.   Accuracy and precision

Probably because there is so little measurement, terms like *accuracy*, *precision*, *resolution*, and *sensitivity* are not often found in the histories of economics. By accuracy is meant the conformity of the statement or measurement to fact.

Precision in measurement means that the rules according to which numbers are assigned are followed exactly as specified. Resolution defines the smallest dimension of the thing being measured. Sensitivity is a measure of the smallest amount of change that can be detected in the thing being measured.

One of the few histories that discuss accuracy that is related to economic thought is Stephen M. Stigler's *The History of Statistics*. He is correct when he says, "Indeed, it could be argued that any measurement that is accepted as worth quoting by more than one person may have some commonly understood accuracy, even if that accuracy is not expressed in numerical terms. But this argument can be an extremely difficult one to apply in historical terms..." (1986, p. 3).

The accuracy required in a measurement depends on the problem. It is important to distinguish the accuracy of the data on which the influential idea is based from the accuracy of the conclusion about the extent of the influence.

Every science and every theory should possess an explanatory power. Mathematized theories often are intended to give predictions as accurately as possible. It is possible that accuracy and explanatory power can sometimes be in an opposing relationship. The history of economic thought has no generally accepted rules about accuracy, precision, or resolution as it pertains to influence.

6.7. The measurement of importance

A general theory of influence ought to include measures of importance. The measures of the importance of a contribution can be thought of as made up of characteristics that are both explicit and implicit. By an explicit characteristic is meant one that can use quantifiable metrics such as statistics and tables, citations, and the like.

Implicit characteristics refer to the traits or attributes or qualities of scientific work. These are manifested in: the method of presentation, e.g., literary, historical, rhetorical; the method of analysis, e.g., approaching a topic in more than one way; the viewpoint, e.g., economic, sociological; the political stance, e.g., left, right center, or none; the approach, e.g., specific concern with ethics and morality. In general, implicit characteristics are identifiable, but not easily measured, attributes of scientific work.

Especially difficult is the case when clusters or groups of features are involved. One way to illuminate these difficulties is to think of influence as being some kind of *Gestal*–a unity or whole of which the parts are both distinguishable and interdependent. Historians of economic thought cannot now apply a numerical value to this kind of situation.

For many other reasons, there is no simple, consistent, or reliable method for measuring the importance of an influence, either relatively or absolutely, of any given contribution that will remain valid for long periods. Keeping all of this in mind, plausible arguments can be made that certain contributions were both important and influential.

7.   OTHER CONSIDERATIONS

7.1.   The extent of influence

Influence varies in extent. Every economics elementary text contains some of the ideas of Smith about markets and competition and the concept of marginal analysis developed by William Stanley Jevons (1835–1882) and others. The spread of these ideas contrasts sharply with the contributions of the majority of economists important in the history of economics. The work of the vast majority is like that of the masons who lay the bricks in a great building. Their work is an absolute requirement for the construction of economics. But the extent of their influence is limited.

7.2.   Uses and misuses of influence

Long ago, Keynes elaborated on Smith's insight when he wrote, "But soon or late, it is ideas, not vested interests, which are dangerous for good or evil" (1936, p. 384). Ideas by themselves neither help nor harm people. It is only when they are put into practice that there are good or bad results.

The overwhelming majority of economists try to exert their influence for what they conceive of are good ends. It is rare when the influence of an economist results in deaths or harm to substantial numbers of people over any long period of time. It is almost unheard of in the history of economic thought for writers on economic subjects to consciously preach evil. The case is different about some of the users and uses of their ideas.

Any tool that is useful can be used for good or evil. So it is with influential ideas that are put into practice. An outstanding example is Marx. The way his ideas were interpreted by Vladimir Ilich Lenin (Wladimir Iljitsch Uljanow, sometimes Ilyich 1870–1924), Joseph Stalin (Iosif Vissarionovich Dzhugashvili, 1879–1953), Mao Tse Tung (1893–1976), and Fidel Castro (b. 1926) led to tens of millions of deaths and untold misery for hundreds of millions of people for more than half a century.

Some economists think that ignorance or inattention to the consequences of ideas has led to social harm when the ideas are made into policy. See Frey for a collection of these views ranging from Keynes through John Kenneth Galbraith (b. 1908) to Friedrich August von Hayek (1889–1992) and Milton Friedman (b. 1912) and others (pp. 2–3).

7.3.   The difficult case of no influence

It is sometimes of interest to examine disputed cases in which influence is claimed but may or may not exist. Friedrich Wilhelm Nietzsche (1844–1900) provides an example of the philosophical complexities when no influence is claimed. Nietzsche is an important figure in intellectual history. He is in at least five histories of economic thought, those by Gide and Rist, Frank Amandus Neff, Karl Pribram (1877–1973), Othmar Spann (1878–1950), and Edmund Whittaker. Does that mean he was influential in the development of economics? No. None of them give Nietzsche credit for any influence in the mainstream economics development.

"Nietzsche did not directly influence the development of economics" is an example of a negative existential proposition. For centuries philosophers have disputed the question of whether such negative propositions can be proved. One argument for the idea that negative existential propositions can be proved to be false is that it may be possible to demonstrate the opposite proposition, "Nietzsche did influence economics." If Nietzsche did influence economics, the negative proposition could be considered disproved or falsified.

If it is not possible to prove the positive proposition, "Nietzsche did influence economics," it does not necessarily mean that the negative proposition holds, only that it is a possibility. One method philosophers use to determine the nonexistence of something is to carefully search for it. If the thing sought for cannot be found, some philosophers accept that as proof that the thing does not exist. Most philosophers accept that not finding something provides, at the least, strong evidence that the thing does not exist. One cannot logically prove a negative proposition. The best that can be done is to search for evidence to disprove it.

7.4.   Fraud

Fraud is the deliberate practice of selecting only the data that support a hypothesis and concealing the rest. I know of no case in the history of economic thought where this has occurred. It is certainly not common in the history of economic thought.

7.5.   Unavoidable "errors"

There are certain kinds of errors in the history of economic thought that are unavoidable. Perhaps it is too harsh a judgment to call it an error when relevant material from languages other than that of the author is omitted. It would be against the experience of science if some ideas now attributed to some writers were not developed independently, perhaps even anticipated in other languages not well known to most economists.

Minor, but leading to inaccuracies at times, are errors about places. Names and classification of places are among the principal items that are subject to factual error. An example is Schumpeter. Schumpeter was born in what is now called Trest in the Czech Republic. At that time it was Trietsch, Moravia or Trešt, part of Austria-Hungary. Someone writing about Schumpeter at different times of his life could be wrong about the name of his birthplace today.

"Errors" resulting from selection and generalization are often necessary results of describing complex phenomena in limited space. Often problems of influence are highly ill-conditioned problems.

8.   ROBUST MEASURES OF INFLUENCE ARE SOMETIMES VERY DIFFICULT

8.1.   Scholarly consensus

At the present time, there are several generally accepted methods of making strong cases for influence in the history of economics. By far the most important of these is scholarly consensus. Smith, Malthus, David Ricardo (1772–1823), Keynes, and Samuelson are example of economists whose names appear in every history that discusses the subjects on which they wrote. This consensus is based on the experience of generations of scholarship.

But the consensus does not go very far. Make a *Gedanken* experiment. Ask one hundred historians of economic thought to compile a list of the one hundred most influential people in the history of economics. It is almost certain that the lists would not be identical. It is very likely that fifty or more of the same names would appear on all of the lists.

8.2.   Other ways

There are other ways to make a strong case that an economist is influential. The best way is to trace what happened to their writing in detail. Who read it? What did those readers write about it? How did it affect their writing? The answers to those questions should be subject to empirical verification or quantification.

It is far more common in the history of economic thought that less than a strong case for influence is possible. Convincing arguments are possible. Such arguments can be made in a variety of ways of which autobiographies are but one. Citation analysis is another. But even if all the citations to an author's works are found, the necessity of assessing the influence of reference on the subsequent development of economic thought remains.

There is no foolproof way to set guidelines for what constitutes all the relevant data for a study of influence. Arguments about the influence of a person on the development of economic thought that would convince every historian of economics are hard to make. Convincing, logical arguments are the best that can be done most of the time.

9.   CONCLUSIONS: THE HISTORY OF ECONOMIC THOUGHT IS GETTING CLOSER TO A THEORY OF INFLUENCE, BUT IS NOT QUITE THERE YET

9.1.   What is needed

Historians of economic thought need to move toward scientifically more respectable and acceptable criteria for analyzing influence. This is required because the term is so important and commonly used.

Historians of economic thought need to search even more intensively for a theoretical matrix that will give both direction and analytical purpose to empirical research about influence. Ideally, this theoretical matrix would draw together all the elements discussed above into a conceptually consistent unity.

9.2.   Why there is no general theory: sources of uncertainty

There are many fundamentally different sources of uncertainty about influence. It is both theoretically desirable and common practice to seek historical truth from a wide variety of perspectives. The criteria used to judge any analysis depend on the goals of the analysis and the theories behind them. A general theory will have to limit these perspectives if it is to be useful.

There are those who argue that all judgments, perceptions, and evaluations of influence in the history of economic thought are related to outside forces such as cultural systems, ideologies, gender bias, and the like. A central problem with this kind of argument is that the passage of time changes ideas about all of these things. One consequence of this kind of analysis is that they are tied to very specific and time-bound notions not suitable for a general theory. Nor is that all. It is easily shown that influence transcends such things as languages, ideologies, cultures, gender, and countries. The screens of time, language, and culture all filter the light of influence somewhat differently.

Measurements of influence are complex not only by virtue of the variety of forms they take but also because of their multiple connections with the whole fabric of economic thought.

There are at least three other fundamental and different sources of uncertainty about influence. One kind comes from accidental or contingent or indeterminate factors which lead to a total or partial breakdown of ways to trace influence.

Another source of uncertainty comes from unpredictable behavior. If a theory is to demonstrate real understanding of influence, it ought to be able to predict at least some kinds of influence.

A third source of uncertainty comes from essential limitations or inherent imprecision in the measurement procedures used.

9.3.   Conclusion

A general theory of influence for the history of economic thought will require limits on the variations allowed to the meaning of the term *influence*. The theory will have to be flexible enough to handle different methodological approaches. It will have to be empirical in the sense that researchers anywhere can confirm its results.

No general theory of influence for the history of economic thought is possible at the present time. A general theory may never be possible because different scholars may continue to interpret and use the term *influence* differently.

It is important to recognize that there are few certain measures of significance. For the time being scholars must rely on conjectures, heuristics, and partial insights. Different authors have different viewpoints, approaches, and emphases. Every study of influence must rely on the judgment of the author of the study because there are no generally agreed-upon measures of influence.

NOTES

1. Acknowledgements: Jürgen Backhaus, Ursula Backhaus, Mark E. Blum, Merle Kingman, Martha Rubenstein, and Leland B. Yeager helped me with useful critiques for which I thank them. I am particularly obligated to Mary Stone Senn who, in addition to making many specialized computer searches, was helpful in countless other ways. Thanks also to Anita Lauterstein who did much of the typing. Any errors are my own.
    Version 1 of the paper presented at the Fourth and Fifth Crossing Bridges Symposium, August 5, 2001, Selma, Alabama. Peter R. Senn is Professor Emeritus in the City Colleges of Chicago. He may be contacted at 1121 Hinman Avenue, Evanston, Illinois 60202. Phone: (847) 328-3767; fax (847) 869-0312. Draft of June 22, 2001. Copyright © April 6, 2000. Printed on 7/16/2007 1:36:00 PM.

REFERENCES

Note: One reason the World Wide Web (Web) is a valuable resource for scholarship is because it contains the full and searchable texts of many important economic publications. The resource is not without its problems, however. One of these problems is the lack of complete source citations, dates, editions, page numbers, and the like. I am confident that the references from the Web that I used are accurate representations of the original sources. For a few references, I have not had the resources to check the original documents. The details that are doubtful are indicated with a question mark.

Aquinas, T. (1964–1980). *Summa Theologiae. Latin text and English translation, intro-ductions, notes, appendices and glossaries.* 61 vols. London: Blackfriars; New York: McGraw-Hill.

Ashley, W. J. (1897). "The Tory Origin of Free Trade Policy." *Quarterly Journal of Economics* Vol. 11? (July). The full text is at http://socserv2.socsci.mcmaster.ca/~econ/ugcm/3ll3/ ashley/toryfree.html

Beveridge, W. H. (1944). *Full Employment in a Free Society: A Report.* London: Allen & Unwin.

von Böhm-Bawerk, E. (1898). *Karl Marx and the Close of His System; A Criticism.* Translated by Alice M. Macdonald, with a preface by James Bonar. London: T.F. Unwin.
The German title is *Zum Abschluss des Marxschen Systems.*

Carroll, L. (1865). "Alice's Adventures In Wonderland." In *The Complete Works of Lewis Carroll.* Illustrated by John Tenniel. Introduction by Alexander Woolcott. New York: The Modern Library. Undated.

Cossa, L. (1893). *An Introduction to the Study of Political Economy.* Revised by the author and translated from the Italian by Louis Dyer. London: MacMillan & Co.
Publication details for the original Italian version are not provided.

Cournot, A. A. (1838). *Recherches sur les principes mathématiques de la théorie des richesses.* Paris: L. Hachette.

Dorfman, J. (1946a). *The Economic Mind in American Civilization: 16061865.* Vol. 1. New York: Viking Press.

———. (1946b). *The Economic Mind in American Civilization: 1606–1865.* Vol. 2. New York: Viking Press.

———. (1949). *The Economic Mind in American Civilization: Volume Three, 18651918.* New York: Viking Press.

———. (1959). *The Economic Mind in American Civilization: Volumes Four and Five, 19181933.* New York: Viking Press.

The two volumes were published separately but with the same title page and index.

Ehrman, H. W. (1964). In Gould, Julius and Kolb, William L. (eds.), *A Dictionary of the Social Sciences. Compiled under the auspices of The United Nations Educational, Scientific, and Cultural Organization.* New York: Free Press of Glencoe.

"Influence." In Chisholm, Hugh (ed.), *The Encyclopaedia Britannica: A Dictionary of Arts, Sciences, Literature and General Information.* 11th ed. New York: Encyclopaedia Britannica, Vol. 14: 552.

Fisher, I. (1904). "Precedents for Defining Capital." *Quarterly Journal of Economics* Vol. 18, 386–408. Full text at http://socserv2.socsci.mcmaster.ca/~econ/ugcm/3ll3/fisher/capital4

Frey, B. S. (2000). "Does Economics have an Effect? Towards an Economics of Economics." Institute for Empirical Research in Economics, University of Zurich. Working Paper Series, ISSN 1424–0459. Working Paper No. 36 (February). The full text, downloadable in PDF format, is online at http://www.iew.unizh.ch/wp/iewwp036.pdf (January 2001).

Gide, C. and Rist, C. (1948). *A History of Economic Doctrines From the Time of the Physiocrats to the Present Day.* Authorized translation by R. Richards. Second English edition, with additional matter from the latest French editions translated by Ernest F. Row. London: George G. Harrap & Company.

The first French edition was published in 1909. The first English edition, which was a translation of the second French edition, was published in June 1915. The 1948 edition was a translation of the seventh French edition. The copy I worked from said it was completely reset in the second English edition of 1948 which was a translation of the seventh French edition of 1947.

Hume, D. (1748). "An Enquiry Concerning Human Understanding." In *The English Philosophers from Bacon To Mill.* Edited, with an introduction, by Edwin A. Burtt. New York: The Modern Library. The Modern Library edition was published in 1939. The *Enquiry* was published as part of *Philosophical Essays Concerning Human Understanding.* The full text is available at http://www.utm.edu/research/hume/wri/1enq/1enq.htm

———. 1769 (1955). Letter from Hume to Morellet, July 10, 1769. In *Writings on Economics.* Edited and introduced by Eugene Rotwein. Madison: University of Wisconsin Press and London: Thomas Nelson and Sons.I worked from the 1970 edition.

Ingram, J. K. (1967). *A History of Political Economy.* New and enlarged edition with a supplementary chapter by William A. Scott, LL.D., Professor of Political Economy, University of Wisconsin and an introduction by Richard T. Ely, LL.D., Professor of Political Economy, University of Wisconsin. New York: Augustus M. Kelley Publishers. The original edition was dated 1888. The edition from which the reprint was made was first published in 1915. The full searchable text is at http://socserv2.socsci.mcmaster.ca/~econ/ugcm/3ll3/ingram/ingram01.html

Katz, E. (1968). "Diffusion: Interpersonal Influence." In Sills, David L. (ed.), *International Encyclopedia of the Social Sciences.* New York: The Macmillan Company & The Free Press. Vol. 4, 178–185.

Keynes, J. M. (1936). *The General Theory of Employment, Interest and Money.* New York: Harcourt, Brace.

Leeson, R. (1997). "Influence (or the Lack of It) in the Economics Profession: The Case of Lucien Albert Hahn." *History of Political Economy* Vol. 29, No. 4 (Winter): 635638.

Levy, D. (1999). "Interview with Arnold Harberger." The Region Magazine. The Federal Reserve Bank of Minneapolis. Vol. 13, No. 1 (March). On the World Wide Web at http://minneapolisfed.org/pubs/region/99-03/harberger.html.

Locke, J. (1691). "Some Considerations of the Consequences of the Lowering of Interest and the Raising the Value of Money In a letter sent to a Member of Parliament." London: Printed for Awnsham and John Churchill, at the Black Swan in Pater-Noster-Row. Full text at http://socserv2.socsci.mcmaster.ca/~econ/ugcm/3ll3/locke/consid.txt

March, J. G. (1955). "An Introduction to the Theory and Measurement of Influence." *American Political Science Review* Vol. 49, No. 2 (June): 431–451.

Marshall, A. (1946). *Principles of Economics: An Introductory Volume.* 8th ed. London: Macmillan and Co. The first edition was published in 1890.

Marx, K. (1906–1909). *Capital: A Critique of Political Economy*. 3 vols. Chicago: Charles H. Kerr & Company. The dates are for the English translation.

Menger, C. (1994). "Carl Menger's Lectures to Crown Prince Rudolph." Edited by Erich W. Streissler and Monika Streissler. Brookfield, VT: Edward Elgar.

Mill, J. S. (1848). *Principles of Political Economy with Some of Their Applications to Social Philosophy*. London: Longmans Green.

Mill, J. S. 1947 (1859). *On Liberty*. Edited with an introduction by Aubrey Castell. New York: F. S. Crofts.

Neff, F. A. (1950). *Economic Doctrines*. 2nd ed. New York: McGraw-Hill.

Newman, P.C. (1952). *The Development of Economic Thought*. New York: Prentice Hall.

Philippovich, E. v. (1893). *Grundriss der politischen Oekonomie*. Tübingen: J.C.B. Mohr.By 1919 there were fourteen editions.

Pribram, K. (1983). *A History of Economic Reasoning*. Baltimore: Johns Hopkins University Press.

Robbins, L. R. (1971). *Autobiography of an Economist*. London: Macmillan.

Roscher, W. (1874). *Geschichte der National-oekonomik in Deutschland*. Munich: R. Oldenbourg.

Samuelson, P. A. (1948). *Economics, An Introductory Analysis*. New York: McGraw-Hill.

Schmoller, G. (1893–4). "The Idea of Justice in Political Economy." *Annals of the American Academy of Political and Social Science* Vol. 4 (March): 697–737. Translated by Ernst L. von Halle and Carl L. Schutz. Originally published in German: *Jahrbuch für Gesetzgebung Verwallung, und Volkswirtschaft*. Vol. 1, new series 1881. Full text at http://socserv.socsci.mcmaster.ca/~econ/ugcm/3ll3/schmoller/justice.

Schmoller, G. (1900–1904). *Grundriss der allegemeine Volkswirtschaftlehere*. 2 vols. Munich: Duncker & Humblot.

Schumpeter, J. A., and Schumpeter, E. B. (eds.) (1954). *History of Economic Analysis*. New York: Oxford University Press.There are several other editions.

Seligman, E. R. A. (1931–1935). *Encyclopaedia of the Social Sciences*. New York: Macmillan Company.

Sills, D.L. (1968). *International Encyclopedia of the Social Sciences*. New York: Macmillan Company & The Free Press.

Smith, A. (1937). "An Inquiry into the Nature and Causes of the Wealth of Nations." Edited, with an introduction, notes, marginal summary and an enlarged index by Edwin Cannan. With an introduction by Max Lerner. New York: The Modern Library. The first edition was published in 1776. The Modern Library edition was taken from the fifth edition of 1789, the last published before Smith's death. Full text at http://socserv2.socsci.mcmaster.ca/~econ/ugcm/3ll3/smith/wealth/wealbk01

Spann, O. (1930). *Types of Economic Theory*. Translated by Eden and Cedar Paul from the Nineteenth German Edition. London: Allen & Unwin.The first edition of the German original, *Die Hauptheorien der Volkswirtschaftslehre*, Leipzig, Quelle & Meyer, was published in 1912. The nineteenth revised German edition was published in 1929.

Stigler, G. (1965). "The Influence of Events and Policies on Economic Theory (1960)." In *Essays in the History of Economics*. Chicago: University of Chicago Press.

Stigler, G. J. with Friedland C. (1982). "The Citation Practices of Doctorates in Economics." In *The Economist as Preacher, and Other Essays*. Chicago: University of Chicago Press. Reprinted from the *Journal of Political Economy* Vol. 83, 1975.

Stigler, G. J. (1988). *Memoirs of an Unregulated Economist*. New York: Basic Books.

Stigler, S. M. (1986). *The History of Statistics: The Measurement of Uncertainty Before 1900.* Cambridge, Mass.: Belknap Press of Harvard University Press.

Thurbsy, J. G. (2000). "What Do We Say About Ourselves and What does It Mean? Yet Another Look at Economics Department Research." *Journal of Economic Literature* Vol. 38, No. 2 (June): 383–404.

Turgot, A.-R.-J., baron de l'Aulne (1766). *Reflections on the Formation and Distribution of Riches.* Translated from the French. London: Printed by E. Spragg, For J. Good, Bookseller, No. 159, New Bond Street; John Anderson, No. 62, Holborn Hill; and W. Richardson, Royal Exchange.1793. Full searchable text at http://socserv2.socsci.mcmaster.ca/~econ/ugcm/3ll3/ turgot/reflecti

Walras, L. (1965). *Correspondence of Léon Walras and Related Papers.* Ed. by William Jaffé. 3 vols. Amsterdam: North-Holland.

Whittaker, E. (1940). *A History of Economic Ideas.* New York: Longmans, Green.

Wiener, P. P. (ed.) (1968). *Dictionary of the History of Ideas*: Studies of Selected Pivotal Ideas. 5 vols. New York: Charles Scribner's Sons.I worked from the 1973 paperback reprint.

3. Gustave Courbet's *L'Origine du Monde* and Its Socioeconomic Implications

Jürgen G. Backhaus

Abstract   This article explores a link between modern painting in the realistic tradition and socioeconomic change. It focuses on Gustave Courbet's famous painting *The Origin of the World* (*L'Origine du Monde*) which has recently been rediscovered after having long been thought either missing or destroyed. The realistic painting is discussed in terms of both its artistic and its socioeconomic impact. The article first discusses the painting in the context of the life and work of its author. It then turns to the extended social policy implications of the work and finally to Courbet's extraordinary propaganda stunt of hiding the message for greater effectiveness.

Keywords: Gustave Courbet (1819–1877), Pierre-Joseph Proudhon (1809–1865), Commune of Paris, family, *Origin of the World*, sexuality

JEL Codes: B14, P26

Gustave Courbet (1819-1877) was a largely self-taught French painter who, after his contribution to the World Exposition in Paris in 1855 had been rejected, organised his own pavilion "Le Réalisme" and thereby founded the realistic tradition of nineteenth century painting which had many followers, in particular in Germany. He combined this approach, however, with a political message in the footsteps of Pierre-Joseph Proudhon (1809-1865), the early socialist who is perhaps best known for the dictum "Property is theft." Courbet left a very large oeuvre, yet one of the most controversial pieces, long thought lost or destroyed, has, perhaps, been also the one that has had its strongest effect on modern society and thereby succeeded in weaving early socialist ideas into the texture of modern society. It is for this reason that this essay explores the significance of Courbet's *L'Origine du Monde*. The essay has three main parts. Part I discusses the author and his painting, part II looks at the extended social

Correspondence to: Jürgen G. Backhaus, Faculty of Law, Economics and Social Sciences, University of Erfurt, 99105 Erfurt, Germany policy implications, and part III turns to the extraordinary propaganda stunt of hiding the message for even greater effectiveness.

1.   INTRODUCTION

One of the most instructive entries on Gustave Courbet can be found in the *New International Encyclopaedia* (New York: Dodd, Mead & Co., 1923, p. 177). The article is still written in the subjectivist style of the turn of the century and therefore does not have the stale prose of politically correct entries as we have them today. "Courbet was of a very independent character and had so little regard for the opinions of the judges of the Salon that he returned for six successive years a picture rejected in 1841. When in the Exposition of 1855 his pictures were refused, he held a separate exposition, which attracted wide attention. In 1870, he returned the Cross of the Legion of Honour to Napoleon with a protest. He was Radical and a Socialist in politics, and under the Commune he was made director of the fine arts. As such he saved the collections of Thiers and of the Luxembourg from the infuriated populace, but he sacrificed the Vendôme Column in order to appease the crowd. For this act he was imprisoned after the downfall of the Commune, and all of his paintings were sold at public auction. In order to avoid the payment of further damages, he went into voluntary exile and died broken-hearted near Vevey in Switzerland, 31 December 1877. He was a strong but rather coarse character, blustering but good-natured–a healthy animal without the lest spirituality."

His painting is characterised in a way that totally abstracts from the political message. "His paintings portray nature exactly as it is without the least addition sentiment or idealism, for he conceived realism to be possible only through the absolute negation of idealism. As he confined himself to the reproduction of nature, there could be no refined composition or real action in his work, for these depend on the painter himself. His figures were no more than mere patches of forest or country taken at random. In figure painting he was partial to the coarse types preferred by the Flemish School, and he always painted them life-size. His colouring was excellent, and in his figure subjects, which are chiefly brushworks, it was pure, strong and mellow. In his landscapes, he used the palette knife very freely, obtaining brilliant and sparkling effects of colour. His chief defect is his lack of strength in drawing. ... Among the best of his figure paintings are *Man with the Leather Belt* (Louvre); the *Stone Breakers* (Dresden), representing two workmen breaking stones, as one can see them in the street; *Les Demoiselles au Bord de la Seine* (Petit Palais), two typical Grisettes reclining in ungraceful attitudes on the grass, yet a picture of great beauty of colour" (p. 177). We shall have to return to these judgements as we discuss *L'Origine du Monde* itself and its context.

Not only in his political actions during the time of the Parisian Commune, but throughout his work, Gustave Courbet has expressed his sociopolitical views forcefully. They stemmed largely from Pierre-Joseph Proudhon, with whom he had a long and close relationship and with whom he shared two characteristics: both hailed from the Besançon area, and both were essentially self-taught. In addition, they shared, of course, the same sociopolitical outlook, socialism, anti-imperialism, radical anticlericalism, and a quest for a total reconstitution of society. In his work, the philosopher quoted Courbet, and the latter "quoted" the philosopher in his work. This shows up in many instances. To begin with, there is the painting *Proudhon and his family* (1865), showing the philosopher deeply entrenched in thought sitting on what may be the doorsteps of his house, his books, writing utensils, and inkpot at his right. Separately and peacefully, the children are playing next to him. Also in 1865, there is the picture of Proudhon on his deathbed, a moving rendition with Courbet's signature very evidently on display on the bottom right-hand side, which occurs only rarely.

A large portion of Courbet's work shows people at work: these are farmers, housewives, or, as mentioned above, the famous stone breakers. They are invariably done with great diligence and respect for the working men and women. This is also true for the famous picture *Les Demoiselles au Bord de la Seine*, where indeed two Grisettes decked out in their colourful Sunday best rest on the riverbank in the middle of the summer; an alternate title is *The Summer*. The girls are clearly from a working-class background and tired. One is sound asleep, the other warily takes a look across the river. In contrast to the general reputation of Grisettes, working-class girls who supplemented their meagre pay on weekends, the picture shows great respect. This is also true for the remarkable work *L'Atelier* (1855), an all-round social criticism with the painter in the middle and a large crowd of detailed individuals looking on. The nude model, however, stands not in front of the painter but in his back, serving as his muse or source of inspiration, while catching many a gaze from the on-looking spectators.

The Origin of the World is part of a long series of nudes, yet they become scandalous nudes around 1865. For instance, *Two Friends* of 1866 shows two naked women in close embrace. One has her hair open, the other, her blond hair carefully coiffured. The setting, the accessories around the bed show great wealth and elegance. A very long chain of very large pearls has been taken off, there is one big beautifully crafted goblet, probably for wine. It is an unmistakable critique of the moral state of Parisian high society, perhaps *les nouveau riches* or even the imperial court, and showing a lesbian couple obviously could not fail to be a provocation.

L'Origine du Monde had been commissioned by a Turkish diplomat based in Paris, Khalil Bey. He had proposed the title and probably also indicated the size of the canvas, which is noticeable because Courbet preferred, in his realism, to reproduce at life-size. We do not know much about the specifics of the order, except for the description (*L'Origine du Monde*), the fact that Khalil Bey accepted the work, and that he mounted it in his residence, but behind a curtain. Only very few selected friends would ever see the painting.

Georges Boudaille (Paris: Nouvelles Editions Françaises, 1981, p. 131) sees the work without any philosophical value, which has an original title and is an excellent piece of painting ("Cet excellent morceau de peinture"). The small painting, oil on canvas, sized 46 x 55 cm, is probably the one that has received the most written attention by commentators of all of Courbet's works. Boudaille speaks of "streams of ink" (p. 131). It shows *Jo, La Belle Irlandaise* (Johanna Hiffernan, born around 1842 or 1843) and was rendered in 1866. About her, we read "this beautiful Irish woman" is Johanna Hiffernan, mistress of the artist James McNeill Whistler (1834-1903), and later of Courbet. In 1865, Whistler, Monet, and Courbet painted together at the French seaside resort of Trouville, where Jo posed for Courbet. What makes *The Origin of the World* different and set off the stream of ink is that the picture shows the extended naked lap of a woman who is still young, the legs spread apart, but only the lap, the belly, and the lower portion of the breasts are visible, the rest being either under a cloth or beyond the picture. Courbet's rendition of the theme, the "origin of the world" is then the inviting lap of a young woman, whose face, head, expression of mind and posture, circumstances, and environment have all been abstracted from.

2.   INTERPRETATION

Does this have to be interpreted as radical materialism, that Courbet saw in a woman only her reproductive capacity emphasising only her lap? After all, I am aware of no culture that emphasises the lap as the sexual symbol of distinction. The predominant distinguishing characteristics tend to be sought in the face, the hands, the posture, and only secondarily other bodily parts. The navel, although clearly worked out in realistic fashion, is not emphasised as in the modern disco scene. In taking this shortcut approach at interpreting Courbet's *Origin of the World*, one would do him grave injustice. Obviously, many interpreters have been at a loss with the picture, trying to diminish its importance in the overall oeuvre of the painter, as they found its interpretation difficult, its rendition offensive to womanhood as such. This interpretation would be a shortcut. First, one has to look at how Courbet saw women in general, and how this view fit in with his peculiar worldview, informed by the discourse of his time.

Women occur frequently in Courbet's paintings, and certainly not only in naked forms as would have conformed to the allegorical school-based mainstream of his time – to which he was opposed. When he engaged in this form, he always gave the rendition a specific twist of social criticism as we had seen in the case of the two lovers. Typically, women are depicted as beautiful, sometimes vain, as proud in their work, as a mother, as a milkmaid, even the Grisettes who are depicted as having honour (a provocation again). Others are differently depicted, and here lies, quite fortunately, the clue to a general interpretation of the underlying worldview that informed Courbet's work. He provided this clue himself, and we can return to the gigantic painting of the *Atelier*. If we look at the rendition of women in this painting, we find at centre stage, of course, the nude model converted muse. Her nudity is compensated for by a large stack of garment – which she has obviously disposed of due to the requirements of her function; however, this large stack of negligently thrown down, yet beautifully arranged garment, right there in the centre of the painting, contrasts positively with the elegant garments others wear. We find other women as well. Still almost at centre stage, there is the wretched Irish mother, trying to breast-feed a baby. This is a reference to the Irish Famine which, having been quite preventable, was seen by the likes of Courbet as a crime against humanity committed by the English landlords and statesmen. In the same painting, but on the right-hand side, we have the very attentive amateuress interested in the work of the painter, accompanied by her equally devoted husband consumed by his effort at watching the painter at work. Next to them, there is a couple in love. The young lady, who happens to be a little bit taller than her lover, is again beautifully dressed in a long white gown. She tenderly embraces her lover and looks into his eyes. We see less of the man.

So far for the depiction of the ladies, in all cases very favourable. On the right-hand side, where the good people are, we also see Baudelaire who pays little attention but reads, and, watching the painter at work, among others of course, Proudhon. As we turn to the left-hand side of the *Atelier* which the painter faces, countered to Baudelaire in the extreme left-hand corner stands the Jewish banker of the corrupt Emperor, who stands right in front of him looking down to his hunting dogs – he is not interested in the painter's work either. Next to the banker, also behind the Emperor, we find a clergyman, a republican, and a hunter. We therefore see the four pillars of the Empire: money and corruption, the support of the Church, the support of the Republican Party on whose ticket the Emperor first ran in order then to turn around and proclaim himself a monarch, and the hunter representing court life.

The Origin of the World, as we know, is either by creation or by evolution. On this topic, as we can now surmise, Courbet put much more stock in the tender love of a young couple and the determination of a starved mother nevertheless to feed her baby than on the precepts of the clergyman who is seen in the direct vicinity of a corrupt court. Hence, the message of the painting is crystal-clear. On the issue of creationism versus evolutionism, Courbet stands firm on Darwin's side.

However, he chose a particular and true to his style provocative form of making this statement, and this form corresponds to the wider issues to which the controversy between evolutionism and creationism refers. Although this dispute has now scientifically been settled, it is still a bone of contention for instance in the political discourse of the United States of America, witness the case of the state of Kansas which does not require questions referring to evolution to be answered on the high school exams on biology. Courbet was, as we have seen in his painting of the *Atelier*, extremely sensitive to political conflicts, contrasts, and tensions. Hence, he would not be surprised to hear, even today, of the Kansas debate. His approach to getting to the core or truth of the matter, quite characteristically, was to divest the relevant figures to their very nakedness. The two men engaged in a fight (*The Fighters*, 1853) are dressed only in shorts, since in this way, the intensity and strenuousness of the fight can be depicted, showing every aspect of muscle movement. In contrast, when he tries to offer praise, there is great attention to details of the dress. This is already much in evidence in the remarkable painting *The Encounter* or *Bonjour Monsieur Courbet* (1854), with *The Young Ladies on the Seine Riverfront* or *Jo, the Beautiful Irish Woman* (1865), which also pointedly shows her as somewhat narcissist. It was probably this trait of hers which allowed the remarkable cooperation between the painter and his model to take the form and execution it took.

3.   CONCLUSION

Courbet's answer to the question about *The Origin of the World* is realistic, plain, and crystal-clear. Human life by necessity has to pass through the female lap by conception and birth.

The answer could not have been more straightforward, but the way it was given certainly was not. The time was not ripe for plain realistic statements such as these, and Courbet did not even make an attempt to send this piece to the Salon, an exhibit, or otherwise publicise it. A more effective way of publicising his view to this important social and also political debate had to be found. And it had been found, witness the "streams of ink" the picture generated. This is all the more remarkable since the writers generally did not see the picture, its fame largely resting on hearsay. Some writers explicitly state so, and then nevertheless go on discussing, and in this case, praising the picture, such as Edmond de Goncourt (29 June 1889), "Cette toile, que je n'avais jamais vue," i.e., This picture which I have never seen. Maxime du Camp describes a naked lady in deep emotion and convulsion. Werner Sombart, in contrast, criticises the painter for reducing the woman to her vagina, or as he puts it in Berlin argot "Fotze." We could go on like this. In fact, the lady is not completely naked. There is no sign of convulsion, either in anticipation of an encounter or due to birth. The picture is entirely placid, Jo might have been asleep on a hot summer day. Since the picture shows only a part of the woman, the question is, what else would one want to see. Clearly, it is the part that has been covered, the upper torso and the face. And here lies a remarkable irony. In giving his down-to-earth answer, Courbet shied away from any pornographic aspect whatsoever, which would have required some motion. Unlike the ascriptions by interpreters who had never seen the painting, it is still. It is almost like a landscape, and rendered in great detail and precision. In rendering *The Origin of the World*, Courbet combined a triple stunt. He gave a clear answer to a controversial question, published it in a way that he could not be attacked as the picture remained part of a private collection, and he avoided compromising his reputation as a painter by reverting to a landscaping style which he imposed on a rendition of the nude body. The painting may belong to those of the *Grands Nus Scandaleux*, this is the title of Chapter 7 in Boudaille, but the scandal must be in the eye of the beholder, it is not with the painting as such.

REFERENCES

Boudaille, Georges (1981). *G. Courbet*. Paris: Nouvelles Editions Françaises. *New International Encyclopaedia* (1923). New York: Dodd, Mead and Co.

FURTHER REFERENCES

The paintings mentioned in this paper can be found at the following websites:

L'Origine du Monde – The Origin of the World

http://www.artchive.com/artchive/C/courbet/origin.jpg.html
http://www.i-a-s.de/IAS/Bilder/COURBET/Origin.htm
http://members.xoom.com/_XMCM/globart/dir001/courbetweb/01/ss1.htm

L'Atelier – The Artist's Studio

http://www.artchive.com/artchive/C/courbet/allegory.jpg.html
http://www.i-a-s.de/IAS/Bilder/COURBET/Allegory.htm
http://members.xoom.com/_XMCM/globart/dir001/courbetweb/02/ss2.htm
http://www.oir.ucf.edu/wm/paint/auth/courbet/allegory.jpg
http://www.hearts-ease.org/gallery/19th-c/realist/courbet/2.html
http://www.cafeguerbois.com/courbet4.htm
http://sunsite.auc.dk/cgfa/courbet/p-courbet7htm

Les Demoiselles au Bord de la Seine – The Young Ladies on the Seine Riverfront

   http://www.artchive.com/artchive/C/courbet/banks_seine.jpg.html
   http://www.i-a-s.de/IAS/Bilder/COURBET/Banks.htm
   http://members.xoom.com/_XMCM/globart/dir001/courbetweb/01/ss1.htm
   http://sunsite.auc.dk/cgfa/courbet/p-courbet5htm

Jo, La Belle Irlandaise – Jo, the Beautiful Irish Woman

   http://www.artchive.com/artchive/C/courbet/jo.jpg.html
   http://www.i-a-s.de/IAS/Bilder/COURBET/Jo.htm
   http://members.xoom.com/_XMCM/globart/dir001/courbetweb/01/ss1.htm
   http://sunsite.auc.dk/cgfa/courbet/p-courbet15.htm

The Stone Breakers

   http://hearts-ease.org/gallery/19th-c/realist/courbet/3.html
   http://www.cafeguerbois.com/courbet8.htm
   http://www2.mmlc.nwu.edu/slidlib/dillon/index.html
   http://members.xoom.com/_XMCM/globart/dir001/courbetweb/02/ss2.htm

Bonjour Monsieur Courbet – The Encounter

   http://www.artchive.com/artchive/C/courbet/bonjour.jpg.html
   http://www.i-a-s.de/IAS/Bilder/COURBET/Bonjour.htm
   http://members.xoom.com/_XMCM/globart/dir001/courbetweb/02/ss2.htm
   http://sunsite.auc.dk/cgfa/courbet/p-courbet8.htm

Proudhon and his family

   http://www.cafeguerbois.com/courbet10.htm
   http://members.xoom.com/_XMCM/globart/dir001/courbetweb/02/ss2.htm

Le Sommeil – Two Friends

   http://www.artchive.com/artchive/C/courbet/sommeil.jpg.html
   http://www.i-a-s.de/IAS/Bilder/COURBET/Sommeil.htm
   http://www.guerbois.com/courbet9.htm
   http://members.xoom.com/_XMCM/globart/dir001/courbetweb/01/ss1.htm

The Man with the Leather Belt

   http://www.cafeguerbois.com/courbet6.htm
   http://members.xoom.com/_XMCM/globart/dir001/courbetweb/02/ss2.htm

PART II

4. Introduction to Blum's Essays

Mark E. Blun

The three essays by Mark E. Blum are a "transgress" of the disciplines that inform his methodology and which are the focus of his application of methodology for several reasons. Most egregiously, he applies methods of inquiry and demonstration to the content of disciplines such as economic history, fine arts, and historiography that have not been applied yet to these disciplines. Secondly, the inquiry methods he selects and develops stem from fields which have neither developed nor applied the methods to such a diversity of disciplines beyond their own boundaries, as Blum's augmentation of the methods are required for the interdisciplinary application. Thirdly, he revives methods of inquiry and demonstration that are a century old, augmenting their still seminal potential. Fourthly, and most significantly, he challenges the very notion of a 'core' discipline that simply adds knowledge incrementally, seeing the 'methodological bridge' of the interdisciplinary inquiry method as a way to change the very parameters of content that are considered the boundaries of a field.

There is a contention that every discipline has a normative 'core' of knowledge that evolves generation to generation incrementally. This view was challenged by Wilhelm Dilthey and Ernst Mach in the nineteenth century. For these German thinkers, how one studies content determines what is known. The notion of paradigms of inquiry transforming what was accepted as the core knowledge of a discipline emerged in their thought. Mach, for instance, spoke of how the concept of acceleration had fallen into disuse in physics because of the failure of methodologies to track variations in speed. He brought photography and new physical demonstrations to physics to develop the facts of acceleration, leading towards what became relativity theory. Mach's concept of changing patterns of knowledge based upon new angles of inquiry is still a contention resisted by positivist science. The same is the case in history, art history, and other fields where the boundaries of what is studied and how it is studied are more than one generation old. Accepted use of that discipline's content and methodologies are well-known by authorities schooled in a field over a career of thought, and thus 'bridging' of disciplines through methodological cross-fertilization is highly suspect. Yet, this is a standard interdisciplinary practice. What startles in Blum's essays is that the 'bridge' becomes a new foundation for knowledge in the field to which it is applied, rather than merely a heuristic to illuminate what is the standard content to be expected in that field.

In all Blum's "bridges" there is a common conceptual thread that brings a new vision of whatever field it enters. That conceptual thread is 'time,' 'time' insofar as it reflects how a thinker experiences what is studied, and how that experience enters his or her judgments, and consequently the evidence and explanation of the evidence. All the arts and sciences have knowledge that is conceived and presented as event-structures, as whether it is study of sub-atomic particles or a landscape, an sequence of data is isolated. Blum brings in each of his three essays the concepts of narrative order to what is judged in fields such as economic history or the history of painting. Narrative order as the temporal experience of the judger in judging does not remove the objectivity of the fact, but it does demand one view this objectivity as a dynamic order that relies upon the attentional focus of the scientist or artist, historian or writer. Knowledge is not formulated in a vacuum. One's attention and judgment is affected by an individual style of knowing and the norms of discerning and formulating judgment in the society and generation in which the person lives.

The individual experiences (erfahren) history within the behavioral and ideational norms of a nation and the broader civilization, as well as the generational norms of a public time. However, the actual living of history in its immediate temporal rhythm (erleben) is an individual, singular foundation. The externally-derived historical norms of knowing and behaving are discerned as a separate envelop of rhetoric from the individual historical logic. The individual historical logic inscribes its characteristic style of expression within the rhetorical norms of expression whereby the nation and the broader civilization in its generation imposes its presence upon thought and speech.

The levels of historical logic in an articulation of events in time and their significance are "historical logic," because they are a distinct ordering of what constitutes and event. There is a "right order" implied by the norms at the generational level, the national and broader civilizational level that constrains the individual level of articulation. These levels of 'right order' are internested within the discursive arguments of one who speaks of events in time.

Discerning these levels of historical order requires an interdisciplinary approach. To recognize the envelop of what is distinct in expression in a generation of a national and wider civilizational set of rhetorical norms necessitates the use of stylistics in addition to what Max Scheler termed "a sociology of knowledge." The relation of idioms and other rhetorical usages to larger ideas of ordering events in time in a society is the amplifying of a sociology of knowledge with stylistics. Formal ideas and informal notions of historical meaning are higher levels of abstraction from the ordinary language of idiomatic meaning imparted by societies in distinct generations. Stylistics as a means of discerning the presence of the rhetorical presence of national, civilizational, and generational historical-logical norms also enables one to appreciate how the preferred ideas of a society, at the highest levels of abstraction, are themselves derived from the norms of idiomatic and informal notions of the what constitutes a historical event in the particular culture.

The three essays by Mark E. Blum take up the rhetorical norms of expression of both nation and the wider civilizational "right order" of historical logic of their time. In his first essay, Blum employs a comparative study of rhetorical norms of expression in his comparison and contrast of German and Austrian-German historical logics as they influence economic historical writings in the late nineteenth and early twentieth centuries.

In his second and third essays on the European "metaparadigm" Blum looks at the wider civilizational movement of generations in the West in the modern age, from the emergence of secular modernism in the mid-seventeenth century into the twentieth century. Using a model first developed by Wilhelm Dilthey, and subsequently by cultural historians such as Ernst Mach (his history of scientific thought) and Thomas Kuhn, Blum shows the manner in which the historical logic of new ideation in a generation is normalized in subsequent generations, affecting not only how an individual expresses his or her ideas, but what inquiry methods are used in differing phases of the new ideation, and thus what outcomes are realized.

Blum's third essay on European painting between 1815 and 1914 is a distinct augmentation and innovation on the work of Dilthey, Mach, and Kuhn. By using the nonverbal evidence of temporal-spatial order, Blum exposes a perceptual basis for event-structures that parallels the verbal bases of a society. Blum argues from the self-evident recognition by art historians since Heinrich Wölfflin that a nation and a generation produces a style of meaning. Blum's argument is new in that it more rigorously examines what Wölfflin sketched– the historical meaning of a time is to be discerned in the logic of composition by the artists of that time.

Within these aspects of the rhetorical envelop of the nation, the civilization, and the generation, the individual, who is singular and unique at an even more foundational level, communicates a vision comprehensible to contemporaries. The painterly style of a Picasso is of its time and nation, but also simply Picasso. The thought of Max Weber is of the German, the West, and the generation of fin-de-siecle Europe, but distinctly Max Weber over his career of expression. In other essays that Blum has contributed one sees the wholly individual level (cf. Mark E. Blum, "Breaks or Continuity in Sombart's Work: A Linguistic Analysis," in *Werner Sombart (1863–1941) Social Scientist,* ed. Jürgen Backhaus, Marburg, Metropolis Verlag, 1996).

Blum's work is also transgressive when he works wholly within the parameters of a field with methods once used in that field, but forgotten. For example, in his use of phenomenological philosophy which does takes seriously the temporality of human judgment, Blum has added the early phenomenological methodology of Wilhelm Dilthey, who used to stylistics to discern the temporal rhythm of thinkers and artists. Blum's taking up the issues of judgment according to the norms of a society and generation with a sociological phenomenology, a practice of Max Scheler, informs Scheler's own methodology with the stylistics Dilthey wished to incorporate into such studies. What Scheler called a "sociology of knowledge" that examined the intentions of persons of a time could only have been improved by attention to the actual statements and creations of persons in the depth and detail that stylistics and semiotics offer.

Finally, Blum's focus on the temporality of judgment in a manner that shows objective norms of judgment over the career of thought of a person, and societal norms of judgment that follow certain patterns over the generations of a society, is a transgress because in this postmodern atmosphere he is demonstrating what he calls a 'neostructuralism,' invariant categories by which any generation in any epoch can be examined. Nietzsche would agree that in this time Blum's transgress is that it is 'untimely'.

5. Contrasting Historical-Logical Narrative Conventions in Germany and Austria and Their Influence upon Inquiry and Explanation in the Arts and the Sciences: An Example from the Economic Inquiries of Gustav Schmoller, Max Weber, Carl Menger, and Ludwig von Mises

Mark E. Blum

Department of History

Abstract   A narrative is a historical order of occurrences that implies relationships, cause and effect, and temporal characteristics such as continuity, discontinuity, change, and duration. Narratives are present not only in novels, stories, and drama, but in any account of an episode in time or state-of-affairs, thus are integral to any art or science. A central premise of this essay is that within a national culture there are certain characteristic patterns of historical order and historical conceptualization shared by all disciplines in the arts and the sciences in an epoch. Europe between the Enlightenment and the present is such an epoch. Normative narrative characteristics form gradually and are slow to change. They are formed in reaction and response to the challenges of that nation's political-social experience, and are imparted through the authoritative persons in the many areas of public inquiry and practice. Significant differences in these narrative norms can be delineated between Western nations, relative to their particular mutual experiences and singular reaction and response to the general political-social-economic challenges of a time–as this essay argues in considering the Germanies and Austria since the Enlightenment. Comprehension of the claims of objective truth or mimetic accuracy in all fields is shown to hinge upon how events are structured in the descriptions and explanations within a national culture. I term these narrative norms the historical-logical perspective of the national culture.

The "national economics" of the Germans Gustav Schmoller and Max Weber and the Austrians Carl Menger and Ludwig von Mises are examined and explicated through attention to the characteristic traits of their respective narratives.

Correspondence to: Mark E. Blum, University of Louisville, Louisville, Kentucky 40292

The guiding concepts of the individuals are seen in their relationship to the manner in which events–in their structure and sequence–are conceived by their national culture.

The German narrative stresses ceaseless change in conditions and institutions. There is a dialectical transformation of the existing whereby higher levels of insight and organization reconfigure history. Encounter is the rule between persons, states, and even natural forces. There is a sense that one principle is at work in a time that subsumes or unifies all others. The Austrian narrative, on the other hand, stresses duration over time in all persons and things: life in the present is a maturation of cultural or natural forms that began or can be identified in previous generations. Interpersonal cooperation is the rule, with an eye toward the entire ecology of interests that must be integrated. Rather than one principle, for the Austrian each single interest in its aggregative sum determines what occurs in history.

The etiology of these narrative characteristics that form the historical-logical "plot" of artistic and scientific description and explanation in the Germanies and Austria is traced to each nation's political-social experience. Adhering to Hayden White's reiteration of Aristotle, essentially the human is a zoon politikon.

Keywords: German historiography, Austrian historiography, narrative theory, Hayden White, historical logic, Gustav Schmoller, Carl Menger, Max Weber, Ludwig von Mises

JEL Codes: A32, B25, B29, Z19

1.   INTRODUCTION

There is a bias given to accounts of findings in the arts and the sciences that stems from the narrative conventions of a political nation. The bias exists in how each nation conceives a "right order" of human and natural events in time, whether these events be studied by inquirers in the natural or human sciences or the humanities. Narrative order is always central to an account of findings. The classical Greek word for inquiry was *historia*, which implied not only research into nature and human affairs, but the explanative story which unified the facts discerned into a comprehension of how natural and human events transpired. One assumed that adequate inquiry would reveal laws that were universal. Nonetheless, many cultural critics since the Enlightenment have been aware of the bias produced by the national traits in depicting and explaining how events occur over time.

The bias of the narrative conventions is created out of the political experience of the nation. Certain ways of articulating the national history protect the national consciousness. The historical-logical conventions are to a great extent rationalizations that secure the trust, faith, and participation of its members. Aristotle's zoon politikon is the foundation for the national style of historical logic. The human as a political animal comprehends the person in time within a historical purview that explains communal experience in its most positive light. Rationalization of national loss or of gain, assertion of national pride, and exculpation of national humiliation are the motives which generate narrative norms of historical explanation. The political bases of a national narrative are ordinarily opaque: the life paths established by institutional authorities for the members of a political nation are so self-evidently a "right order" that the traverse of them discourages self-criticism. The national narrative norms arise through all public media, schooling, and institutional decision-making, through familial values and the manner in which religious authorities explain life in this world. Times of turmoil in which the "right order" is challenged can lead to a discernment of the very ground of normal historical perspective. The constant change in the political alignments of the Germanies produced cultural analysts who became aware of the shaping force of political life upon a national consciousness. From Hegel's vision of the human as a zoon politikon into Max Scheler's sociology of knowledge, which sought to explain and transcend the formal causal presence of political forms in culture, German minds began to clarify the nature and effects of the very narrative through which they thought and spoke. Austrians, from Nestroy through Karl Kraus, from Freud through Wittgenstein, were even more effective in creating tools for the careful analysis of motives and nuanced expression which might lead to a self-consciousness of their narrative norms.

In this essay, I show the bias of the distinct, singular national conventions of historical thought as they exist in the separate narrative conventions of Germany and Austria in the nineteenth and twentieth centuries. The political experience that created the respective narrative norms are sketched: the German narrative taking shape in the late medieval struggles between aristocracy, the urban patricians, and the suburban third estate; the Austrian narrative norms arising in the late medieval ascendancy of the dynastic family of the Habsburgs as Holy Roman Emperors. The political life of the Germanies, in the ceaseless strife of principality, suburb, and town, led to documents averring clear demarcations of rights and responsibilities between all parties. The German populations generated accordingly narrative conventions that underscored the didactic clarity of principle. The Austrian Habsburgs, on the other hand, were successful in using their authority as Holy Roman Emperors and as overlords in their own family lands to quell resistance. The medieval freedoms of the town disappeared, and administrative justice according to the will of the Habsburg rulers became a norm. Historical life in the Habsburg realms took on the character of an extended family, which in their historical narrative conventions became the historical logic of interdependence.

My demonstration of the differences in the German and the Austrian historical narrative is drawn from the discipline of economics, although any field of knowledge would illustrate the same historical-logical narrative conventions. The Germans Gustav Schmoller (1838–1917) and Max Weber (1864–1920) and the Austrian-Germans Carl Menger (1840–1921) and Ludwig von Mises (1881–1973) each are known for distinctive approaches that while sharing principles to some degree differ greatly in their individual contributions to economics. I show what is common to the Germans in contradistinction to the Austrians. The economic principles of these men that were developed out of their research into the economic events are shown to be influenced by the respective national culture's manner of relating a "right order" to events in time.

Events in time in the German culture are shaped into a narrative Gestalt (or "plot") that can be broadly understood as dialectical. The narrative Gestalt is adapted as illustrative and explanatory in the field of inquiry one pursues as a guide for explicating the narrative topics of time, place, manner, cause, and meaning. The German narrative plot as essentially dialectical treats time as always in ceaseless motion, yet characterized by stages that have a qualitative sameness. Time moves dialectically, in that the qualitative stages of its movement culminate in a period of resolution that reflects upon the times that have passed as its progenitors, but progenitors that have been surpassed. Consequently, one is shown changes in place, with an evaluation of the present state-of-affairs as being emergent and progressive. The manner of individual or group action reflects adherence to a consistent idea that in its didactic univocality encounters resistance from opposing ideas. The manner is that of encounter and resolution. Personal agency in its manner of motive and praxis is uncompromising: there are winners and losers in this "plot." Cause in time is seen as the dominating law, force, or condition. One can label cause as both the Aristotelian final and efficient causes: final in the telos suggested by idea; efficient in the willed agency of the individual in service of the idea or principle. Meaning then is essentially the idea that is pursued. This idea subsumes all persons, being an overarching unifier that coheres the heroes, villains, and incidental persons in its scope.

Events in the Austrian narrative can be understood as contributing to a morphological Gestalt or "plot." The Austrian narrative Gestalt can be broadly understood as morphological. Time is treated as a durational present that has emerged from a past whose fundaments are still within that present. Rather than ceaseless change and transcendence, as in the German plot, time for the Austrian is felt and known as a fulfillment of its ancestral beginnings–the oak that has emerged from the acorn, the adult who has grown from an infant.

Although changes are apparent, these changes are merely greater recognition of what has existed, what are one's roots. Places remain and are revisited. The present emerges out of the past as does the German, but for the Austrian this emergence is not a transcendent progress, rather a predicted development of what was. Manner is an interdependent, mutual and reciprocal interaction, where the separate acts of individuals in their aggregate effects complete common forms of existence and solve problems in-common. Thus, there are no winners or losers, only the whole "family" of Austria dwelling together, their very lives completing cultural forms that define and empower their coexistence. The Aristotelian formal and material causes comprehend the shape and dynamics of their narrative Gestalt: formal in that all individual and group striving is in service of a pattern that will configure the mutual forms of existence; material in that fulfillment requires close attention to the empirical facts of coexistence so that they can be cultivated without the vacillation and strife that come from merely an individual point-of-view. Meaning, then, is found in the aggregate of all individual actions, where a common whole becomes merely by the facts of coexistence, rather than a meaning that subsumes everyone under a univocal principle, as in the German plot.

The economic theories of Schmoller and Weber adhere in their meanings to univocal principles that define a milieu. Although the economic vision of Schmoller and Weber differed in many ways, the essential "plot" of their vision was the same because of a transgenerational historical logic shared by both men. Time, place, and manner focus upon the personal agency of individuals who through conflict-dominated encounter impress their truth upon a time. These narrative topics help these men and their readers comprehend certain facts in the history of economic practice, while at the same time limiting what can be comprehended because of the narrative stress upon encounter and resolution, change over time, and transcendence beyond what has been. The same is the case for the Austrians Menger and von Mises, whose economic theories seem vastly different and whose lives were separated by profound distances. The Austrian economic theories of Menger and von Mises in their national narrative structure, if applied to the same sets of data as the Germans, would yield other kinds of facts. Interdependence in economic cause and common practice tells a nondramatic story. Whether the social equity realized through Menger's marginal utility theory or the benefits of the wholly free market economy of von Mises, public policy needs no conflict preceding resolution or aspirations of transcendent purpose. What is in its complex interdependence is what becomes. The Austrian can point the way to civil peace, but the dark side of this vision is a curtailing of independent action or a realization that some conflict, some winning and losing, is necessary among ideas and the praxis they inform.

The duration of national historical logics is long and often warping in relation to an adequate grasp of contemporary realities. The transgenerational logic of history I present in each culture offers, respectively, truths that only that culture could reveal on the strength of its guiding concepts, but whose shadow side was the very bias, i.e., measure, that could generate such significant perspectives. National historical conventions arise slowly and pass away long after their time as adequate concepts for actual experience have gone.

2. HISTORICAL-LOGICAL NARRATIVE CONVENTIONS THAT DIFFERENTIATE HOW THE GERMAN AND AUSTRIAN-GERMAN ARTS AND SCIENCES CONCEIVE EVENTS IN TIME

> Language expresses thought and its perceptions as objects, but it also by following thought's rhythm...its pace, the continuity and discontinuity of its flux imparts the characteristic affinities by which differing nations order thought and perception.

> Wilhelm von Humboldt, *The National Character of Language* (c. 1823)

> The integration of the individual with the reinforcing stimulus and energy of the nation is the critical point in the spiritual economy of the human race.

> Wilhelm von Humboldt, *The Integration of Individuals and Nations* (1827–1829)

I selected two citations from Wilhelm von Humboldt as epigraphs for this contribution to the Crossing Bridges Conference as Humboldt's lifework remains fecund for contemporary historiography and the history of science. Humboldt asserted the centrality of language and its operations for any inquiry whatsoever, moreover how the rhythm and order of expression in itself creates temporality. Humboldt restated, if you will, the Greek root for inquiry which is historia.[1] All inquiry in its conduct and findings is in part an expression of a temporal order. Herodotus, credited as the first historian by Werner Jaeger, earned that title because of the "dramatic" element that showed the sequential order and consequent effects of human interactions (Jaeger 1974, 382). I bring to this conference a consideration into how the rhetorical narrative of any report of findings in the genres of the arts and the sciences of a nation is conditioned by the narrative conventions of that nation–and how that national style imparts a singular conception of time that colors its findings. I call this orientation an attention to a "national historical logic." Humboldt has been an inspiration to my research into historical logics since my work on linguistics and historiography began. In the recent past I have established forms of invariant historical logic that order the career of thought of individuals. A chapter in *Werner*

Sombart (1863–1941) Social Scientist that tracked the career of thought of Werner Sombart and Max Weber was illustrative of this concern with individual style.[2] The invariant personal logic I have found to be transnational and trans-generational. Since then I have focused upon the rhetorical conventions which are an additional layer of language and thought in any personal expression. These rhetorical conventions I have found to be identified with specific nations, at least since early modern Europe, as Humboldt so clearly saw.

Humboldt's concept of the "inner form" of thought and language, a logical-grammatical Gestalt which prereflectively imparts its form to each sentential judgment, is central to the evidence I examine of a lifelong style of historical logic in each individual, and a national historical logic, present in every generation, that plays its role in individual historical thinking.[3] A historical logic, as I will argue, is how one orders the succession of events or event-moments in one's experience. Historical time, as well as our immediate sense of time's passage, is generated by the continuities and/or discontinuities imparted to events and event-moments in our judgment. Humboldt emphasized the determinative influence of a national culture as it lends us the language to express our historical judgment.

As Humboldt suggests in the first epigraph, how one structures events imparts the rhythms of temporal succession to our vision of events. There is no cosmically uniform, qua objective, historical time. Historical time differs with each person judging the event in question. Historical time as a product of human cognition varies according to styles of temporal judgment. This is not a novel claim. Since Immanuel Kant, Western approaches to historiography have deepened our understanding of the cognitive complexities of historical judgment. The phenomenological and linguistic bases of my theory are linked to the history of analyses into the "deep structure" of cognition. I consider the historiographical heuristic I offer in this work to be within the phenomenological project begun with Immanuel Kant's views of the constitution of temporality in forms of cognition, and continued through Edmund Husserl's views of the logical-grammatical constitution of time. In my current work, however, I augment these linguistic-philosophical studies with contemporary investigations of narrative conventions in differing cultures. The second epigraph of Humboldt strengthens my resolve, as well as contemporary inquiry into narrative theory by Paul Ricoeur and Hayden White.[4]

Nationally, the conventions of a historical logic are known both informally in everyday expressions and in the more formal genres that govern the historical aspects of inquiry and expression. The genres of literature, historical writing, and scientific explanation into event-structures are composed intuitively out of the lexicon of temporal constructs provided by the individual historical logics. This intuitive construction is generated by the private as well as public demand for forms of narration that communicate a succession of events comprehensible to all parties. A narrative is a style of articulating the succession of events and event-moments of human experience.

A national historical logic will create a distinct schema of continuity and discontinuity, duration and change in what transpires. The schema of the national historical logic is not to be found within the single sentential judgment as is the schema of the individual historical logic. Rather, the national historical logic occurs over an entire narration, over the diachronic development of an exposition, explanation, or argument. All persons who mature in that culture take on this schema. As one becomes a professional, the genres which guide the professionalization carry the schema of the national historical logic. The closing decades of the nineteenth century marked the inception of a metacognitive awareness in the Western arts and sciences that laid the foundation for an assessment of the generational arbitrariness of disciplinary "logics," and the role of a disciplinary manner of ordering events in the inquirer's appreciation of temporality. Friedrich Nietzsche's criticism of historical consciousness was among this pioneering self-assessment. Astute critics within particular disciplines began to comment upon expository styles and changing generational norms in how historical evidence was presented. Ernst Mach revealed that the historical order of cause and effect in physics has had generational emphases in its exposition. Friedrich Meinecke gave his nation a detailed overview of its national historical logic of historicism. Nonetheless, the insights were limited to the disciplines. Awareness that both professionals and laypersons within a national culture in a particular generation were educated into the same "right order" of historical succession by the very forms of popular culture of a generation, and, in that generation, a metaparadigm shared among all the special fields of inquiry has remained an opaque reality. National standards of historicality are "opaque" because culture has as yet not demanded that one become aware of how time is stylized in either popular or scientific discourse, or how the national characteristics of historical judgment are wedded subtly to one's own invariant historical logic in every episode of historical judgment.

A national historical logic is a normative manner for that nation's populace of conceiving the nature and meaning of the historical flux of events. A national historical logic becomes a narrative, as through its accounts it orders the actions and interactions of individuals into sequences of behavior and issue resolution. A national historical logic in its variety of public expressions provides a model for not only interpreting the historical experience of what has been, but a model of normative historical order for one's contemporary public and private activity. It is created in response to the contingencies of historical experience. A national historical logic will change in its characteristics over time as a consequence of the nation's changing history. A national historical logic is not only the formal historiographical creations of those who practice the discipline of history. It is also the historical perspective of novelists, dramatists, journalists, and other professionals who contribute to the historical understanding of the nation's populace. The dissemination of a national historical logic is a combined effort of the many institutional expressions of the nation's culture–the press and other communications media, the schools, and other private and public organs.

My demonstration of the enduring national historical logics of Germany and Austria that can be traced to the early modern conceptions of change over time in the Germanies and in Austria rely not only upon the self-conscious conceptions of the people of these cultures. To be sure, the narrative constructions of historical experience by members of each nation were to some degree self-conscious artifacts of deliberation. Styles in their standards are explicable, but why these delineations of knowing and not others are less transparent. The cultural concept of "right order," found in every world culture, helps explain the intuitive limits of what makes sense in that nation's historical logic. Each discipline in its procedures and explanations within that culture's arts and sciences, every religious expression in its liturgical and ceremonial emphases, and even the common-sense norms of its everyday transactions will exhibit its cultural "right order." All world cultures have concepts that underscore the idea of a "right order" of things in time–in Greece it was the concept aidios, in Egypt maat, in China the tao.[5] The "right orders" change as the underlying values and intentions of a nation change. At times there is a general agreement, at times competing "right orders." One is educated into national historical-logical norms as one learns to communicate in written (and oral) expression. An example of the logical-grammatical presence of such a norm in the English culture of the Tudor and Stuart era is that of antithesis, a pervasive tropic figure in the construction of the sentence of that time. This semantic style, with its syntactical structuring, may have been how the political-social tensions were sustained.[6] Arthur Joseph Slavin has written of the Tudor-Stuart generations as a time of "permanent crisis" in which conflict was normative.[7]

3.   THE POLITICAL HISTORY OF GERMANY AND AUSTRIA OVER THE CENTURIES, AND THE NORMS OF "RIGHT ORDER" THAT CORRESPOND WITH THAT HISTORY

There was always a cleft between German and Austrian political history, before and after the Enlightenment, that had an influence on how citizens of each nation perceived the nature of their historical experience. While both the

German and the Austrian political tradition have favored a strong centralist presence in governance, the relation and practice of the ruler to the ruled within the centralist aegis differed markedly. Reviewing each nation's practice of cameralism between the seventeenth and nineteenth centuries provides a basis for discerning the differing "right orders" in regard to governance of the two nations. Correspondingly, I will derive the historical-logical norms of the two nations out of these differences in governance. Cameralism was a mode of governance that justified aristocratic executive leadership of all interests, groups, and classes of the nation.[8] Since Jean Bodin's writing in 1576 on the res publica (the republic) as the public space of all best served by an aristocratic ruler,[9] German and Austrian political thought justified the respective "right order" of their stewardship within this perspective. Bodin had challenged John Calvin's earlier notion that the "natural law" of God in regard to the self-governance of humankind did not distinguish between aristocrat and commoner. Calvin held that every responsible citizen regardless of family heritage had the right to be an executive authority in the community if he was a presbyter, a wise one who was an elect of God and thereby suited to establish his community of saints.[10] Calvin's notion led to government by councils of the people, and subsequently to legislatures where every presbyter could voice an individual point-of-view. Calvinist governance ideation became a justification for republican principles of government by the seventeenth century.[11] The Calvinism of the Hohenzollerns and other aristocrats, as I will discuss below, adopted Bodin's notion of "natural law" whereby the stewardship of the community of saints remained in the authority of aristocrat executives. Bodin's thought supported the forms of administrative leadership of the King's ministers, administrative leadership that became known as cameralism by the seventeenth century. Cameralism set itself against the republican principle of the majority will, a will criticized by those in sympathy with cameralism tenets as the will of the common, propertied person.[12]

Despite their mutual adherence to cameralist doctines, the practice of German and Austrian cameralists differed, the differences lying in the normative relations between ruler and ruled that had developed over centuries. The half-millenium Habsburg dynasty gave a paternalistic pattern to Austrian political life. The strength of this "family-oriented" norm was in the highly interpersonal tone of political life. Austrian cameralism at its best was a benign outreach by bureaucratic officials into the daily lives of its charges, in a face-to-face encounter that legislative governance could not so equitably match. The practical outcome of legislative governance is largely the will of majority interests; cameralism is even-handed case-by-case decision. German cameralism leaned toward governmental structures and statute law, more impersonal and principle-based than the practice of Austrian cameralism

(Sommer 1967, 6, 12).[13] The Austrian personalism is evidenced in the stress by their cameralist theorists on the "style" of face-to-face intersubjectivity between the administrative official and the client.[14] Both Austrian and German cameralism, however, conceived the authority of the central government as a nonpartisan force that cared for the interests of all in the state, favoring no group or class interest. Indeed, the Austrian and German political ethos into the twentieth century depicted the best political leader as above party interest, a person who was the Führer of all the people. The profound contributions in interpersonal understanding that arose in the forms of practice in Austrian psychiatry, law, drama, literature, and the fine arts in nineteenth and early twentieth century fin-de-siècle culture can be linked to this stress on reaching cooperative, common practices. Faust had no place in Austrian culture.

The problem of a "'family-oriented" norm in governance was in the inevitable weakening of a self-directed, assertive political will among the members of the society. Kant's recognition that one cannot be "given" freedom perhaps stemmed from his observation on the discontent of many freed serfs, and the discomfort of religious minorities with the new public schools in Joseph II's Austria. The self-concept of individual Austrians never freed itself from the presence of others for whom one must care or whose care one must recognize. The strengths of this interpersonal world were in its cultivation of an accurate recognition in the arts and the sciences of interdependence and its facilitating forms of empathy. From the early eighteenth century Hanswurst through Kafka's Momus in *Das Schloss*, the rough humor of another's barbed penetration of private aims and a too self-absorbed project will bring the Austrian individual back to the gravity of an interdependent world. The weakness of this embeddedness among others was in a discomfort with the final responsibility and aloneness of selfhood that bred for the German the Faustian paradigm. The Austrian political horizon will never leave its past behind to start fresh, no more than the prodigal son could ever fully distance himself from his parents. The Austrian selection of a morphological logic as the dominant form of national historical norm contributes both to the collective, i.e., interdependent, and to the conservative quality of its historical thought. In a morphological logic, all facts contribute to the form, each individual action plays its role in the mutually shared form to which all contribute. While a morphological thinker need not be a political conservative, there is a "conserving" aspect to all morphological thinkers in that historical forms never completely disappear, and for the most part are always in a phase of becoming.

The Germanies, on the other hand, had norms for historical life that for each individual stimulated more public assertion. The ceaseless competition that existed among the princes in the hundreds of principalities, a competition that was dynastic and religious, set a conflict-oriented model of public life. Moreover, the patriciate of the towns were in conflict with the princes since the late middle ages. The suburban artisans and peasants were milieus that gravitated between alliances or conflict with the urban patriciate and the lower aristocratic landowners of the surrounding country. Every social class knew that only self-assertion could protect its rights. Thus arose an active citizenship in the Germanies, even against the aristocracy's continual attempts to frustrate the sharing of public power. In most German states administrative governance did not even have the mask of benign interest. The government as an extended family was not the norm. German historical norms also isolated the individual, not cultivating that state as an "extended family." The individual as an isolate will who found community only through common principle made law more salient than in the patrimonial state of Austria. In the years between 1200 and 1500 when citizen rights flourished in the German cities, the constant, often conflicting claims of autonomy, rights, and responsibilities between the city and the aristocratic ruler became normative. In that same time, citizen rights ended in Austria. The burghers of the Austrian cities from the rule of Emperors Rudolf I through Maximilian gradually lost all the medieval privileges they had gained by the end of the Hohenstaufen Emperors. The proximity of the Habsburg Dukes, the Luxemburg focus upon the Eastern Empire, and then the Habsburg residence in Bohemia and Austria contributed to this steady dissipation of burgher privileges.[15] Justice was increasingly a product of the Emperor's goodwill, rather than as became the Germanic bourgeois norm, justice wrought by the fair application of an impersonal law.

While the period between 1500 and the Enlightenment in Austria brought increasing control of every facet of public life by the Habsburg Emperors, in the Germanies Calvin's vision of "natural law," which bound ruler and ruled by contractual clarity, grew in its influence. Frederick William, the Great Elector of Brandenburg-Prussia, became a Calvinist, and his attention to the highly differentiated rights and responsibilities that already existed in the Hohenzollern domains was underscored by the Calvinist emphasis upon natural law,[16] albeit interpreted from the point of view of the tradition of Bodin (a perspective soon to be formulated for the Prussian rulers by Samuel Pufendorf).[17] The educated commoners of Brandenburg-Prussia and the other Germanies gravitated toward a natural rights conception of membership in the state that even more radically conceived the distribution of political authority than Frederick William's circumspect understanding of the rights and responsibilities of ruler to ruled. Johannes Althusius articulated a natural rights individualism that enhanced the already existent norms where each social group asserted its traditional autonomy and rights.[18] Kant's fourth thesis in his essay on an Idea for Universal History restated this natural law emphasis for the bourgeois classes in its stress on individuality and law: "the means employed by Nature to bring about the development of all the capacities of men is their antagonism in society, so far as this is, in the end, the cause of a lawful order among man."[19] Individuals kept their own counsel, and acted as a rule with great self-direction. Ideas were more of a helpmeet than other people. Ideas gave justification for going it alone, publicly and privately. Principles were the best company. Where Germans formed associations so that common, collective action could be made, these associations were organized in their means and ends with clear role and scope so that an individual knew his or her place within them, and could differentiate this engagement from the other aspects of their private and public commitments.

The weakness of the German norms lay in the very strengths of their individual self-direction that was justified by idea, for it led to an overweening individualism taken to extremes of imbalance. One might compare Kleist's Michael Kohlhaas or Goethe's Faust to Austrian heros such as the civil servant in Grillparzer's *Ein treuer Diener seiner Herrn* or Kafka's counterexample to the Kleis or Faustian heroes, in his Karl Rossman of *Amerika*, Josef K. of *Der Prozess*, or K. of *Das Schloss*, all individuals who learn difficult, but necessary lessons of interdependence. A healthy democratic society requires cooperative models as well as individualistic models. Individualistic self-assertion is reinforced for the Germans by a historicism whose expression sharpens individual encounter, contrast, and contradiction. The Austrian historical narrative norms will be muted by a stress on the cooperative aspects of an encounter, a reflection of the omnipresent "family-oriented" background of their dynastic public world. And, thus, the weakness will be in an overdetermination of the individual by his or her milieu and other determining factors that subdue individual will and idea. For the Austrian, every new beginning was weighted with the past and its own finite possibilities. For the Austrian, mortality was an omnipresent aspect of new beginnings, a fact which the seemingly eternal round of birth and death within the Habsburg dynasty seemed to verify, and perhaps to which it contributed. State sovereignty had a very human proportion in the Habsburg state. The Austrian concern with death that William M. Johnston has discerned in almost every field of the arts and the sciences, as well as in everyday expression of cultural life, may be rooted in this dynastic model.[20] Germany and Austria can be said to have engendered in their historical attitudes vastly different normative Weltanschauungen, even upon the same historical-logical bases.

**4.   THE PERSISTING CHARACTERISTICS
OF GERMAN AND AUSTRIAN NARRATIVES
IN THE ARTS AND THE SCIENCES FROM
THE ENLIGHTENMENT TO THE PRESENT**

A narrative is an account of events that can be considered to convey a meaning that grows out of the what, where, when, why, and how of the events, but a meaning that is also generated by the temporal-spatial order these events constitute in the narrative account. My thesis is that the temporal-spatial Gestalt of the narrative as a whole reflects a temporal-spatial order that has a unity rhetorically configured by the historical logic of national conventions (even as individual differences exist imparted by the character of the individual author). The national norms will be shown to be a temporal-spatial Gestalt that conditions narratives in the sciences as well as the arts. There is a normative Gestalt that is more primary and pervasive than even the paradigmatic genres which exist in specific disciplines. The disciplinary genres themselves, within which an individual must communicate, are formed within the temporal-spatial design of what might be called the metaparadigmatic Gestalt which is the deep background of how time is experienced in the culture. The metaparadigmatic Gestalt consists of temporal-spatial properties that can be found in the disciplinary paradigms of all fields within a given generation or more.

The genres within a discipline adapt themselves to the temporal-spatial metaparadigm of the culture in a given time, the persistence of a particular genre in a field contemporaneous with the persistence of the metaparadigm. Thus, in German literature, for example, the Bildungsroman and the novelle are two genres which come to be in the late Enlightenment, in a time when the German arts and the sciences were guided by a temporal-spatial narrative metaparadigm that imparted progressive development (the Bildungsroman) through transvaluative understandings that guided actions into new directions (the novelle).

German and Austrian political-social realities between the Enlightenment and the present have created conditions in which the narrative designs of account and explanation in the two cultures' arts and sciences have preserved several essential temporal-spatial characteristics.

The model narrative is explicated as a "plot" in that time, place, manner, cause, and the rhetorical mode by which causation and meaning are explained within the narrative form a coherent Gestalt in which each of these categories reinforces the other. I use "plot" in the traditional sense of a narrative schema constructed of the unities of time, place, and manner, and the variations that offer meaningful departures from these unities.

Table 1. Historical Narrative Structure

German

1. Configuring Gestalt or plot: time, place, and manner:
   a. time: the past ceases to be as significant as the present; however, the past is preserved by being reconceived or refigured as a surpassed ancestor of the present.
   b. place: changes as action or motive changes.
   c. manner: form imposed by concept; concept frames beginning and ending; single voice, dominant character.
2. Cause in history:
   a. one dominating cause of a state of affairs.
   b. cause is idea or other intangible that can never be completely known empirically.
   c. conflict and contrast of defined realities, potentialities, etc.
3. Personal agency and the historical event: individual will dominates; intersubjectivity is mediated by a personal point of view: inspired or in service of the one law, force, or condition.
4. Historical meaning/explanation:
   a. Dialectical and didactic certainty: thesis posed, defended, and elevated as principle or law.
   b. The one and the many: the parts are at once individuals, yet members that are comprehended by an overarching whole.

Austrian

1. Configuring Gestalt or plot: time, place, and manner:
   a. time: the past is continuing matrix of the present; the past remains the leaven of meaning for each new moment.
   b. place: perduring; remains a present, revisited, or absent context.
   c. manner: form cohered from tangible events and interactions; sensual image, rather than concept, frames beginning and ending; multiple voices; no character dominates without a dialogical participation with others.
2. Cause in history:
   a. many mutual interacting causes.
   b. psychic or physical causes empirically discoverable.
   c. integrative unity among defined realities.
3. Personal agency and the historical event: intersubjectivity dominates; each point of view has its own just authority; individual destiny never isolate.
4. Historical meaning/explanation:
   a. Morphological and problematic certainty: questions posed and deliberated.
   b. The one and the many: the parts while individuals are simultaneously parts that cumulatively constitute a whole (rather than being comprehended by an overarching whole).

The German national "plot" institutes a temporal-spatial thesis at the onset of any account, and a concluding temporal-spatial reconfiguration, whose symbiosis imparts a phenomenal time that is strikingly different than the temporalization of similar events in any other national culture. German temporal-spatialization initiates in its alpha, or opening statement, the temporal rhythm and sequence that governs all events and relationships in its account, which finally in its omega remarks creates a revisioning of all that has transpired, inviting the audience to revisit its understandings. The alpha is a didactic conceptual overview of the issue at hand that functions as the overarching concept in continuity logic. The omega is the type of transvaluation of what has transpired that is akin to the orthodox dialectical synthesis. This temporal-spatial model seeks to impart clarity concerning any immediate orientation to what is at issue, and to encourage a change in how the state of affairs is conceived after presenting the events under discussion. There is an intention in the "plot" to encourage sameness among individuals so that a national effort can be cohered.

The Austrian "plot" assumes a pervasive form that coheres a common national effort no matter how many individual differences are expressed in the historical flux. The Austrian "plot" seeks conservation of the past, preservation of the ground that has existed, articulating in its temporal-spatial model a design that reflects its half-millenium dynastic governance of a multinational population. Austrian temporalization is an unfolding of a time defined initially, with what I will call "problematic certainty." There is not the clarity of purpose and meaning announced in the German narrative. What overarches for the Austrian is the formal cause dimly perceived by a citizenry who must fathom the dynastic state of an ancient family, the Habsburgs, whose public realms express the omissions, commissions, and difficult-to-discern direction of its public policies. The enduring issues of the realm and the sameness of how these issues were addressed through public policy bred a morphological logic in which the end is foreseen in the beginning, but the whole only metaphorically intuited. The actions of public authorities that seem consistent, as well as those that are contradictory to what has been the case, generate for the Austrian questions and problems rather than measurable outcomes (as in the German narrative). There is a conclusion to an Austrian narrative, but even in that coming to be of the form articulated, the conclusion reiterates the issues, problems, and deliberations that began the narrative–as if the aporias that generated inquiry, and consequently story, will continue despite the conclusion. Rather than reconfigure time in a dramatic transvaluation, the Austrian absorbs all events into the initial temporal design, demonstrating the perdurance of that temporal rhythm and sequence. The Austrian alpha and omega are the same: a protean form established by metaphorical intuition whose image is sufficiently permeable to entail all passing circumstances in its locus, a protean form restated in a metaphorical recapitulation of what has transpired. The Austrian does not wrap up history in a didactic package of episodic accounts that exemplify the point and purpose first drawn–as does the German. Rather, the Austrian recognizes the riddle-like nature of the public realm in all its historical life. This riddle-like beginning and ending of the Austrian narrative metaparadigm infuses its aporetic structure into the sciences and the arts.

Temporal and spatial configurations normative in the narratives of the German or Austrian culture are the foundation upon which certain causes are discerned in human and natural events. The German stresses successive cause-effect sequences generated by the immediacy of historical agents overarched by a final cause that informs rather than compels. The Austrian stresses a formal cause that makes the historical agent one who finds accord with a preexisting form, rather than as the Germanic individual who being but informed by abstract final causes is freer to interpret and to innovate how historical forms express those realities.

The event-structure of the narrative in Germany or Austria is generated and bounded by their respective temporal-spatial foundations. The event-structure is expressed within the beginnings, associations, and endings of the persons, places, and things according to the temporal-spatial design as a whole, which Hayden White and Paul Ricoeur have called "deep temporality," the summative design functioning as a formal causal pattern, and the phases that mark the development of its narrative progress, which Hayden White and Paul Ricoeur call its "historicality," those temporal-spatial conceptions which generate the pattern.[21] The concept of "manner" enters into my explication at this point. How the interrelations of the several temporal-spatial components which constitute the event-structure occur, especially as comprehended by the German and Austrian humanities and the social sciences, give a human proportion to the "plot." "Manner" in the national narrative model is understood as not only the kind of action, but how the character of the historical agents, and the cause and meaning their actions are explained, and assessed (which have been part of "manner" since Aristotle).[22] Aristotle refers to "thought" which "is shown in everything to be effectedby (the protagonist's) language" (Poetics, 1456a, 37) as the basis for comprehending the "qualities of their action" (Poetics, 1450b, 38+). Aristotle calls the discipline which can identify and explicate this narrative thought, rhetoric (Poetics, 1456a, 35).

The characteristics of "plot" indicated in Table 1 remained the same over the centuries of German and Austrian narrative design because of the long-term constancies of political-social experience. As I have asserted, the political authority of the nation, and the effects of that authority on the social life of the populace, are the most definitive single factor in generating the normative historical narrative that presumes to explain and guides one's interactions. Even when the aristocratic authorities of King and Emperor were replaced by democratic republics in Germany and Austria, I will indicate how features of the political-social contingencies warranted the maintaining of the by then traditional "plot" characteristics for the respective cultures.

Hayden White supports Hegel's assertion that a "genuine historical account" has "to display not only a certain form, namely, the narrative, but also a certain content, namely, a politico-social order" (1987, 11). The politico-social order is the contingent cause of the narrative structure for Hegel (and White) because "it is only the state which first presents subject-matter that is not only adapted to the prose of History, but involves the production of such history in the very progress of its own being" (1987, 12). In other words, a common, objective public world is the basis of a unified history for a populace. White goes on in his explication of Hegel's insight into the roots of narrative by pointing to the forms of authority in a culture that give definition and design to its historical narrative.

But once we have been alerted to the intimate relationship that Hegel suggests exists between law, historicality, and narrativity, we cannot but be struck by the frequency with which narrativity, whether of the fictional or the factual sort, presupposes the existence of a legal system against which or on behalf of which the typical agents of a narrative account militate. And this raises the suspicion that narrative in general, from folktale to the novel, from the annals to the fully realized "history," has to do with the topics of law, legality, legitimacy, or, more generally, authority (1987, 13).

White's reaffirmation of the Hegelian doctrine that the presence of a particular form of political state legislates what the historical narrative structure of a time is to be, includes also the assertion (with which I concur) that all the narrative forms of a culture, not only the historiography proper, owe their shape to the influence of this comprehensive authority. White does not argue that the authoritative persons in charge of the state create the narratives, rather that what is law, legitimate and authoritative, influences what the narrative becomes. Rebels too can write the narratives because they address the legitimacy which they wish to change. Thus, political-social reality in its "legality, legitimacy, ... authority" gives its slant to what becomes the conception of temporal-spatial events no matter who within that state seeks to affect how events transpire within the authoritative order.

A political authority must affect the concept of historical flux to preserve its own dominance in how public events are conceived and treated. Opponents of the legitimate order must affect its existing definitions if they are to gain public power. A populace that has a public life in common must insist upon commonly understood time, place, and manner to effect comprehensible solutions in its address of its diverse needs. To ignore the common narrative, or to insist on a separate narrative, is either to declare civil war or to retreat into public anomie.

The characteristics of the national "plot" listed for Germany and Austria in Table 1 are a "plot" for any sequence of events deemed sufficiently meaningful to relate, whatsoever. Contrary stories concerning a common issue by members of the national culture will be organized, regardless of the differing values and even cause-effect implications, according to the existing national plot. Any story–that of the life of a plant, a diplomatic mission, or the plight of an abandoned child–is fit within the temporal-spatial narrative design of "how" this story is told. The rebel, the scientist, the historian, the politician–all narrate the content pertinent to them in this narrative model. In the arts or "human" sciences, this narrative model offers a vision of cause and effect, and import, that has the singular insight only its narrative Gestalt can impart. In the natural sciences, the narrative model likewise imparts a singular truth: what is shown depends upon the style of revelation, and that style opens aspects of natural phenomena that no other discursive account can exactly replicate. Moreover, there is no account of objective facts in any culture that does not reflect the angle of understanding that a national narrative provides.

Although proofs of the enduring German and Austrian narrative model will have to await my more thorough discursive accounts and illustrations of the artistic and scientific narratives in my ongoing work, I can offer a list of short explanations at this point from the aspect of contingent political cause that account for the characteristics I assert gave shape to the essential "plot" of German and Austrian narratives from the Enlightenment until the present.

5.   CONTINGENT POLITICAL-SOCIAL REASONS THAT GAVE RISE TO THE GERMAN AND AUSTRIAN NATIONAL NARRATIVE MODEL

5.1.   Historical meaning/explanation

1. Germany opens and closes every narrative with a didactic definition of what is the true or false state of affairs because in its political-social culture, the existing authority and those who abided by or challenged the authority, adhered to or strove to effect their will by legal processes that required clear discrimination of rights and responsibilities. The tradition of conflicting interests in the Germanies required an even-handed scale for decision-making and public order. Kleist's Michael Kohlhaas is a tale that exemplifies this didactic clarity as a private individual seeks public justice (which one can contrast with the Austrian

problematic/riddle-like mode of beginning and ending accounts of private individuals who seek public justice, for example, Grillparzer's Ein Treuer Diener Seiner Herrn or Kafka's Das Schloss). Since the Enlightenment, the natural law premises of equality before the law required rational and scientific justification of authority. Dynastic rulers gave credence to these concepts. The Weimar Republic and post-World War II Germany maintained this emphasis upon law, and circumstances throughout the twentieth century have kept its culture so conflict-ridden that rights and responsibilities were and are constantly an issue.

2. Austria opens every narrative with a statement of "problematic certainty," either a pregnant question or a state of affairs that is to be addressed or solved. The closing statement is a reiteration of the question or even an assertion that nothing will ever be settled definitively. This raising of the question to a higher status than an answer can be tracked within the Austrian mode of governance to the access to and exercise of public authority through and by fallible individuals–the Habsburg dynasty and their administrative appointees. Administrative decision-making was always more important than equality before the law. In the absence of a tradition of public conflict, the Habsburgs were unchallenged in their administrative governance, where personal contacts and contexts were the bases of justice. Intensifying this emphasis on contextual reality that made law and justice a human artifact rather than natural law was the ambiguity attached to the Habsburg authority over many of their lands. Since Frederick III, the Habsburgs considered their lands Austrian and dynastic property, while others saw many of these lands as Imperial property merely to be governed by the legally elected Emperor. This arguably paradoxical status of the realm was finessed by the Habsburg assertion of dynastic authority where justice and truth emanated from the person, rather than the more abstract bases of natural law. The Habsburg Emperors traced their station to Rome, and even before the Caesars to Aeneas.[23] Historical circumstances generated a continuation of this essentially patrimonial governance in the First Republic, by political groups whose authority was centered in personal vision of a leader who headed a hierarchical party, dedicated to the welfare of their "extended family," the nation. Even today Austria has the most cameralist, qua corporate form of public governance in the West.[24]

   Patrimonial wisdom is explicitly or tacitly recognized as an attempt to master destiny. Its decisions are by their very nature more fallible, even when more humane, than transcendental principles.

3. The Germanic "one and many" has its ideological beginnings in the nature of the German communities themselves, where individuals had radical

autonomy, yet were also envisioned as integral members of the whole they comprised (cf. Otto von Gierke, Das deutsche Genossenschaftsrecht (Graz: Akademische Druck u. Verlagsanstalt, 1954)). The one, yet the many was a principle of political-social reality, although these dual poles of identity created no problems, and preexisted philosophical principles within the culture. The encounter of the separate Germanic communities with Charlemagne and the formation of an Empire based on Roman Law created a more conscious awareness of the one and the many. The encounter generated the need for a synthesis between two conceptions and codes of law: the Roman and the customary law of the German communities. Charlemagne's "personality principle" enabled the gradual integration of the two legal systems in each of the separate Germanic communities. The encounter of the idea of Empire and Roman Law with German community law (which in itself harbored a vision of the one and the many that composed a community) transmitted this ideational model in subsequent cultural thought.

4. The one as a cumulative product of the many in Austrian thought, in contradistinction to the Germanies' vision of the many comprehended by the one, is differentiation that grew out of the multiethnic composition of an Austrian Empire, controlled by one family, whose pragmatic control removed the kind of political-social autonomy that enabled the other Germanies to see the separateness of the many more clearly. The ancient German community in its seamless shift from the one to the many among its members was more evident in Austrian political life than in the conflict-ridden distance between the one and the many of the German model.

5.2.   Cause in history

1. Germany perceives a single, dominant cause in history as a consequence of its particularistic heritage. Ridden by conflicts among estates and interest groups within the small principalities in which these differences must coexist and cooperate, the Germanies preferred solutions that insisted upon a commonalty. Ethnic and regional homogeneity supported the desire for univocality. Winners and losers in this conflict were inevitable, but were a more realistic solution for the geopolitical reality than a multiplicity of truths in one realm.

   Moreover, the many states sought a unity beyond themselves that might cohere them into one nation–thus, the continual dream of a Reich. Abstract concept was a standard that gave unity to diversity. The cause can never be known completely as an empirical phenomenon because it is idea, rather than fact (one thinks of Schiller's remark reminding Goethe that an Urpflanze is a genus idea, not an actual plant). The fact that the Germanies were always subject in some respect to the Imperial throne, if only the feudal authority to grant titles, contributed to the sense of an omnipresent, yet invisible higher authority which stood for common standards. The greater reliance on law than upon cameralist personalism (as in Austria) was a reflection of the need to ameliorate differences that seemed otherwise unbridgeable. The extreme individualism, and lesser concern with interpersonal realities, also contributed to the habit of mind in the individual of believing one's own idea unified everyone.

2. Austria recognizes many interacting causes, all of which can be brought fully to empirical demonstration (think of Austrian phenomenology). The good administrator has such a purview. The inclination to see events as constituted by many, reciprocal causes, i.e., capable of being integrated into a system, is reinforced by an awareness of the interpersonal, multi-sourced bases of political-social realities.

All aspects of the reciprocal, binding causes can be known when all are shown in their interrelated system. In a dynastic, personalized governance there are no hidden or intangible unifiers.

5.3.   Personal agency and the historical event

1. German narratives give "just authority" to one protagonist, and possibly his or her adherents. The justifying idea forms an arena within which the protagonist must move to be hero. Without the efficient cause whereby the hero "wills" that idea there is no coherent plot. Act knits thought into historical fact. German political-social history has been an arena of contested ideas, a constant address and redress of a population's cultural life. A political-social leader can make a significant difference in the name of this idea in his or her lifetime.

2. Austrian narratives, as the cameralist governance that serves as their model, have no place for protagonist-heroes who overcome their enemies. Everyone is a member of a system of just interactions in Austria, where everyone receives a due measure of support and criticism. There is no tragedy; rather, tragicomedy. The forms of interpersonal inter-actions are more significant than an individual will. Actions should integrate everyone, rather than extirpate someone. Actions self-evidently carry historical truth or error: they need no ideological setting. The self-evidence comes from what an audience knows to be normative.

The historical event, as in Austrian political-social history, is a conservation and readjustment, rather than the definitive change of the German historical event.

5.4.   *Configuring Gestalt or plot: time, place, and manner*

1. Time, place, and manner change constantly for the German, but always within a single idea or purpose established in the initial statement of the narrative account. The governing agent who sets the purpose, with its concomitant rhythms of change in time, place, and manner, is the authoritative individual. Change is constant from the political-social perspective because all citizens strive to realize purposes. The unifying idea or purpose which informs individual action is perceived as a universal idea. Kant's categorical imperative is one of the clearest articulations of the German relationship between the individual and the collective in the nation. One knows unity with others best through the idea one pursues, for that idea is a potential guide for everyone.

   "Place" changes constantly for the German, because life is oriented to modifying any moment in the service of the goal to be realized. The German "manner" of action is infused with self-reflective commentary in every moment because consideration of one's purposes is the most salient medium for binding the constantly changing movement of one's course of life. The revisioning of the course of events offers the protagonists as well as audience one more opportunity as well as an alternative understanding in attributing purposeful significance to what has transpired.

   The Peace of Westphalia which gave each Prince the right to define the purposes and manner of life within his principalities is an ideal-typical standard for authority in a life for the German individual. (There were many political statements of this type of political-social autonomy in German history before 1648–The Golden Bull of 1356 and the 1231 Statute of Cividale are examples.) Extreme autonomy is enabled by a common system of rights and responsibilities. The narrative of Goethe's Faust is the fictional equivalent of the Peace of Westphalia. An ideal-typical life of a self-defining individual is the alpha and omega of public, as well as private meaning.

2. Interactions generate the configuration of a plot for the Austrian. No single motive or rationale dominates in an action, rather each action produces overtones of reciprocal and mutual interests. The Aristotelian notion of actions as the formative medium of plot, rather than character serving as a cohering medium, is particularly true for the Austrian.

A character's actions for the Austrian are never solely to individuate his or her character, rather each action is an interaction designed to facilitate an occasion for the fate or individuation of everyone touched by that action. Moreover, since in Austria so many ethnicities existed with differing folkways that any public interaction begun by public policy had many unintended ripples in many directions. The questions addressed by public policies remained questions even after much decision-making and interaction.

Aristotle tells us that an action does not so much contribute to the character of the agent, as it does to a quality of life. An action is a certain kind of activity that facilitates life (Poetics, 1954, 230–231 [1450a], 17–21). If he had specified "life among others," then it would be cast more as an Austrian insight. For the Austrian administrator a political decision must facilitate life among others. It can do that well or poorly, but in any event a decision has a ripple effect on many.

The past remains as the source of meaning as every present action positively or negatively facilitates what has been begun already by others, both present and absent from view. Environments change hardly at all in the Austrian narrative because the focus is upon the evolving form of the interacting lives.

The narrative characteristics of Table 1 pervade the sciences as well as the arts. One need only substitute for persons flora and fauna: the individualism of the German in contradistinction to the interpersonal understandings of the Austrian are translated, respectively, into attention to salient, single efficient causes and transforming states in contrast to reciprocal causes and ecologies with more duration.

6. NATIONAL HISTORICAL NARRATIVE CONVENTIONS IN THE POLITICAL ECONOMICS OF GUSTAV SCHMOLLER, MAX WEBER, CARL MENGER, AND LUDWIG VON MISES

A short review of the historical narrative structures of the German and Austrian-German istoria introduces a more careful analysis of specimen works of Sombart, Weber, Menger, and Mises. The German "plot" is unified by the ideas that are salient among the persons of a generation, with a protagonist that exemplifies the key idea, and an antagonist that exemplifies what must be and is overcome. Historical meaning is the unity of idea under which all persons, places, and things are subsumed. The unity of idea as idea is a general truth that the modest honesty of its norms allows to be an ideal type, rather than exhaustive. The German preserves a degree of mystery in the presentation of its narrative realities–that which cannot be completely discerned or understood. The pressure of time and change contribute to this narrative convention (the Austrian will always have time to thoroughly reveal what is problematic) .For the German, the unities of time, place, and manner stress ceaseless change, with past principles being refashioned to become again dominant under new conditions or to be overcome by competing principles. History can veer in differing directions, so that the Aristotelian efficient cause–personal agency–is more significant than the Austrian preference for determinative interdependent patterns–the Aristotelian formal cause–which manifest reciprocal effects. For the German there are winners and losers in history; for the Austrian only differing saliences generated by a multiplicity of individuals, with "winner" or "loser" not in the cultural vocabulary.

The Austrian cultural whole is the human family with its sons and daughters and parents being that whole. There is nothing other than the human family or "the family of humankind." Historical time is human time. Time is the mortal life in all its stages and phases, and it is relative to each who experiences it. The Austrian does not speak of a "Zeitgeist." If there is a Zeitgeist, it is always an ambiance that is difficult to define, nonetheless empirically describable as a phenomenal reality–as problematic as the atmosphere of a family. Robert Musil's much-reported characterization of his "age" captures the Austrian problematic certainty that is like a member of a family describing the holiday dinner: "The time was on the move. But in those days no one knew what it was moving towards. Nor could anyone quite distinguish between what was above and what was below, between what was moving forwards and what backwards."[25] The Austrian has been accused of having no "Übergeschichte" ("conceptual overview") like the German.[26] History is merely how people live and what they are. The German cultural whole, on the other hand, is that of the abstract unity that is greater than the sum of its parts. There are generational divisions and Zeitgeists: the German individually is always affected by the unity of the time. Humans first and foremost must accommodate themselves to the univocality that is the time, not to the diverse temporalities of each other.

Gustav Schmoller's 1884 chapter on The Mercantile System and Its Historical Significance in his *Studien über die wirthschaftliche Politik Friedrich des Grossen*, reproduced in English in 1897 as a self-contained essay, will serve as an example of the Germanic narrative "plot" in his works.[27] The "plot" of Schmoller's text is in its comprehensive meaning the univocal idea of mercantilism, a concept for Schmoller that aside from its name as a European system of economics between roughly 1500 and 1800 was a principle that even earlier and later described "the aegis of government authority in economic planning."

Schmoller used the term "mercantilism" ("mercantilismus"), but his intended meaning is more political than merely the economic meaning the term took on in the English-speaking world (cf. note 13).

One is immediately struck by the ages of ceaseless development and reconfiguration through which the mercantilist idea emerged, each age reconfiguring its meaning.

> In association with the tribe, the mark, the village, the town (or city), the territory, the state, and the confederation certain definite economic organisms have been successively evolved of ever wider scope: herein we have a continuous process of development, which, though it has never accounted for all the facts of economic life, has, at every period, determined and dominated it (1967, 3).

Each of these political units, dominating in its respective times, was considered a whole. The economic developmental principle that ran through all these political units differed in small, but in large the principle was that of "the sole agency of governing body in its functional representatives to stipulate the economic life." The policies of this whole subsumed all citizenry to its purpose. Otto von Gierke has helped us understand how this whole was an "undivided unity," more than the aggregative sum of each individual, in his Genossenschaftsrecht.[28] Schmoller states:

> The citizen body looked upon itself as forming a whole, and a whole that was limited as narrowly as possible, and for ever bound together (1967, 7).

The unity was a political/economic principle of association which might change, and with it its form, but always that principle cohered the criteria for the unity.

Schmoller creates an adversary in each phase of the mercantilist principle. The parent political unit had to be ever vigilant against other political units and miscellaneous strangers. Encounter was the rule. In speaking of the towns, for example, Schmoller creates the vision of a ceaseless war against nonmembers:

> The omnipotence of the council ruled the economic life of the town, when in its prime, with scarcely any limit; it was supported in all its action by the most hard-hearted town selfishness and the keenest town patriotism,–whether it were to crush a competing neighbour or a competing suburb, to lay heavier fetters on the country around, to encourage local trade or to stimulate local industries (1967, 8).

Schmoller's adjectives and adverbs adhere to the "town" and its institutions, not individuals directly. All persons will take on these characteristics. The "manner" is a single voice possessed by all. Personal agency is apparent in its many actions, that is, an efficient causal incrementalism, but it is a personal agency writ large that is assumed to be shared by all, with no individual variation:

> Market-rights, toll-rights, and mile-rights are the weapons with which the town
> creates for itself both revenue and a municipal policy. The soul of that policy is
> the putting of fellow-citizens at an advantage, and of competitors from outside
> at a disadvantage.

Schmoller's plot culminates with Frederick the Great who uses these tools, but to further trade for everyone, even those beyond the state (1967, 79–80). Frederick the Great, the first servant of the state, adhered to the principles Samuel Pufendorf made clear to his Hohenzollern ancestors–the "state" is a natural law phenomenon that must be the highest principle for whom even the King is but a function. The mercantilist principle will live on in ever-new and productive forms, with enemies nonetheless who fail to live within or grasp its rules.

Throughout his essay, Schmoller qualifies the degree of certainty of evidence or the variable he employs. In this he articulates the Germanic narrative convention of a degree of mystery that in an exposition is never resolved. This is markedly clearer in the Germanic belles lettres or fine arts; in the sciences, where certainty is prized the convention is more subtle. Max Weber's "ideal type" is an example of how this degree of uncertainty is finessed conceptually. Weber, like Leibniz before him, expresses the "identity of indiscernibles'"– the principle or evidence stated is sufficient even when one must recognize its incompleteness. The German physicist Heisenberg articulates this qualified evidence in his "indeterminacy principle." This treatment of evidence is not to be confused with the Austrian "problematic certainty," which is the recognition of the difficulty of complete evidence, but only a delay in finding it.

Max Weber's *The Protestant Ethic and the Spirit of Capitalism* written in 1904–1905 serves as an example of a "plot" that shares the same major characteristics as Schmoller's, even as it departs in many, but not all, of its economic premises from him.[29] Conceptual premises within a disciplinary paradigm are greatly influenced by the metaparadigmatic assumptions of a national culture. Weber's univocal principle that changes its shape as it is reconfigured through periods of history, the univocal principle that characterizes the Western world more than any other culture, and which is the efficient cause of all distinctive Western contributions, is "a rational, systematic, and specialized pursuit of science, with trained and specialized personnel, [that] has only existed in the West in a sense at all approaching its present dominant place in our culture. Above all is this true of the trained official, the pillar of both the modern State and of the economic life of the West" (1958, 15–16). The motor of this pursuit is the "rational, systematic" principle in itself, regardless of where this rational systematization is applied. Capitalism is a subprinciple within economics, per se. Yet, its chief principle as an efficient cause is this "rational systematization":

> The impulse to acquisition, pursuit of gain, of money, of the greatest possible amount of money, has in itself nothing to do with capitalism...and is still less its spirit. Capitalism may even be identical with the restraint, or at least a rational tempering, of this irrational impulse. But capitalism is identical with the pursuit of profit, and forever renewed profit, by means of continuous, rational, capitalistic enterprise (1958, 17).

The immediate ancestor of "capitalism" is found by Weber in the same principle of "rational systematization" that recurs again and again in public and institutional manner within Calvinism. Capitalism is the secularization of Calvinism, the religion of successful businessmen in the sixteenth and seventeenth century. That principle can be conflated with Calvinist "piety," or how one is justified before one's fellows in the eyes of God (1958, 45). Ben Franklin's maxims are the evidence of this piety become economic theory (1958, 48–54). Weber takes pains to discriminate the phases and stages of this reconfiguring of religious doctrine between Europe of the Reformation and Franklin's Enlightenment America (1958, 43–45). Nonetheless, the motor that empowers the historical continuity through its changes is the inexorable ethos of rational systematization.

There are adversaries all along the way. The principle creates enemies in its wake who fail to comprehend its claim to exclusive truth. Each age has a defender or an opponent of "rational systematization" as the foundation of capitalist enterprise. Depending upon the age, sometimes even capitalists themselves fail to grasp what is in their best interests, while those not quite benefactors from capitalist enterprise do:

> Some moralists [of the Italian Renaissance]...accepted developed capitalistic business forms as inevitable, and attempted to justify them, especially commerce, as necessary. The industria developed in it they were able to regard, though not without contradictions, as a legitimate source of profit, and hence ethically unobjectionable. But the dominant doctrine rejected the spirit of capitalistic acquisition as turpitudo, or at least could not give it a positive ethical sanction. An ethical attitude like that of Benjamin Franklin would have been simply unthinkable. This was, above all, the attitude of capitalistic circles themselves. Their life-work was, so long as they clung to the tradition of the Church, at best something morally indifferent....

> Now, how could activity, which was at best ethically tolerated, turn into a calling in the sense of Benjamin Franklin? The fact to be explained historically is that in the most highly capitalistic centre of that time, in Florence of the fourteenth and fifteenth centuries, the money and capital market of all the great political Powers, this attitude was considered ethically unjustifiable, or at best to be tolerated. But in the backwoods small bourgeois circumstances of Pennsylvania in the eighteenth century, where business threatened for simple lack of money to fall back into barter, where there was hardly a sign of large enterprise, where only the earliest beginnings of banking were to be found, the same thing was considered the essence of moral conduct, even commanded in the name of duty (1958, 73–75).

Weber describes how educational institutions came to instill this principle as both an explanatory and effective means of living a life. Speaking of his own time, Weber points out that the moiety of capitalist "winners" economically in their degree of wealth and power were educated into these principles through their formal education (1958, 35–38). These "winners" are Protestants; the "losers" are Catholic. One can differentiate their respective educations by the treatment of the principle of "rational systematization" as a principle for life (1958, 37–38). Historical culture always has the convergence and conflict of cultural/ethical choices. The "either/or" choice (which Sombart saw in mercantilistic and nonmercantilistic practices) Weber discusses as "probability" theory in human decision-making in an essay that more than any other imparts succinctly his vision of the essential cultural-historical "plot." Weber uses the Battle of Marathon as an example of how two distinct cultural principles met each other, and how one had to succeed while the other failed.[30] Weber is noted for his "decisionism" in formulating the *topos* of an issue. Jürgen Habermas points out how Weber's penchant for juxtaposing variables in a manner that imposes an "either-or" choice is specious. Citing Weber's delineation of the mutually exclusive claims of the political and technocratic sectors that strive to govern public policy, Habermas points out that logically this juxtaposition need not hold–that problems can be construed without this juxtaposition of interest being considered the primary ground of the problem. He remarks: "[This juxtaposition] is a noteworthy social fact explicable on the basis of objective constellations of interests. But it is not something that necessarily follows from the nature of real problems."[31]

What stands out in my presentation of Schmoller and Weber is the omnipresent agency of principle as it is conceived in the former as a public expression of law, and in the latter as a set of ethical intentions. All who grasp this principle or who are under it express it. There are those who are included within the scope and those who are either attacked by or in their turn attack this principle as it is exercised univocally by everyone who is its adherent. The constant change of its forms speaks of its live essence. Manner remains characteristic within the grasp of principle even as times and places vary.

Principle as a univocal higher ordering premise protects the German against the factual contingencies and uncertainties of their history. Weber, himself, expresses the allowance for a degree of mystery in affairs that can never be solved because of the lack of past facts–even when one must assume such facts existed (Weber, "Objektive Möglichkeit und adäquate Verursachung," 271–272, 289). Indeed, Weber's notion of "ideal type," like his compatriot Leibniz's notion of the "identity of indiscernibles" contains the premise that a generalized principle is sufficient to cover minor unknowns or disparities in the evidence. As I now delineate the Austrian "plot" over roughly the same three-quarters of a century from Menger to von Mises, the samenesses of the German in its contradistinctiveness to the Austrian "plot" will become apparent.

Carl Menger's "marginal utility theory" clearly does not pose "either/or" choices, rather asks for all possible interests to be rank-ordered and included in public economic policy.[32] The historical meaning is in fact that any "one" is an aggregate of the many. Every human being is a composite of needs (Bedürfen), which vary in each individual and among individuals. Although preferences gave more salience to some in a time, this always varied. The state itself is a similar composite of persons, each having a differing and legitimate presence. There are never winners and losers, only existents. Menger's economic principles make clear both the composite nature of economic and societal reality. The common denominator is the "composite human." The alpha and omega of all history in its many institutional forms are each human in his or her complex nature. Society is the complex, composite human family or family of humankind. History is the story of the family of humankind repeating in differing arrangements its solution to the same finite, yet complex needs.

Seeing the foundation of history as the wants of being human, rather than the principle or idea that impels humans, as in the German, gives a conservative, anthropological turn to Austrian ideation. History is the partial or more complete fulfillment of a milieu's needs: it is not the embodiment of idea. Ideas may be vital in solving needs, but the interpersonal praxis is more evident than its rational. There is a formal causal pattern each individual enters in his or her maturation; and, society itself advances or declines against the measure and within this pattern.

In his *Principles of Economics*, Menger begins by establishing a formal causal pattern for human economic praxis, that is, the search for the satisfaction of needs by creating goods:

> If a thing is to become a good, or in other words, if it is to acquire goods-character, all four of the following prerequisites must be simultaneously present:
>
> 1. A human need.
>
> 2. Such properties as render the thing capable of being brought into a causal connection with the satisfaction of this need.
>
> 3. Human knowledge of this causal connection.
>
> 4. Command of the thing sufficient to direct it to the satisfaction of the need.
>
> Only when all four of these prerequisites are present simultaneously can a thing become a good. When even one of them is absent, a thing cannot acquire goods-character, and a thing already possessing goods-character would lose it at once if but one of the four prerequisites ceased to be present (1981, 52).

Besides exemplifying the Austrian narrative convention of a unity formed out of a multiplicity, Menger's above remarks give evidence of the "problematic certainty" that pervades knowledge. One can never be certain what an immediate state-of-affairs might be in this four-dimensional grid. One can theoretically state what the criteria for certainty are, but in examining a specific historical state-of-affairs only a case-by-case personalism, not a univocal general rule, can be articulated. Thus, when one looks at Sigmund Freud's comparable human causal complexity, his manner of inquiry and report is the personalist case study, and his therapy the personalist praxis. Similarly, Austrian governance was administrative personalism, rather than the impersonalist formal truth of the written law. Austrian historiography stresses the details of human practice, and tends to be in its anecdotal detail antiquarian (in Nietzsche's sense of the term). Detail gives the direction to the potential "certainty" even when it is a problematic pursuit.

Menger then speaks of the interpersonal bases of all individual life. The individual never is an isolated entity, rather always in the midst of interactions and relationships. History is not as in Schmoller's Frederick the Great or Weber's Ben Franklin the exemplary personal agent carrying forward himself and others with the motor of principle. Rather, individual reality is the outcome of interacting needs in oneself and between oneself and others:

> From an economic standpoint...what are called clienteles, good-will, monopolies, copyrights, trade marks, etc., are the useful actions or inactions of other people, or (as in the case of firms, for example) aggregates of material goods, labor services, and other useful actions and inactions. Even relationships of friendship and love, religious fellowships, and the like, consist obviously of actions or inactions of other persons that are beneficial to us (1981, 55).

There is never a monumentality in history in the Nietzschean sense. No one wins at the expense of the losers: rather even "inactions" benefit reciprocally.

Time and history for the Austrian is an unfolding and evolving of categorial constants, and thus is experienced as a sense of enduring, if improving relationships of constant character. Absent is the "historicist" sense of periods changing the quality of historical life in a radical manner. Menger was the critic of Schmoller who condemned his economics with the label "historicist."[33] There must be a sense of the absurd for a German who reads an Austrian account of economic "history," so different is its treatment of things in history. Menger, for example, speaks of the constant value of the cow in history through the changes that spanned the nomadic to the early urban classic cultures because of the categorial properties of durability and transportability. Even after the rise of the commercial city, Menger points out the gradualism of the shift in the bases of economic value away from cattle to the intrinsic value of metallic coin because of these constant valuable characteristics of the cow (Menger, 1981, 263–264). Compare the German economist Wilhelm Roscher's treatment of cows in history. Roscher subsumes the value to the cow not to its inherent, categorial properties, rather to the stage of societal civilization in which it is bred, that is, to a higher unity of principle that pervades the general character of a time:

> Cows are primarily milk-producing animals…. It is indeed possible by its transformation into butter or cheese to preserve milk and make it capable of transportation. But to carry on such a business for the purposes of trade, a care and a cleanliness are needed which are national characteristics only of a highly civilized people…. Hence their price, as a rule, rises later than that of oxen, but, in the higher stages of civilization, it rises much more surprisingly.[34]

Ludwig von Mises's *Human Action, A Treatise on Economics*, written and first published in Geneva, Switzerland, in 1940 under the title *Nationalökonomie, Theorie des Handelns and Wirtschaftens*, founds its principles within enduring, categorial human attributes, in the spirit if not letter of Menger.[35] Again, one cannot say that von Mises was in the school of Menger, rather that as an Austrian, certain enduring historical narrative conventions were almost inevitably central to one's istoria. I say "almost inevitable" as my concluding remarks will touch upon the atavistic influence of national historical conventions that when perceived can be addressed and even changed.

Von Mises calls his economic theory praxeology, the science of human action. Human action is treated in an "ahistorical" manner, much as Menger's array of goods that recur in varying saliences as constants in human history. The "ahistoricality" is like that of the human family over generations of ancestry: practices recur because of the nature of that family, and time seems to dissolve as the practices are recounted. There is no apology for this ahistoricality as von Mises treats the theme in a chapter that deliberates praxeology and history. He deliberately refers to "the formal and aprioristic character of praxeology":

> The problem of whether there are or whether there are not a priori elements of thought–i.e., necessary and ineluctable intellectual conditions of thinking, anterior to any actual instance of conception and experience–must not be confused with the genetic problem of how man acquired his characteristically human mental ability. Man is descended from nonhuman ancestors who lacked this ability. These ancestors were endowed with some potentiality which in the course of ages of evolution converted them into reasonable beings (1949, 33).

Although there is change in time, for Homo sapiens it is for at least hundreds of thousands of years a question of morphological fulfillment of potential powers within environs, rather than radical or ceaseless changes of the human community in its essential political and economic nature.

Von Mises's treatment of capitalism reflects this sense of morphological time, where a seemingly a priori category unfolds and is moved towards mature fulfillment:

> All civilizations have up to now been based on private ownership of the means of production. In the past, civilization and private property have been linked together. Those who maintain that economics is an experimental science and nevertheless recommend public control of the means of production, lamentably contradict themselves. If historical experience could teach us anything, it would be that private property is inextricably linked with civilization. There is no experience to the effect that socialism could provide a standard of living as high as that provided by capitalism.

> The system of market economy has never been fully and purely tried. But there prevailed in the orbit of Western civilization since the Middle Ages by and large a general tendency toward the abolition of institutions hindering the operation of the market economy. With the successive progress of this tendency, population figures multiplied and the masses' standard of living was raised to an unprecedented and hitherto undreamed of level (1949, 264–265).

Historical periods do not have principles that subsume the category of private property, rather this category is an a priori essential to being human, but its strength and promise develop alongside other forces.

Von Mises's morphological temporal perspective helps us to see the dynastic influence upon normative national time. Just as a dynasty unfolds as it matures in the life of the ruler of the time, and cumulatively, so does capitalism or other fecund categorial realities that are the essence of being human. One is reminded of Franz Grillparzer's character in his play about Rudolf I, the first Habsburg Holy Roman Emperor–*King Ottocar, His Rise and Fall*–who admonishes a courier to give his vote to the Electors in time, since "one day too late is thirty years too soon."[36] Time is measured by the span and course of a lifetime. Von Mises generalizes this vision of morphological time in a chapter entitled "Action in the Passing of Time," which gives his "Perspective in the Valuation of Time Periods":

> Acting man distinguishes the time before satisfaction of a want is attained and the time for which the satisfaction continues.

> Action always aims at the removal of future uneasiness, be it only the future of the impending instant. Between the setting in of action and the attainment of the end sought there always elapses a fraction of time, viz., the maturing time in which the seed sown by the action grows to maturity. The most obvious example is provided by agriculture. Between the tilling of the soil and the ripening of the fruit there passes a considerable period of time. Another example is the improvement of wine by aging (1949, 476).

Time is a formal causal pattern that recurs. Change is measured by the fulfillment of the pattern. Austrian institutions are such morphological constants. The recurrent nature of unchanging human nature, and in terms of Austria's political sociology, the recurring presence of authoritative structures such as the Habsburg monarchy, are examples of formal causal pattern in existence. Even after the demise of the Habsburgs, the Austrians created a "corporatism" that mirrored Habsburg cameralism. Austrian corporatism from 1918 still exists, a mirror image of the cameralist heritage of that monarchy (cf. Bischof and Pelinka 1996).

Austrian corporatism's key premise is that the nation is the extended human family whose individuals may have distinctly singular lives, but who are nonetheless the state as family. One is never alone, even in a political-economics that adheres to the English premise of benign egoism. Von Mises departs from Menger's state guardianship of social concerns by emphasizing the English tradition of individual "benign" selfishness, but when he expresses this, the Austrian historical narrative topic of interdependence as the complex structure of the whole is unmistakable:

> If praxeology speaks of the solitary individual, acting on his own behalf only and independent of his fellow men, it does so for the sake of a better comprehension of the problems of social cooperation. We do not assert that such isolated autarkic human beings have ever lived and that the social stage of man's history was preceded by an age of independent individuals roaming like animals in search of food. The biological humanization of man's nonhuman ancestors and the emergence of the primitive social bonds were effected in the same process. Man appeared on the scene of earthly events as a social being. The isolated asocial man is a fictitious construction.
>
> Seen from the point of view of the individual, society is the great means for the attainment of all his ends. The preservation of society is an essential condition of any plans an individual may want to realize by any action whatever. Even the refractory delinquent who fails to adjust his conduct to the requirements of life within the societal system of cooperation does not want to miss any of the advantages derived from the division of labor. He does not consciously aim at the destruction of society. He wants to lay his hands on a greater portion of the jointly produced wealth than the social order assigns to him. He would feel miserable if antisocial behavior were to become universal and its inevitable outcome, the return to primitive indigence, resulted (1949, 164).

"Problematic certainty" as a narrative convention enters von Mises's *Human Action* in the initial paragraph, cautioning readers that even in praxeology a difficulty will exist in establishing purposeful from involuntary behaviors:

> Conscious or purposeful behavior is in sharp contrast to unconscious behavior, i.e., the reflexes and the involuntary responses of the body's cells and nerves to stimuli. People are sometimes prepared to believe that the boundaries between conscious behavior and the involuntary reaction of the forces operating within man's body are more or less indefinite. This is correct only as far as it is sometimes not easy to establish whether concrete behavior is to be considered voluntary or involuntary. But the distinction between consciousness and unconsciousness is nonetheless sharp and can be clearly determined.

> The unconscious behavior of the bodily organs and cells is for the acting ego no
> less a datum than any other fact of the eternal world (1949, 11).

With diligence, islands can be raised from the stream. The Austrian always allows empirical facts to be discovered that potentially can elucidate a phenomenon totally. Whether the Austrian be Franz Brentano, Sigmund Freud, Edmund Husserl, or Ludwig Wittgenstein, the problematic nature of human variables in their interaction must be considered, but for all including von Mises, elucidated certainty is a possible outcome. Unlike the German who preserves a degree of mystery, the Austrian political sociological causality grows from the lifetime and continuity of ancestry in its rulers. Over a lifetime, all is possible. The German requires the Nietzschean carte blanche at times in order to be fresh in its next political constellation.

Von Mises himself has contributed important work to the definition of national characteristics, especially in the discipline of economic history, because of his exercise of what I term the Austrian historical narrative convention of tracking durations over centuries, coupled with the exacting empiricism that is able to discern a priori aspects that recur over time. His bias (in the best logical sense of measure) is the longue durée, as is the wont of his fellow Austrians. Von Mises himself, by dint of this eye for the longue durée, had a keen appreciation of the presence of national ideological conventions in economic thought. His essays in *Nation, State, and Economy* attest to differentiations between German and Austrian national economic practice whose causation lay in their respective political experiences.[37] Von Mises's comprehension of the existence and causes of a national style of public policy in history reinforces my own perspective.

7.   CAN THE NATIONAL HISTORICAL NARRATIVE BE CHANGED?

All national historical narratives offer insights through the norms of their genres in the arts and sciences that are singular and valuable. Even the bias of the historical narrative is a measure. Nonetheless, the evidence of the national historical narrative illustrates how certain topics are inadequate for the changing demands of the time. The "family' model of the Austrian is socially responsible, but suffocating in a country that no longer has to convince twelve differing nationalities that they are Austrian. In populations that are more homogeneous in language and background, the part-whole paradigm should be less demanding of familial cohesion. Germany, in its historical narrative bias, creates adversaries unnecessarily. One wonders if the quickness that brought unity in 1990 was but another way of sustaining the polar tensions of friend/enemy that is now the bitterness of "those of the east and those of the west."

Insight into the existence of a historical "plot" that configures premises and measures outcomes would have to become a national consciousness guided by a new, corrective heuristic. Interestingly, it is Austria whose national historical narrative is most resistant to change because of its nature, but whose very "pathology" (understood in the Kantian sense of a logic that violates the rules of adequate deliberation of experience) has spurred its greatest minds to insights that can accomplish this heuristic.

The Austrians who have seen the depth of narrative "plots" in their fundamental shaping of human existence include Ludwig Wittgenstein and his insight into "language games" that function as a priori formal causes. The mathematician Gödel in his delineation of the essential assumptions in scientific inquiry that are axiomatic rather than demonstrable has penetrated the lazy nature of the a priori in cultural thought. Sigmund Freud and his Viennese followers, in particular, have revealed the pathological assumptions which limit and give authority to our imputations of authenticity, functioning as illusive "problematic certainties." My own research has leaned heavily on Franz Brentano and Edmund Husserl, the Austrian-German phenomenologists who have exposed the deep structures of linguistic judgment that build narrative designs.

The German historical narrative almost always has been able to find principles that were in accord with events. The pathological aspect of the German narrative is to subsume all events and agents to that public principle, its agents rarely heeding their own caveats that other lines of inquiry are possible. Nonetheless, the German mind is more prone to find ideas that respond to cultural changes. Germans initiated modern heuristic studies in the eighteenth century largely because of their inclination to the reconfiguration of principles over time which could be more in accord with the character of a time.

NOTES

1. See Werner Jaeger, *Paideia: The Ideals of Greek Culture*, trans. Gilbert Highet (New York: Oxford University Press, 1974), 155, 179, 294, and 382.

2. Mark E. Blum, "Breaks or Continuity in Sombart's Work: A Linguistic Analysis," in *Werner Sombart (1863–1941) Social Scientist*, 3 vols., ed. Jürgen G. Backhaus (Marburg: Metropolis Verlag, 1996), 3: 11–109.

3. Wilhelm von Humboldt, *Schriften zur Sprachphilosophie*, in *Wilhelm von Humboldt Werke in Fünf Bänden* (Stuttgart: J.G. Cotta, 1963), 3: 463–475.

4. See Hayden White, *Metahistory: The Historical Imagination in Nineteenth Century Europe* (Baltimore: Johns Hopkins University Press, 1973), and *The Content of the Form, Narrative Discourse and Historical Representation* (Baltimore: Johns Hopkins University Press,

1987). See Paul Ricoeur, *Time and Narrative*, trans. Kathleen McLaughlin and David Pellauer, 3 vols. (Chicago: University of Chicago Press, 1984–1988).

5. See Joseph Campbell's discussion of the Egyptian concept of maat in *The Masks of God: Oriental Mythology* (New York: Viking Press, 1962), 54ff. The equivalent Greek concept is aidios or "right order" in time; see F. E. Peters, *Greek Philosophical Terms: A Historical Lexicon* (New York: New York University Press, 1967), 7. The Chinese concept of the tao as the "right order" is also discussed by Joseph Campbell in *Oriental Mythology*, 23–25, 28, 446–447.

6. See Walter J. Ong, *The Technologizing of the Word* (London: Methuen, 1982), 115. Ong believes that one's being schooled in the rhetoric of antithesis contributed to attitudes and behavior that fueled conflict; Ong, *Rhetoric, Romance, and Technology* (Ithaca: Cornell University Press, 1971), 66.

7. Arthur Joseph Slavin, *The Tudor Age and Beyond* (Malabar, Fla.: Robert E. Krieger, 1987), viii ff.

8. See the discussion of German and Austrian cameralism as a political-economic system in Albion W. Small, *The Cameralists: The Pioneers of German Social Polity* (Chicago: University of Chicago Press, 1909); Erhard Dittrich, *Die Deutschen und Österreichischen Kameralisten* (Darmstadt: Wissenschaftliche Buchgesellschaft, 1974); and Louise Sommer, *Die Österreichischen Kameralisten in Dogmentgeschichtlicher Darstellung* (Wien: Carl Konegen, 1920; Aalen: Scientia Verlag, 1967). Further reference will be to these texts and editions.

9. Jean Bodin, *The six Bookes of a Commonweale, based on the English edition of 1606* (Cambridge, Mass.: Harvard University Press, 1962), 8–10.

10. John Calvin, *Institutes of the Christian Religion*, trans. Ford Lewis Battles, 2 vols. (Philadelphia: Westminster Press, 1960), 1: 846–849 (Book III, Ch. 19) , 2: 1485–1495 (Book IV, Ch. 20).

11. See John T. McNeill, *The History and Character of Calvinism* (New York: Oxford University Press, 1954), 347–348.

12. One of the clearest arguments in this respect is made by Henry St. John, Viscount Bolingbroke in the eighteenth century. Public reality in England led Bolingbroke to counterpoint cameralism and legislative Republican governance. There had been overt public strife between those of Republican principles, like John Locke, and the aristocratic sympathizers, which had given rise, respectively, to the Whig and Tory parties. The emerging power of Parliament as a counterforce to the King or Queen led to Bolingbroke's essay *The Patriot King* in 1749. In Germany and Austria, Republicanism as a political reality or even public expression was virtually nonexistent in the Enlightenment era. See Bolingbroke, *The Patriot King* (Indianapolis: Bobbs-Merrill, 1965), especially pp. 45–48.

13. See also Louise Sommer, "Cameralism," in *Encyclopedia of the Social Sciences*, Vol. 3 (New York: Macmillan, 1951), 158–160.

14. See Joseph von Sonnenfels, *Über den Geschäftsstyl; die erste Grundlage für angehende österreichische Canzleybeamte* (Wien: Kürzbock, 1784/1820), especially on the principle of intersubjective decorum "Anstandigkeit," pp. 45–53.

15. See Heinrich Schuster, "Die Entwicklung des Rechtslebens, Verfassung und Verwaltung." In *Geschichte der Stadt Wien* (Wien: Adolf Holzhausen, 1897), 361ff.

16. See Ferdinand Schevill, *The Great Elector* (Chicago: University of Chicago Press, 1947), especially pp. 96–97 for the traditional awareness of legal limits to authority in the Hohenzollern lands, and pp. 249 and 409ff. for the impact of Calvinism on Frederick William.

17. See Leonard Krieger, *The Politics of Discretion, Pufendorf and the Acceptance of Natural Law* (Chicago: University of Chicago Press, 1965).

18. See Otto von Gierke, *Natural Law and the Theory of Society, 1500–1800*, trans. Ernest Barker (Boston: Beacon Press, 1957), 70ff.

19. Immanuel Kant, "Idea for a Universal History from a Cosmopolitan Point of View," *On History*, trans. Lewis White Beck (Indianapolis: The Bobbs-Merrill Company, 1963), 15.

20. See William M. Johnston, *The Austrian Mind: An Intellectual and Social History 1848–1938* (Berkeley: University of California Press, 1972), 165ff.

21. See Hayden White, *The Content of the Form, Narrative Discourse and Historical Representation* (Baltimore: Johns Hopkins University Press, 1987), 51. Further reference is to this text and its included articles.

22. Aristotle terms explanation and assessment of the action of a plot, as this explanation is articulated as an integral factor in the plot, the "thought." See Aristotle, *Poetics*, 1449b, 38+; 1450b, 4, 11; 1456a, 34+.

23. A discussion of this habit of mind in the Habsburgs warranted an entire text; see Marie Tanner, *The Last Descendant of Aeneas: The Hapsburgs and the Mythic Image of the Emperor* (New Haven: Yale University Press, 1993). Further reference is to this text and edition.

24. See *Austro-Corporatism, Past, Present, Future*, Günter Bischof and Anton Pelinka, eds. (New Brunswick: Transaction Publishers, 1996). The historical roots of Austria's existing corporatism are discussed in articles by Andrei S. Markovits, "Austrian Corporatism in Comparative Perspective," 5ff., and especially by Emmerich Tálos and Bernhard Kittel, "Roots of Austro-Corporatism: Institutional Preconditions and Cooperation Before and After 1945," 21ff. Further references are to these articles and edition.

25. Robert Musil, *The Man without Qualities*, trans. Eithne Wilkins and Ernst Kaiser (New York: Coward-McCann, 1953), 3.

26. See Günter Fellner, *Ludo Moritz Hartmann und die Österreichische Geschichtswissenschaft, Grundzüge eines paradigmatischen Konfliktes* (Wien-Salzburg: Geyer, 1985), 93.

27. Gustav Schmoller, *The Mercantile System and its Historical Significance* (New York: Macmillan, 1897; reprinted New York: Augustus M. Kelley, 1967). Further reference is to this text and edition. The original German edition of the chapter was published in *Studien über die wirthschaftliche Politik Friedrich des Grossen und Preussens überhaupt von 1680–1786* (Leipzig: Duncker und Humblot, 1884), 1–60.

28. Otto von Gierke, *Das deutsche Genossenschaftsrecht*, 3 vols. (Graz: Akademische Druck- u. Verlagsanstalt, 1954), 1: 39ff.

29. Max Weber, *The Protestant Ethic and the Spirit of Capitalism*, trans. Talcott Parsons (New York: Charles Scribner's Sons, 1958). Further reference is to this text and edition.

30. Max Weber, "Objektive Möglichkeit und adäquate Verursachung in der historischen Kausalbetrachtung," *Kritische Studien auf dem Gebiet der kulturwissenschaftlichen*

Logik in Gesammelte Aufsätze zur Wissenschaftslehre, 2nd ed. [Tübingen: J.C.B. Mohr (Paul Siebeck)], 276–277.

31. Jürgen Habermas, *Toward a Rational Society*, trans. Jeremy J. Shapiro (Boston: Beacon, 1970), 65–66.

32. Carl Menger, *Principles of Economics*, trans. James Dingwall and Bert F. Hoselitz (New York: New York University Press, 1981), 122–128.

33. William M. Johnston, *The Austrian Mind: An Intellectual and Social History 1848–1938* (Los Angeles: University of California Press, 1972), 79.

34. William Roscher, *Principles of Political Economy*, trans. John J. Lalor (New York: Henry Holt, 1878; republished New York: Arno Press, 1972), 397–398.

35. I use von Mises's English transcription of *Human Action: A Treatise on Economics* (New Haven: Yale University Press, 1949). Further reference is to this text and edition.

36. Franz Grillparzer, *King Ottocar, His Rise and Fall*, trans. Henry H. Stevens (Yarmouth Port, Mass.: The Register Press, 1938), 8.

37. Ludwig von Mises, *Nation, State, and Economy: Contributions to the Politics and History of Our Time*, trans. Leland B. Yeager (New York: New York University Press, 1983).

REFERENCES

Bischof, Günter and Pelinka, Anton, eds. *Austro-Corporatism, Past, Present, Future.* New Brunswick: Transaction Publishers, 1996.

Blum, Mark E. "Breaks or Continuity in Sombart's Work: A Linguistic Analysis." In *Werner Sombart (1863–1941) Social Scientist*, 3 vols., ed. Jürgen G. Backhaus. Marburg: Metropolis Verlag, 1996. 3: 11–109.

Bodin, Jean. *The six Bookes of a Commonweale, based on the English edition of 1606.* Cambridge, Mass.: Harvard University Press, 1962.

Bolingbroke, Lord. *The Patriot King.* Indianapolis: Bobbs-Merrill, 1965.

Calvin, John. *Institutes of the Christian Religion.* Trans. Ford Lewis Battles. 2 vols. Philadelphia: Westminster Press, 1960.

Campbell, Joseph. *The Masks of God: Oriental Mythology.* New York: Viking Press, 1962.

Dittrich, Erhard. *Die Deutschen und Österreichischen Kameralisten.* Darmstadt: Wissenschaftliche Buchgesellschaft, 1974.

Fellner, Günther. *Ludo Moritz Hartmann und die Österreichische Geschichtswissenschaft, Grundzüge eines paradigmatischen Konfliktes.* Wien-Salzburg: Geyer, 1985.

von Gierke, Otto. *Das deutsche Genossenschaftsrecht.* 3 vols. Graz: Akademische Druck- u. Verlagsanstalt, 1954.

———. *Natural Law and the Theory of Society, 1500–1800.* Trans. Ernest Barker. Boston: Beacon Press, 1957.

Grillparzer, Franz. *King Ottocar, His Rise and Fall.* Trans. Henry H. Stevens. Yarmouth Port, Mass.: The Register Press, 1938.

Habermas, Jürgen. *Toward a Rational Society.* Trans. Jeremy J. Shapiro. Boston: Beacon, 1970.

von Humboldt, Wilhelm. *Schriften zur Sprachphilosophie. in[0] Wilhelm von Humboldt. Werke in Fünf Bänden.* Stuttgart: J.G. Cotta, 1963. 3: 463–475.

Jaeger, Werner. *Paideia: The Ideals of Greek Culture*. Trans. Gilbert Highet. New York: Oxford University Press, 1974.

Johnston, William M. *The Austrian Mind: An Intellectual and Social History 1848–1938*. Berkeley: University of California Press, 1972.

Kant, Immanuel. "Idea for a Universal History from a Cosmopolitan Point of View." *On History*. Trans. Lewis White Beck. Indianapolis: The Bobbs-Merrill Company, 1963.

Krieger, Leonard. *The Politics of Discretion, Pufendorf and the Acceptance of Natural Law*. Chicago: University of Chicago Press, 1965.

McKeon, Richard, ed. *The Basic Works of Aristotle*. New York: Macmillan, 1941.

McNeill, John T. *The History and Character of Calvinism*. New York: Oxford University Press, 1954.

Menger, Carl. *Principles of Economics*. Trans. James Dingwall and Bert F. Hoselitz. New York: New York University Press, 1981.

von Mises, Ludwig. *Human Action: A Treatise on Economics*. [0]New Haven: Yale University Press.

———. *Nation, State, and Economy: Contributions to the Politics and History of Our Time*. Trans. Leland B. Yeager. New York: New York University Press, 1983.

Musil, Robert. *The Man without Qualities*. Trans. Eithne Wilkins and Ernst Kaiser. New York: Coward-McCann, 1953.

Ong, Walter J. *Rhetoric, Romance, and Technology*. Ithaca: Cornell University Press, 1971.

———. *The Technologizing of the Word*. London: Methuen, 1982.

Peters, F.E. *Greek Philosophical Terms: A Historical Lexicon*. New York: New York University Press, 1967.

Ricoeur, Paul. *Time and Narrative*. Trans. Kathleen McLaughlin and David Pellauer. 3 vols. Chicago: University of Chicago Press, 1984–1988.

Roscher, William. *Principles of Political Economy*. Trans. John J. Lalor. New York: Henry Holt, 1878; republished New York: Arno Press, 1972.

Schevill, Ferdinand. *The Great Elector*. Chicago: University of Chicago Press, 1947.

Schmoller, Gustav. *The Mercantile System and its Historical Significance*. New York: lMacmillan, 1897; reprinted New York: Augustus M. Kelley, 1967.

———. Studien über die wirthschaftliche Politik Friedrich des Grossen und Preussens *überhaupt von 1680–1786*. Leipzig: Duncker und Humblot, 1884.

Schuster, Heinrich. "Die Entwicklung des Rechtslebens, Verfassung und Verwaltung." In *Geschichte der Stadt Wien*. Wien: Adolf Holzhausen, 1897. 293–498.

Slavin, Arthur Joseph. *The Tudor Age and Beyond*. Malabar, Fla.: Robert E. Krieger, 1987.

Small, Albion W. *The Cameralists: The Pioneers of German Social Polity*. Chicago: University of Chicago Press, 1909.

Sommer, Louise. "Cameralism." In *Encyclopedia of the Social Sciences*. Vol. 3. New York: Macmillan, 1951.

Sommer, Louise. *Die Österreichischen Kameralisten in Dogmentgeschichtlicher Darstellung*. Wien: Carl Konegen, 1920; Aalen: Scientia Verlag, 1967.

von Sonnenfels, Joseph. *Über den Geschäftsstyl; die erste Grundlage für angehende österreichische Canzleybeamte*. Wien: Kürzbock, 1784/1820.

Tanner, Marie. *The Last Descendant of Aeneas: The Hapsburgs and the Mythic Image of the Emperor*. New Haven: Yale University Press, 1993.

Weber, Max. *The Protestant Ethic and the Spirit of Capitalism*. Trans. Talcott Parsons. New York: Charles Scribner's Sons, 1958.

Weber, Max. "Objektive Möglichkeit und adäquate Verursachung in der historischen Kausal-betrachtung." In *Kritische Studien auf dem Gebiet der kulturwissenschaftlichen Logik in Gesammelte Aufsätze zur Wissenschaftslehre*, 2nd ed. Tübingen: J.C.B. Mohr [0](Paul Siebeck). 266–290.

White, Hayden. *The Content of the Form, Narrative Discourse and Historical Representation.* Baltimore: Johns Hopkins University Press, 1987.

———. *Metahistory: The Historical Imagination in Nineteenth Century Europe.* Baltimore: Johns Hopkins University Press, 1973.

6. The European Metahistorical Narrative and Its Changing "Metaparadigms" in the Modern Age (Part I)

Mark E. Blum

Department of History

1. INTRODUCTION

The historian Ortega y Gasset called for a "metahistory," a field of study that analogically would be as physiology for medical science.[1] "Metahistory" would enable us to discern in the panorama of history the invariant categories of judgment that led to differing historical understandings of human experience. "Metahistory" would include such categories as change, duration, development as well as those categories which focused upon historical cause. Theories of history depended upon the metahistorical categories as medical science upon physiology in that "history" might have many theoretical approaches in its conceptualization, but its range of concepts were determined by how the mind functioned as it judged temporality. The concept in my title of "changing metaparadigms" is temporal in the idea of change, but also in the idea of a "metaparadigm." Ortega y Gasset explains how in each generation the movement of life and thought is guided by generally shared assumptions. Nothing is ever still: existence is temporal and thus changing. I will discuss the concept of "metaparadigm" as a set of general assumptions spanning several generations that govern the conduct of inquiry in all the arts and sciences of a time, as well as the manner of life in popular culture. A "metahistorical" understanding enables me to look at the diverse events of scientific, artistic, humanistic, and popular culture in a given period of time and elicit from this welter of differing activities a coherent sense of the basic temporal-spatial assumptions that were opaque to most persons, but nonetheless guided their activities. I will in this discussion show how Thomas Kuhn's notion of the

Correspondence to: Mark E. Blum, University of Louisville, Louisville, Kentucky 40292 "paradigm" included this overarching sense of generalized assumptions that subtly guided one or more generations of scientific activity before a change in these overarching assumptions. Kuhn will not be the major focus of my essay, but his thought will help a contemporary audience grasp my line of argument which draws more from late nineteenth century and early twentieth century thinkers, such as Wilhelm Dilthey, Max Scheler, Edmund Husserl, Ernst Mach, and Ortega y Gasset, than it does from Kuhn.

Ortega y Gasset, whose theory of a metahistorical knowledge is vital in much of my work, could be considered a philosophical phenomenologist and his historiographical work phenomenological history in the spirit of Max Scheler, who was his intellectual mentor.[2] Time was a cognitive product for this post-Kantian philosophical school whose most renowned twentieth century philosopher was Edmund Husserl.

The Kantian/Husserlian/Schelerian consideration of historical time in its cognitive genesis is central to my historical theory and method. As a cultural historian, I will present certain basic assumptions in Western culture that can be described as metahistorical assumptions held by thinkers in the arts and the sciences, assumptions held to be true for all time as they entered the historical judgment of these individuals, yet were actually points of view that were quite relative to the time in which they occurred, generated by generational preferences in the categorical lexicon of human time-consciousness. Among the metahistorical categories I will elucidate that created major changes in the arts and the sciences from generation to generation are:

1. historical time as either a gradual (incremental or evolutionary) or a radically discontinuous, changing process;
2. the agency of historical cause being either a group or centered in individuals;
3. historical effects as either highly determined for all events within the compass of their cause or highly accidental, never predictable; and
4. the content of historical cause and its most significant effects to be found in the materiality of persons, places, and things in their mutual interaction or, in contradistinction, to be found in the mutual reciprocity of ideas and intentions of persons as they are directly communicated or through their artifacts in systems of technology or institutional practice.

Ortega y Gasset recognized several of the metahistorical categories in their generational changes I will track in Western culture. He saw the pendulum shift from a collective to an individualistic perspective over generations, as well as the sense of enduring time associated with the collective in contrast to quantum changes with spontaneous suddenness associated with the individualistic perspective (*Gesammelte Werke*, 1950, 1:533–537; 2:112115, 455–460, 462466).

The polar differences within each of these four categories I listed created generational differences as they found expression in each of the arts and sciences of the time. I will describe a period of thought in Western culture from 1815 until the mid-1860s that grasped time as a gradual evolution of persons, places, and things, wherein collective cause created determined effects, and material realities were more evident as causal than the variety of ideas and intentions that attended them. Karl Marx whose thought was of that period called ideas the superstructure of more foundational material relations. Gustav Fechner in psychophysics and physiology spoke of the duality of mind and body as controlled by body, the mind being its dependent variable. I will counterpose that time with a period that stretched from the late 1860s until World War I in which time was seen as a radically changing phenomenon in history and ordinary life, wherein a variety of individual causes created a plethora of differing effects in human as well as natural history, none absolutely predictable. Human history ceased to be considered from the point of view of group causality, individual historical agency became more evident. Human ideas and intentions played a greater role than human physical needs in this era, as well as the artifacts of those ideas and intentions to be recognized in technologies and preferred methodologies in the arts and the sciences. In organic nature, mutation and polycausal perspectives replaced the causal univocalities which characterized humanistic and scientific explanation of 1815 to the mid-1860s. Freud turned Fechner on his head, declaring the mind as the determiner of effects in the body in mental illness. Even Marxists became concerned with ideation and intentionality, the Austro-Marxists Max Adler and Friedrich Adler, for example, considering the cognitive and linguistic bases of differing forms of class-consciousness.

Ortega y Gasset called such shifts as I have delineated in the basic assumptions of change in time as "rhythmic" changes:

> One of the most interesting metahistorical investigations would be in inquiry into the great historical rhythms (*The Task of Our Time*, 1950,84)

Ortega y Gasset was influenced in his notion of historical rhythms by Friedrich Nietzsche. Nietzsche's *The Birth of Tragedy* and *Human, All too Human* breathe through Ortega y Gasset's essays–either cited or implicit (cf. his reference to Nietzsche's vision of historical rhythms in *Gesammelte Werke*, 1950, 2:114–115, 127128). Ortega y Gasset, as Nietzsche, identified the metahistorical rhythms as a species rhythm. In *Human, All too Human* Nietzsche referred to the 80,000 years within which human categories that guided the shaping of historical culture recurred. The human character within these cycles was to all extents and purposes invariant.[3] This could change, and

Nietzsche, Max Scheler, and Ortega y Gasset seemed to think that a transcendence of existing, seemingly invariant characteristics of shaping history would be transcended in their own time.[4] My treatment of the metahistorical rhythms does not postulate this transcendent present or future although I concur with all three men that new species self-understandings are possible, and consequently an altered human praxis, by dint of new insights into the nature of being human.

Ortega y Gasset used the term Homo sapiens when he spoke of "the human as a maker of history" ironically, for the human was an adventure to him, an action in time and space where knowledge was always partial, incomplete.[5] The range of being human historically was a "rhythmic" process in which each phase of the rhythm offered differing forms of human praxis, viewpoints and methodologies of inquiry concomitant with that praxis, and consequently a circumscribed knowledge in accord with the nature of that rhythmic phase (*Gesammelte Werke*, 1950, 1:15–19). Each generation had its rhythm of knowing and acting. Each generation took up tasks in that rhythm of knowing and acting it inherited from the previous generation. A generation could fail to satisfactorily realize their particular task in the metahistorical rhythm of history; Ortega y Gasset thought his own generation had experienced such failure in adequately meeting the required rhythm of his time (*The Task of Our Time*, 1950, 85). The historian would show what was called for in the rhythm of historical creation, and how and why the generation succeeded or failed its species mission.

Most important in Ortega y Gasset's vision of metahistorical rhythmic change is "why" that occurs. Why does the collective move to the individual and back to the collective? Why is time experienced as enduring, and then suddenly quantum spontaneity? Why is material existence emphasized, and then human intention and will? Why is there an assumption of completely determined fate and then an emphasis upon free will? Ortega y Gasset speaks of a teleology in culture that begins with fresh insights by the individual genius, followed by an augmentation of those ideas by cultural agents who create out of them a "socialized" or collective expression that as normative can guide all who exist in that culture. The mass of persons come to see the new normed notions as the "right order" of things, leaving past norms behind (*Gesammelte Werke*, 1950, 3:466). The pendulum shifts from individuality to the collective as guiding assumptions in the cultural activity of a time are actually stages of a teleology of cultural formation. For example, Ortega y Gasset speaks of the innovative age of individuality that brought the idea of science and rationality into being as 1550–1650, ideas with attendant values that gradually became the cultural system of the modern world (*Gesammelte Werke*, 3:439). Undoubtedly, Ortega y Gasset came upon this idea in Wilhelm Dilthey, whose theory of generational change is cited by him (*Gesammelte Werke*, 1950, 2:457, fn 1). Dilthey spoke in his vision of cultural systematization through a movement from individual genius to collectivization of the modern scientific age from pantheism through secular rationality.[6] He is far more detailed in terms of generational stages and contributions than Ortega y Gasset. There is not a straight line in the cultural systematization of science and rationality, rather a spiral development where augmented ideation interrupts collectivization between the sixteenth and the nineteenth centuries, so that a pendulum from individuality to the collective occurs several times over these three centuries.

I depart at this point from Ortega y Gasset and take up Dilthey as my next mentor. Ortega y Gasset has reinforced my discovery of well-articulated metahistorical rhythms in Western history, that move in their inception of new ideas and values bred in individuality to their norming as a collective "right order," from a sense freedom in human praxis to the determinative standards that constrain innovation but guarantee generalized meaning, from a focus upon will and intention to the material realities which seem the time-honored foundation (yet were in themselves merely institutionalization of the new ideas and values). Dilthey's theory of cultural systematization is more detailed than Ortega y Gasset's. William Kluback synthesizes Dilthey's theory of generational change in the service of the cultural systematization of new ideas and values in his study of Dilthey's historical thought:

"He sketched the pattern of development (of new ideas and values in culture) in four stages. In the beginning a new outlook grew primarily out of a new life-relationship which no longer fitted within the old categories. The new life-relationship then expressed itself in new concepts and in fragmentary systems in poetry and unsystematized thought. Out of the early studies there grew up comprehensive, systematic metaphysical constructions. Finally, the new world-view reached maturity when critical investigations laid the epistemological bases for these systems. Only in this final stage, said Dilthey, could lasting progress be made toward understanding the phenomena of historical reality.[7]"

Linked to this four-phased theory of new cultural systematization is Dilthey's concept of the Weltanschauung–the product of the final phase of the new cultural systematization, and the enabling Weltbilder, which provide the kinds of concepts and values that inform the cultural agent's activity in each of the stages. Dilthey's theory of cultural systematization over generations will enable me to not only speak of the metahistorical rhythm, but of "metaparadigms" in the basic assumptions of the culture which guided how inquiry was conducted in the individual "paradigms" of the arts and the sciences in each generational phase of the multigenerational systematization of new ideas and values.

I differ with Dilthey's insights to some degree: I find that each of the four stages generates coherent views of historical reality, not solely in the fully developed cultural-historical ideas of Dilthey's fourth phase that guide long-term historical life. Also, the critical investigations Dilthey sees as the final phase are of what I term the inductively oriented third phase in which a concerted deconstruction of the older system occurs, and a focused, indeed pragmatic reconstruction of the culture's institutions and mores within the aegis of the new ideas and values. I see the fourth phase as a creation of an architectonic of principles built from the previous activity, which are then applied more or less deductively as policies that norm and maintain the cultural system. The collective perspective is the metahistorical rule informing all assumptions in governance and the arts and the sciences. Historical time is now viewed as a gradual, enduring character in which change is not foreseen. Gradual "evolution" enters this fourth of the cycle in the early nineteenth century, but it is an evolution that occurs after ages. There are advances in knowledge, as well, in this fourth phase that are guided by the collective perspective which normalizes the earlier three phases.

Regardless of this difference I have in the staging of the new cultural systematization, Dilthey's concept of the Weltanschauung which emerges out of the Weltbilder "pictures of the world" associated with each stage throughout the system's development provide me with epistemological guidance. The Weltbilder are concepts and images of reality that become the lexicon of each particular stage of cultural systematization. There are particular kinds of Weltbilder for the inception in new ideas and values, other "pictures of the world" for the next phase where differing models of the impact of ideas upon the institutional and informal life of persons, other "pictures of world" for the deconstruction and reconstruction of actual systematic elements of the society, and then "pictures of the world" in that cultural system's final norming. Attention to what constitutes a Weltbild provides me with a conceptual structure that links my current phenomenological historical methodology to its progenitors. The rich heritage of Wilhelm Dilthey and others of his time, such as Edmund Husserl and Max Scheler, exists still in their ever-relevant inquiries into the genesis of historical time in individual human consciousness. The evidence of these stages in the systematization of new cultural ideas, values, and practices is also ever-extant in their artifactual presence in the public culture of a nation as well as in what can be seen as common among the nations.

Dilthey's Weltanschauung was both a philosophical orientation to existence in its more articulate historical consciousness and an ingrained common-sense understanding in the broader popular culture that absorbed these guiding ideas without the theoretical underpinnings (*Gesammelte Schriften*, 1960, 8:13). The concept included three aspects of historical consciousness in any particular generation which guided that phase of cultural systematization: (1) a totality or system of concepts and images that assigns meanings and significance to human existence (called by Dilthey the Weltbild because of the empirical, imagistic content which its concepts order and explain); (2) the psychic laws that structure how this ideation occurs, including the spiritual-emotional responses that in accord with the Weltbild orient the person's praxis; and (3) the praxis of the person which fulfills or avoids the meaning systems of the Weltbild. History is experienced and made within the governing point d'appui and inclinations of the Weltanschauung, as these inclinations are expressed in the linguistic and imagistic guidance of the Weltbild (1960, 8:13). Dilthey states that a Weltanschauung is "bildend, gestaltend, reformierend," that is in constant movement because the individual is situated in the flux of events, which creates the need to transform and change one's system of ideas and actions to adequately respond to this flux (1960, 8: 84, 13). Nonetheless, despite its constant movement, a Weltanschauung has a coherent identity, until events radically change the individual's or the culture's meaning systems. Dilthey allows a Weltanschauung to individuals, to nations, and to the broader culture of a society such as the West or the East (1960, 8:47–67).

The concept of Weltbild as "empirical, imagistic" content became increasingly a manner of understanding how opaque assumptions created selectively one's imagistic understanding of a time and place and condition. Dilthey's late nineteenth century historiographical innovations entered a wedge in the sense of "one objective reality" each person in any time could access; rather, given the same circumstances, differing Weltbilder harbored by differing individuals could generate differing facts that supported differing meanings in those same circumstances. Indeed, what were the circumstances themselves would vary for each person. On the other hand, in a certain generation there were generally shared assumptions that generated approximate samenesses in how a state-of-affairs was examined, especially in the disciplines of the arts and the sciences in that particular generation. I begin here to show the European, indeed Germanic ancestry of Thomas Kuhn's concept of the "paradigm" and the "metaparadigm." A paradigm, equivalent to the Diltheyan Weltbild that governed the conduct of inquiry in a discipline of a generation, would be the assumptions that governed problem or hypothesis articulations, methods of inquiry into the problem or hypothesis formulations, and the favored principles that provided explicative and explanatory expositions of the conduct of inquiry. The paradigm as Weltbild is not philosophical, rather tangibly present in workable hypotheses, methods for gathering empirical evidence, and responsible in its rational explications and explanations to the rules of logic, even new logical formulations capable of demonstrating new insights. Kuhn explicates this quite clearly. He dwells on the tangibles of problem formulation, method of inquiry, explications, and explanations in his *The Structure of Scientific Revolutions*. One of Kuhn's interpreters, Margaret Masterman, makes a strong case for this pragmatic, procedural focus of the Kuhnian paradigm.[8] She speaks of the "paradigm" in Kuhn's "concrete" application: "as an actual textbook...supplying tools, as actual instrumentation"

of how science was practiced according to normed procedures in one or
more generations (Masterman, 1970, 65). A metaparadigm, on the other hand,
as equivalent to the Diltheyan Weltanschauung is philosophical–an array of
principles, values, theses, and the like that are the entry to and outcome of
a multigenerational departure from how the world had been addressed in a
previous cultural systematization, and what the new horizons of the individual
disciplines of the arts and sciences will be over several generations as the new
cultural assumptions are made into a concrete system of institutions and daily
life.

Kuhn articulates the concept of a metaparadigm several times in his *The
Structure of Scientific Revolutions* according to Margaret Masterman, who uses
this term for the first time in describing Kuhn's theory in the above-cited 1965
colloquium dedicated to Kuhn's work. Masterman says that Kuhn saw not only
change over time in the basic assumptions of a discipline, but in a broader
world-view shared more generally across a scientific culture: "For [Kuhn's]
metaparadigm is something far wiser than, and ideologically prior to, theory: i.e.
a whole Weltanschauung" (*The Nature of a Paradigm*, 1970, 67). Masterman
states that one can read of the metaparadigm, rather than the mere paradigm on
many pages in *The Structure of Scientific Revolutions*–pp. 2, 4, 17, 102, 108,
117–121, and 128 of the first edition (*The Nature of a Paradigm*, 1970, 65).[9]
Kuhn speaks for example, according to Masterman, of the metaparadigm shared
across many fields because of the "shift of vision" generated by a crisis in
cultural understanding that effects over time a new cultural systematization of
science. The crises recur over centuries introducing new ideas and values. Such
a crisis occurred according to Kuhn in the late sixteenth and early seventeenth
centuries. Harbingers of the new cultural vision (Dilthey's initial stage of
genius) were, for Kuhn, Galileo, Descartes, and Newton:

> Aristotle and Galileo both saw pendulums, but they differed in their interpreta-
> tions of what they had seen.

> Let me say at once that this very usual view of what occurs when scientists
> change their minds about fundamental matters can be neither all wrong nor a
> mere mistake. Rather it is an essential part of a philosophical paradigm (read
> according to Masterman "metaparadigm") initiated by Descartes and developed
> at the same time as Newtonian dynamics. That paradigm has served both science
> and philosophy well. Its exploitation, like that of dynamics itself, has been fruitful
> of a fundamental understanding that perhaps could not have been achieved in
> another way. But as the example of Newtonian dynamics also indicates, even the
> most striking past success provides no guarantee that crisis can be indefinitely
> postponed. Today research in parts of philosophy, psychology, linguistics, and
> even art history, all converge to suggest that the traditional paradigm is somehow
> askew (my emphases) (*Structure of Scientific Revolutions*, 1962, 119–120).

As I have suggested, Wilhelm Dilthey's second volume in his *Gesammelte Schriften* which charts carefully the new cultural systematizations of rationalism and science since the 1500s through the Enlightenment in the West could have been a model for Kuhn. I doubt that Kuhn ever consulted Dilthey, as his tentative insights into the history of science are far less thorough than Dilthey in their development of the metaparadigmatic assumptions of each century.

Kuhn is best in reviewing the "concrete" level of the "paradigm" that guides a discipline within a metaparadigmatic set of assumptions. One can abstract at least twenty-one "concrete" characteristics of the procedures of disciplines that erect an emergent new paradigm and then establish it as a normed conduct of inquiry in Kuhn's *The Structure of Scientific Revolutions*:

Characteristics of an emergent paradigm

1. New paradigms are conservative: they preserve most of the terminology, examples, and methods of previous views (1962, 7, 141–142, 168).
2. The emergence of a new paradigm is a slow process (where new problematic insights and methods incrementally replace traditional procedures among an increasing body of inquirers) (1962, 84–85).
3. The emergence of a new paradigm is accompanied by the creation or adaptation of new methods for collecting and analyzing data (1962, 84–85).
4. New paradigms explain existing anomalies (better, more simply, more completely than did previous views) (1962, 154).
5. In new paradigms explanation generally runs ahead of proof–the details which provide firm support for arguments must be filled in (1962, 44, 46).
6. A new paradigm appeals to others (i.e., those working in other fields) because it offers illumination and confirmation of their assumptions and insights that have begun to changes their paradigms) (1962, 120, 166).
7. Popular acceptance of a new paradigm requires that it be consonant with deeply held self-evident beliefs (i.e. with the metaparadigm which exists at the time) (1962, 127).
8. A new paradigm must be seen as culturally useful if it is to stimulate "normal" scientific activity (1962, 23–24). Characteristics of a normalized paradigm
9. A paradigm is characterized by the use of distinctive methods–methods accepted by all those carrying out research within the paradigm (1962, 47–48).
10. A paradigm produces a standard stock of demonstrations and examples used to illustrate basic methods and prove basic principles (1962, 46–47).
11. A paradigm recognizes a limited number of valid sources for data (1962, 4, 24).

12. A paradigm insulates researchers from distracting problems and phenomena (1962, 37).
13. A paradigm guides researchers in choosing activities and problems for investigation (1962, 24).
14. A paradigm limits the range of hypotheses which can be offered as explanations for problems (1962, 24).
15. Those sharing a paradigm uses uniform language (1962, 127–128, 135).
16. Those working within a paradigm must meet rigid standards for orthodoxy (i.e. to be accepted as members of the community of researchers) (1962, 167–168).
17. Researchers within a paradigm never question its foundations–its basic hypotheses, methods, categories of acceptable evidence, etc. (1962, 47).
18. Researchers sharing a paradigm are often unable to articulate the foundations on which the paradigm is built (1962, 47).
19. A paradigm produces data which lasts even when the paradigm is replaced as the previous concepts and methods when rigorously applied generated actual facts (that the new paradigmatic methods might ignore) (1962, 139–142).
20. Most paradigms use books only as texts for teaching new researchers; active communication between or among established researchers is carried out through highly specialized short reports (1962, 135–137).
21. All of the paradigms which are widely accepted in any period by a culture share many common features of problematizing, methodology, and acceptable evidence (1962, 120).

Kuhn's specificity gives a rich basis to the concrete aspects of the conduct of inquiry that have a paradigmatic coherence. He had a predecessor in this specificity a century before, Ernst Mach, an Austrian-German physicist who saw how through the assumptions that undergirded certain scientific practices the concepts and procedures of the sciences changed and were normalized. Mach wrote the scientific histories of several fields elucidating how they developed around a new conception that guided explication and explanation. In his introduction to the *Principles of the Theory of Heat, Historically and Critically Elucidated* (1986), Mach describes the evolving emergence, normalization, and deconstruction of paradigmatic approaches:

> Historical studies are a very essential part of a scientific education. They acquaint us with other problems, other hypotheses, and other modes of viewing things, as well as with the facts and conditions of their origin, growth, and eventual decay. Under the pressure of other facts which formerly stood in the foreground other notions than those obtaining to-day were formed, other problems arose and found their solution, only to make away in their turn for the new ones that were to come after them.[10]

In his *Popular Scientific Lectures* (1894), Mach describes how the ideas from past paradigms could still be of value if reapplied in innovative ways. As an Austrian, Mach's national narrative stresses that no past reality ever ceases entirely to be of living value if consulted; Mach incorporated this understanding in treating the seminal ideas of past paradigms, even after their dissolution (cf. my first paper in this journal The Austrian and German Historical Narrative). Mach testifies to the continuing value of Newton's concept of attraction and repulsion in physics, even as Mach himself borrows the concept of acceleration from medieval physics to begin a new vision of measurement in physics (which leads to the measure of the speed of sound).[11] Ideas in a science (or art) guide how one sees a phenomenon. Ideas can be used to redirect knowledge gathering. A physical idea is a guide to "measuring" physical phenomena:

> our ideas must be based directly upon sensation. We call this measuring (*Popular Scientific Lectures*, 1943, 206).

What serves as a measure, however, most often becomes elevated to the status of a universal, unchanging truth. Mach's awareness of changing paradigmatic assumptions in a discipline made him sensitive to this distortion of the locus of validity of an idea:

> All physical ideas and principles are succinct directions, frequently involving subordinate directions, for the employment of economically classified experiences, ready for use. Their conciseness, as also the fact that their contents are rarely exhibited in full, often invests them with the semblance of independent existence. Poetical myths regarding such ideas,–for example, that of Time, the producer and devourer of all things,–do not concern us here. We need only remand the reader that even Newton speaks of an absolute time independent of all phenomena, and of an absolute space–views which even Kant did not shake off, and which are often seriously entertained to-day (*Popular Scientific Lectures*, 1943, 204).

Mach infers that paradigm development itself becomes a belief in a set of assumptions held to be the only objectively real address of the content studied. Ironically, Mach's new departure in physics had a family resemblance methodologically to many other disciplines in the arts and the sciences of his time–which I will address in my study of the metaparadigmatic assumptions and shared methodologies of the arts and the sciences between the late 1860s and World War I. Mach too was blind to the shared assumptions that cued him toward "acceleration" as a counter-concept to Newton's "attraction."

Mach's Weltbild like others of his generation in differing arts and sciences was a "way of seeing" that had undergirding concepts, forms of measurement and explication, and even explanatory principles in common. Ludwig Wittgenstein, a fellow Austrian German of a younger generation, dwelled at length on the manner in which a "picture of the world" preceded theory, indeed was a visual understanding whose generating assumptions and attendant lines of inquiry were usually unrecognized. While Mach appreciated these deeper geneses of a way of seeing in past science, he did not fully comprehend how his "accelerative" view of reality shared the metaparadigmatic assumptions of the present. The "image" of reality was seen, but its roots were not fully appreciated. Wittgenstein writes, for example:

> A picture held us captive. And we could not get outside it, for it lay in our language and language seemed to repeat it to us inexorably.[12]

> How do I know that this line of thought has led me to this action?–Well, it is a particular picture: for example, of a calculation leading to a further experiment in an experimental investigation. It looks like this–and now I could describe an example [*Philosophical Investigations*, 1958, 137 (Prop. 490)].

> One wants to say that an order is a picture of the action which was carried out on the order; but also that it is a picture of the action which is to be carried out on the order [*Philosophical Investigations*, 1958, 141 (Prop. 519)].

Wittgenstein filled a large part of his text with these incisive investigations into the nature of immediate perception and the concept of "Bild" "image/picture." I include one more which is a challenge I have taken up; that is, to examine one's picture of the world as it occurs in both verbal and nonverbal judgment. Each picture is a completed predication whose verbal or nonverbal grammatical style[13] reveals the hidden assumptions and rules to be enacted in praxis by the perceiver:

> To have an opinion is a state.–A state of what? Of the soul? Of the mind? Well, of what object does one say that it has an opinion? Of Mr. N.N. for example. And that is the correct answer.

> One should not expect to be enlightened by the answer to that question. Others go deeper: What, in particular cases, do we regard as criteria for someone's being of such-and-such opinion? When: he has altered his opinion? And so on. The picture which the answers to these questions give us shows what gets treated grammatically as a state here [*Philosophical Investigations*, 1958, 151 (Prop. 573)].

How does one "freeze" a picture of reality so as to examine it? The picture of reality can be discerned in the artifacts of judgment. One can see in a conceptual choice, in a selection or even construction of a method by which one examines and analyzes, the picture of reality that offers itself as the bases for inquiry. My approach is to use the sentential judgments (and pictorial judgments) of persons as that frozen, artifactual image. My approach to using the "picture of the world" contained in a verbal or nonverbal (pictorial) judgment may or may not have been accepted by Wittgenstein. Nonetheless, I will explicate the judgment as in its grammatical structure as an artifact of the meaning imparted by the individual in what now is taken up as an artifact of that person's intent and comprehension. Almost all artists, humanists, and scientists work within the norms for the conduct of inquiry within their disciplines. These norms in their prescriptive lexicon are a public leaven for that individual's intent and meaning. Wittgenstein asserts above that these rules are within their very images of reality, to be seen in the artifacts of their predication. Prescriptive reality is engendered in and through their actions–actions initiated by a "picture of a state-of-affairs" in the moment. The order generated in the acts of a person is not a consequence of the formal rules in an external form they attend, but inherently in the self-generation of the pictures of reality which are every waking (and sleeping?) judgment. These Weltbilder are engendered subtly every day by teachers in many fields, popular media, and other sources, besides their disciplinary leaders, and come to be the narrative guide whereby each judgment is shaped. There is a deeper narrative guide that is a highly personal historical logic. I will touch on that below. However, the region, the nation, and the larger societal culture (i.e., the West; East Asia, etc.) are also present in each judgment as part of the grammar which shapes the guiding prescriptive picture, accompanying syntactic elements of the deeply personal. How can that be? I will address that below as I discuss the complex layers of the Weltbild.

Since it is in the very picture of reality in a judgment that an artist, humanist, or scientist works, Kuhn is correct in his above claims:

17. Researchers within a paradigm never question its foundations–its basic hypotheses, methods, categories of acceptable evidence, etc.
18. Researchers sharing a paradigm are often unable to articulate the foundations on which the paradigm is built.

Praxis in the real world does not often refer in a deliberative manner to theory, rather to what is actually seen as the appropriate move, and each next step emerges in the same immediate manner. This leads critics of paradigm theory to assert that all that exists is individual creativity at the level of procedure in the conduct of inquiry, not paradigmatic, prescriptive rules. What such critics fail to realize is the imagistic locus of the paradigmatic influence–in the Wittgensteinian sense. Margaret Masterman emphasizes the origin of prescriptive paradigmatic practice in the very procedures: "A paradigm has to be a [concrete] 'picture'...because it has to be a 'way of seeing'" (*The Nature of a Paradigm*, 1970, 59); "A (concrete) paradigm is less than a theory, since it can be something as little theoretic as a single piece of apparatus: i.e. anything which can cause puzzle-solving to occur" (*The Nature of a Paradigm*, 1970, 67).

Kuhn's twenty-first characteristic "All of the paradigms which are widely accepted in any period by a culture share many common features of problematizing, methodology, and acceptable evidence" (*The Structure of Scientific Revolutions*) will be integrated by me into how I describe the "metaparadigm" that is the aegis of commonality of one or more generations of inquiry. Yet, I will adhere to Margaret Masterman's insistence that the "concrete" level of procedure is closest to empirical evidence of a model in operation. I will point out how certain conceptual perspectives, modes of inquiry, kinds of content explicated, and explanatory forms of rhetoric are "concretely" a metaparadigm of a generation in the sharedness of the manner of conducting inquiry among the arts and sciences of the time. Margaret Masterman emphasizes that the difference between a metaparadigm and the paradigm is in the philosophical abstractness of the former and the empirical means of the inquiry of the latter, which enables the ideas and values of the metaparadigm to actually become a factual discovery or a solved problem. Her distinction is useful, but it makes a distinction that can interfere with the recognition of shared procedural aspects across disciplines that must be considered metaparadigmatic if one is to appreciate the concrete conduct of inquiry pervasive as a cultural systematization.

Dilthey's concept of the Weltbild, the conscious meaning systems that are the basis of historical conceptions of existence, will be augmented in my usage. I will incorporate his notion of psychic laws that create the parameters for the Weltbild into the Weltbild itself. This integration of Dilthey's first and second aspects of historical consciousness enables me to discuss the close relationship between the concepts and images of historical meaning and the generative psychic activity. Dilthey discriminated between the Weltbild and its psychic rules so as to isolate that which is empirical from that which is an unseen set of intellectual operations. However, in my vision of the Weltbild, the logical/psychic operations that impart an order to events are empirically present in every artifact of a thinker. The rules of psychic activity can be found in their products. This premise will be explained in my second section: it is the heart of what I mean by phenomenological history. The rule-giving operations that constitute the logic and grammar of the surface sentences, and the design of the more extended passages of thought, are also present as a semantic-syntactical content in that manifest thought. The images wrought by the fine artist or anyone in command of representational and nonrepresentational artistic rules are also forms of judgment that can be explicated in the manifest depictions of nonverbal statements. This paper will depict the "concrete" metaparadigmatic aspects of written thought in the arts and the sciences in one metaparadigm– that of the 1750s through the middle 1860s. My second paper will take up the nonverbal artifacts of painting that are evidence of the metaparadigmatic shift from that metaparadigm to a new one that begins in the late 1860s, culminating its fourth phase in the mid-1960s.

2. PHENOMENOLOGICAL HISTORY: REVEALING THE FOUNDATIONS FOR HISTORICAL TIME IN HUMAN JUDGMENT

What constitutes in the mind of cultural-historical agents the Weltbilder which impart form to the public institutions which carry the historical rhythms of a culture over time? If it was truly a physiology of the human as a creator of history, a *zoon historion*, then the metahistorical science would speak of structural constants of historical understanding over time that varied in their expression, in their differing emphases–invariants whose manifest forms generated the differing rhythms of history. I term the generating forces of a historical rhythm invariants in the spirit of Max Scheler, a friend of Ortega y Gasset, who while he saw history as in part the real interests and forces of a time, on the other hand as a philosophical phenomenologist described how these real aspects of life were co-conditioned by cognitive forms of understanding, factors of consciousness that affected the actual praxis of historical life. How humans ordered and valued their image of the political-social interests and forces of a time determined the activity of a generation. The metahistorical rhythm for Ortega y Gasset and Max Scheler was an intergenerational schematic, generated from generation to generation by the complex of recurring cognitive organizers as they structured the material content of societal experience. Issues and material circumstances of persons and societies might change constantly, but under-girding how they were perceived and organized into institutional realities were the invariants of historical knowing. Max Scheler had written:

> The sociological character of all knowledge, all thought-, intuitional-, and knowledge-forms is indisputable: that does not mean the content of knowledge and still less its validity, rather the selection of the objects of knowing according to the prevailing social-intentional perspective. Further, the "forms" of the spiritual acts in which knowledge is acquired, always and necessarily socio-logical, that is through the structure of the society, are co-conditioned. I say co-conditioned. I reject the "sociologism" (a pendant of psychologism) which differentiate neither the thought- and intuitional-forms from the "essential-forms" "Seinsformen", nor the successive reflective knowledge of both forms from the forms themselves. The essential-forms (with Kant) can be found within the thought- and intuitional-forms, but (in contradiction to Kant) these subjective forms themselves are derived (by sociologism) from the work- and language-forms of "society." This kind of origin theory corresponds to a conventionalism in logic and theory of knowledge like Thomas Hobbes first taught ("truth and falsity is only within human speech").[14]

A phenomenological history explores two sources of an event-structure according to Scheler–the invariant laws of judgment whose temporality gives rise to the "A ⊃ B" which is an "event," and the lexicon of the culture that offers the semantical terms by which that succession is named. Scheler has defined this duality in the phenomenological historical enterprise as one that attends both the contingencies of a culture's political sociology and their "co-conditioning" by invariant cognitive structures of the individual which shape this experience.

The pre-World War I generation of intellectuals had deepened epistemo-logical understanding of how human consciousness gives form to human experience, particularly the Germans and Austrian-Germans whose Enlight-enment breakthroughs from Kant through Hegel were revisited. Thomas Mann, imbued with this spirit, identified two invariants of historical consciousness that will be central to my own approach to the nature of the metahistorical knowing, stating that "epochs of individualistic and of social thought alternate in history."[15] I have discussed in Section 1 above how Ortega y Gasset and Dilthey saw a teleological movement from an individualistic age to that which was collective. Each Western nation evidences this shift in its new cultural system-atizations. Yet, Mann's grasp of this variance in cultural-historical emphases also grasped a purely national level to metaparadigmatic formation. Mann's insight was immediately qualified by the assertion that the German could in any generation contribute to both the individualistic and the social, i.e., collective perspective, because his or her historically formed orientation is to see the most radical individuality simultaneously as a functioning unit in a common whole with others (thus supporting my initial paper in this volume on the contrasts between German and Austrian-German historical logic) (*Reflections of a Nonpolitical Man*, 1983, 201–202).

What I present in this second essay is the broader commonality of shared generational metaparadigms across all Western nations. In my first paper in this journal The Austrian and German Historical Narrative, I subsumed the metahis-torical invariants to how the German and the Austrian nation shaped them into distinctively national narratives. In this paper, I will expose the invariants themselves as they exist in every national experience in West as undergirding structures for each particular national narrative in a given generation. Although I stress the West in this paper, my knowledge of world cultures allows me to surmise that these invariants undergird societal historical self-understandings in all world cultures, to be sure, each society and culture shaping out of these invariants its own vision. My premise of cross-cultural categories rooted in the human cognitive manner of organizing historical temporality is akin to Noam Chomsky's premise of a universal grammar. Out of these finite invariants an infinite number of cultural-historical organizations of temporal experience can occur.

The invariants of historical consciousness involve how time and movement in space are conceived. How does movement through space over time constitute event? The English historian G.R. Elton succinctly defined history as "the movement from A to B."[16] To translate this broad metaphor into epistemologi-cally fecund categories one turns first to Kant who showed how all inner sense and understanding is subject to time: "All our knowledge is thus finally subject to time, the formal condition of inner sense."[17] Kant demonstrated this premise by elucidating how in every organization of a person, place, or thing in human attention, there is a movement between parts and parts, parts and wholes, and wholes and wholes. Kant clarified how the part-whole successions as quanti-tative structure create a temporal series that can vary as kinds of qualitative temporality. Temporality in its qualitative variations is created by the relations and corresponding movement perceived between the parts and wholes in a state-of-affairs, the parts and wholes called by Kant extensive magnitudes that "flow" (*Critique of Pure Reason*, 1968, 204 [A 170, B 212]). The relationships and "flow" were generated by how the human judgment was constructed–not in the state-of-affairs "in itself." Every human judgment was essentially a historical judgment as it organized the temporal series of extensive magnitudes in some order of relationship, i.e., occurrence. To experience "change" is occasioned by the disjunctive flow from whole to whole; to experience "duration" is the continued governance of every partial moment by the one whole which is being formed or which maintains its authority over every augmented part. These differences in part-whole structure and the movement that constitutes that structure are a qualitative temporality. The quality is always expressed by empirical content, but actually as history its quality is in its "enduring," "changing," "emerging," "dissipating," or other manner of temporal relation as an event-structure. Edmund Husserl has taken up this Kantian understanding in the twentieth century, focusing upon how each sentential judgment itself is a creator and conveyor of an inner sense of time.[18] The syntax of the sentence–the placement of phrases and clauses and their mutual relations–forms the temporal event. Husserl speaks of a new form of grammar that can reveal how the connectedness and flow of time-stretches (Kantian extensive magnitudes) are formed by syntactical relations (*Logical Investigations*, 2:507–522). Thus, time is not merely a verbal tense or a semantic noun that imputes qualitative tempo-rality; rather, it is the experience of whole separated from whole in a sentence where the placement and punctuation give one the inner sense of discontinuity, or the experience of part to whole that carries connectedenss and continuity, such as a subjective complement.

There is, of course, actual movement in the environment, that is, actual time. Not that cognition created the movement which is time, rather as a series of locks on the river of time, a certain order is given to the flux. Picture time as the water in a river, as Heraclitus had it, flowing constantly, and ostensibly changing each moment. Now picture that river channeled by a set of locks in each person's cognition. The cognitive "locks" perform a "diairesis,"[19] i.e., "dividing according to a thing's natural joints."

History, then, in the Kantian and Husserlian phenomenological understanding is the human judgment that delineated what was an event. The judgment generates time through its form of order as attention depicts movement as connected or unconnected among its parts and wholes: whether the event was a continuity of extensive magnitudes that were related, or whether it was a discontinuity between separate wholes, whether there was duration of the same parts and wholes, or whether one could see an incremental change that allowed a relative continuity within increasing discontinuities. In our common-sense comprehension of history, these variations in change and duration, continuity and discontinuity are "self-evident." Yet, despite the self-evident, matter-of-fact acceptance of such differentiations, how these perceptions are generated and how they subtly affect each sentential judgment or larger theory of history has not been explored in a focused manner. There are three levels in my studies of human historical cognition that explore these differing manners of diairesis in comprehending events–the personal, the national, and the continental (the West, South Asia, East Asia, Near East, etc.) or more recently, the world culture.

The diaireses are the manner in which parts and wholes structure change or duration over time. One can broadly differentiate between a diairesis that shows rapid change and another that shows gradual change. Change in time can never be denied, although some forms of diairesis depict recurrence. The prereflective processes which constitute historical order through part-whole alignments become an overt grammatical order as one uses language to predicate the nature of the event. The Weltbild is not simply a set of finished concepts, rather a sentential undergirding of syntax and semantics that is the trace of the psychic operations that formed it. Realizing these traces through the empirical analysis of the Weltbild enables one to more consciously and finely educate a historical logic, in the individual as well as in the nation. Becoming aware of how one thinks historically can enable one to cull the literature and language of culture to enrich one's lexicon so as to better articulate that historical logic. Knowing the dynamic form of one's historical vision through the evidence of the manifest content enables one to use the Bild more carefully as a guide for one's Bildung–as the German might put it.

Within each sentential judgment of a person educated into his or her culture one can find three levels of diairesis–the personal, the national, and the world-region, i.e., the West, East Asia, etc. The personal is the most fundamental in that its diairesis guides one's development of sentential judgment as one matures.

2.1.   Personal historical logic

One can discern the presence of a singular syntactical style of historical judgment in a person over a career of thought in each sentential judgment that is a "well-formed" sentence. In earlier publications I have detailed how the personal style of conceiving history is imparted in each "well-formed" sentence as it conveys that person's recurrent part-whole diairesis. Among the great thinkers in history I have explored over a career of thought were Paracelsus, Johann Wolfgang von Goethe, Carl Gustav Jung, Werner Sombart, and Max Weber.[20] This personal historical style of judgment is of psychogenetic origin; its invariant expression in each sentential judgment a necessity of how the singular ideation of the person occurs.

2.2.   National historical logic

The presence of national conventions of conceiving and articulating historical events by individuals, regardless of their personal style which are never in complete accord with these cultural rules, can distort individual judgmet The national convention is a narrative order of utterances and concepts that buttress the semantic meaning of this narrative. Personal logics must always speak through the norms of the narrative order of the wider public, as it exists in differing disciplines and the genres of popular culture. Idioms are an additional feature of national conventions. Personal conversations between individuals that do not require the narrative order of the national conventions are experienced in the idiomatic expressions that enable colloquial informality.

The national conventions are amalgams that integrate several kinds of the personal historical logic into a narrative diairesis that can be discerned in the semantic and syntactic conventions which establish the narrative sequence or "plot" of how relationships are to develop. Although they are structured within the full design of the sentential judgmental style of the person, an overlay of the national conventions is recognizable in certain recurring concepts shared among the populace of a generation and in the idioms most salient. These national conventions of viewing history are created by the political-social experience of the nation (cf. my initial article in this publication, "Contrasting Historical-Logical Narrative Conventions in Germany and Austria and Their Influence upon Inquiry and Explanation in the Arts and the Sciences"). The national conventions of conceiving historical events are purely arbitrary, derived out of the accidents of historical experience, and the perceived "necessity" of explaining and organizing a historical life so as to reassure a citizenry of the stable continuity of how a life is to be conceived and lived.

The epistemological bases of these rhetorical and semantic conventions are the same invariant manners by which extensive magnitudes (parts and wholes) are connected in a personal historical judgment, forms of relatedness which generate and convey temporality (the movement of attention guided by these alignments of parts and wholes). In the national narrative order, the relationships of part-whole extend over utterances which encompass paragraphs, creating a plot-like convergence in the story of events. The personal logic, on the other hand, is a recurrent temporal picture in each sentence that more rigorously presents an event, staying closer to the particular facts than the rhetorical, plot-like picture of the national conventions. Thus, the national conventions as arbitrary constructs most often create a competing picture of events with one's own actual historical logic. A discerning mind can see this disparity. The salient concepts and idioms of the national historical logic steer personal understanding toward the national Weltbild, but the personal is there for a more authentic personal comprehension if one is aware of how it either conflicts or supports the national. For example, the Tudor-Stuart national historical convention of seeing events as antitheses was a seemingly unavoidable understanding,[21] but minds such as Francis Bacon could comprehend how rhetorical "icons" so characterized what might be other than that premise.[22]

I will call these national historical conventions metahistorical in that they offer the basic assumptions of a time. These assumptions are always embedded in the rhetorical conventions and idioms of the popular culture, and in the explication and explanation of the arts and the sciences of their time. The metahistorical conventions are not imposed at a theoretical level in a discipline, rather as Margaret Masterman emphasizes, out of the concrete practices where innovators intuited the next step. Nonetheless, these insights in each separate discipline are subtly guided by the political-social national experience through its infusion of life meanings, values, and expected temporal rhythms and outcomes. The sense of a complete life in its seasons imbued and fostered by the national historical forms that have been constructed from the cognitive invariants of temporal-spatial experience are translated largely unknowingly into the paradigmatic tenets of a field of inquiry or popular entertainment and reciprocally reinforce the national assumptions. The national historical narrative is not noticed; it works its influence upon individual creativity in a discipline person by person.

Francis Bacon's insight into the "icons" of judgment in a given time was among the first socially astute comprehensions in the early modern age into idiomatic and narrative bias that skewed personal judgment. Plato's analogy of the cave in which the shadows of the manufactured objects were projected into one's field of vision is the oldest comprehension of this process in the

West. Out of the overview by an interdisciplinary mind may come a new general philosophy of the time. The cultural historian who has a sound grasp of the range of disciplines of a culture can then generate a cultural theory of history for that society–albeit influenced by his own personal historical logic. Most "authorities" in a discipline never rise to the clarity that permits insight into the distorting role of national convention. Most authorities in the differing disciplines never see their relationships to other disciplines. The authorities, by dint of the political-social influences that led them intuitively to make certain changes or preserve certain constancies in the fields, will never come to see the metahistorical family resemblances that link them to other disciplines in their common culture.

Mann's testimony to the individual as simultaneously a link in an organic whole is an expression of the national German historical convention. I have shown how within the German notion of an event there is "the many as the one," that is, the many individuals of the nation are comprehended by the homogeneous unity they strive to configure. Such a time is convergent, but discontinuous, a dialectic of thesis and antithesis that seeks a common synthesis. A radical individuality is favored that has been connected with Luther, but always existed in the German spirit: only by the "encounter" of person and person can these contrasting individualities achieve the unity which is an ideal. Historical time thus is filled with conflicting wholes, but transcendent moments of unity among them. The Austrian "soft law" of historical judgment, in contradistinction, is one in which 'the one is the many," where an inter-dependence of cooperating persons generates a whole out of their separate, yet intersubjective integrities. The experience of such a time is that of a continuous flow of coexistent moments, and a continuing development over time–much different than the German sense of an event as either conflict or transcendence.

The authority lent to the imparting of the national historical convention in one's own rhetoric with its larger genre-based structures of "plot" and explicative and explanatory rules, as well as its semantic metaphors, analogues, and other habitual expressions, lies in the claim of these forms of explication and explanation to "objectivity." In truth, the individual may accept these forms, but the perspectives created may conflict with how persons actually see events immediately in an actual perception. Perception is often replaced, especially for events at a distance, by the normative modes of the culture. As I have demonstrated in my attention to German and Austrian-German economists, even a "science" is not immune from the subtle public pressure of the explicative and explanatory guides of how the nation wills to see the structure of events.

The personal conflict that exists between personal and national norms of historical understanding is rarely thought through. Each sentential judgment is a personal vision. The adoption of genre-based norms of rhetorical exposition and explanation, and other cultural semantic expressions, can blunt or obfuscate one's personal understanding. Nonetheless, as I explore in the first article, the very institutions and problem-formulations of one's culture are also historical experience. Thus, while one's immediate vision may be considered what actually occurs to that person, the national cultural-historical conventions are as real in their impact upon that person's reflections of his or her cultural experience. Obviously, a new personal dialogue must be encouraged that separates how one's personal logic operates in the face of the rhetorical and semantic conventions which so strongly influence what is judged.

2.3.   The Western (and world) metaparadigms in their individual and collective aspects

The regional or world metaparadigm arises among the several or many nations of the world who engage in mutual political and economic activity, particularly among those who have had this interaction over centuries. The regional or world metaparadigm harbors assumptions that are deemed necessary for the development of knowledge into those relations which are between nations and regions. Indeed, inquiry in the arts and sciences of a nation most often has to do with the interdependencies that are more extensive than nation. The metaparadigm of regional and world interdependence generates in its assumptions questions to be explored by inquiry. This metaparadigm is as contingent upon the events of experience as the national narrative, and as arbitrary in that it isolates only certain perspectives in a time that appear most salient. Moreover, there is a defensive linguistic posture in the metaparadigm that aims to protect and to preserve integrities in the culture that seem the bases of a normal existence. Certain assumptions arise of a generation that affect how culture and society in that time should address its public and private activities. Institutional and personal aspirations and order emerge, structured as historical organizations through the same cognitive, invariant organizers as the personal historical logic, but partaking in the rhetorical narrative plot, idioms, and concepts that as the national historical conventions impart the orientation to inquiry as well as to defensive, maintenance-oriented meanings that enable groups of individuals to coexist despite their singular personal understandings.

3.   THE CATEGORICAL ASSUMPTIONS
     THAT UNDERLIE THE FOUR-PHASED
     CYCLE OF CULTURAL SYSTEMATIZATION
     SPANNING THE WESTERN NATIONS
     (EUROPE AND NORTH AMERICA)

I rely on Aristotle and Kant in confirming certain basic categories of judgment organize human experience into qualitative meaning. All the topics of Aristotle or the categories of judgment of Kant can be seen as derived from the relationships of part to part, part to whole, or whole to whole that I have shown as generating the temporal flux in human judgment. Kant makes this appreciation in *The Critique of Pure Reason* where he derives any concepts that result from a judgment from the succession of part-whole relationships [1968, 134 (A 104)]. Kant points out that the articulation of concept is an act based upon the product of the succession of part-whole extensive magnitudes, yet he states that this connection of product to the temporal concretum formed of part-whole relationships in the act of predication remains opaque for most thinkers (including Aristotle)[23]:

> This consciousness may often be only faint, so that we do not connect (the concept) with the act itself, that is, not in any direct manner with the generation of the representation, but only with outcome (that which is thereby represented). But notwithstanding these variations, such consciousness, however indistinct, must always be present; without it, concepts, and therewith knowledge of objects, are altogether impossible [1968, 134, (A 104)].

Even before names fix these relationships into concept (topic, category, name, etc.), the existence of the relationship is discerned in the part-whole flux. The matter of existence in its part-whole relationships "flows" past one's attention as connected, disconnected, enduring, or changing [*Critique of Pure Reason*, 1968, 204 (A 170, B 212)].

Enabling the analyst to see the relationship between a person's concepts of history and their temporal experience is addressed by me in other publications (see footnote 20). In my first article in this publication on Austrian and German historical logics I worked only with the concepts which formed each nation's typical narrative of events in time. Now that I have introduced the notion of the flux of extensive magnitudes that form a discrete event in time (Kant) or the time stretches whose sentential form is the temporal concretum of a discrete event (Husserl), I will refer to both the qualitative temporality and its related historiographical concepts as I demonstrate the shift in generational metaparadigms of the West that enabled cultural systematization.

The cultural systematization of new ideas and values in the West is a four-phased cycle. The initial phase is an emergent new idea and/or value; the second phase is a model for all the significant individual and institutional changes; the third phase is a pragmatic deconstruction of the older system and a construction of the new one; the fourth phase is a normalization of the new system so that it becomes a habitual right order for all its participants. There are four categorical assumptions which underlie the development and implementation of cultural activity in the first three phases that precede the fourth phase of normalization:

(1) the complex individual differences of all integrities (person, place, or thing) that participate in an assumed common totality;
(2) the freedom of intelligent beings or accident/chance for things without mind or will;
(3) quantum change in states-of-affairs;
(4) mind rather than matter as the chief content of judgment.

The fourth phase presents the converse of these concepts: one sees

(1) the collective expression of persons, places, and things, that is, having the totality formed by them in common by dint of shared characteristics;
(2) determinism in the laws of function in intelligent beings and in things without mind or will;
(3) a conception of duration of states-of-affairs;
(4) matter rather than mind is the chief content of judgment.

The temporal experiences or more accurately the qualitative temporalities which give rise to the metahistorical categorical assumptions of the initial three phases and then the fourth phase of cultural systematization can be seen in Immanuel Kant's recognition of the essential difference between an "aggregate" comprehension of the diverse elements in states-of-affairs and the quantum cohesion which assumes the common identity of all particulars; A quantum is a unity of particulars in which discontinuities are obliterated in favor of cohesive continuity: a mark of fine silver (in which the thirteen thalers that lie on the table are subsumed into a unity by a productive synthesis). An aggregate is the thirteen thalers, seen separately that make up the mark of fine silver (in which each thaler is separated from another by the repetition of "an ever-ceasing synthesis" (*Critique of Pure Reason*, A 171, B 213).

The emergent reality of a new cultural systematization is an "aggregate," where attention is given to each existing integrity that constitutes the present collective whole, challenging that whole initially (first phase) in its very assumption of normality and inclusiveness. The qualitative temporality of this first phase for the person or persons whose acts most constitute it in a public manner is an attention to every moment of life in its discrete content, weighing the validity of that discreteness on the judgmental scale of a new rule of existence, in comparison to how that discrete reality has been considered by the extant collective measure. The person who is the agent in the first phase, to use the Kantian analogue, sees that there are twelve coins on the table, not thirteen–he or she has attended each coin's presence with diligence; and, he or she finds the assumption of a commonality that transcends in value each separate coin is false. A sudden or quantum change is demanded; and, the person's praxis is conducted with the authority of one who has seen how the complex individuality of the collective proved the rule of the whole false. An intuition of a new totality is suggested that better suits the aggregate characteristics of each coin (or entity). Qualitative time for those who agree with the demand for quantum change is experienced as an "ever-ceasing" event that leaves no record of moments, for each moment is lived to erase the public reality which oppresses one's everyday. There is a freedom of will known in rejecting the extant "right order" that compensates for its challenge in every detail of everyday life.

The historical agent of the second phase builds a new model from the particulars, suggesting how or where that new totality may be formed given the aggregate characteristics of participating entities. Qualitative time for that person as well as for others who live under the cultural qualitative time thus imparted is that of transcendence. The present gives way in each moment to the sense of an ending and a new beginning. Attending to the model allows one's day to be filled with the abstract "right order" rather than actual realities one disdains.

The qualitative time for the third phase's cultural agents as well as those who adhere to the vision that guides these agents is that of everyday change in its pragmatic work. One does not look at the mountain–to put it in a Taoist analogue–rather, one sees only each step on the path. The deconstruction and reconstruction of society's institutions keep one in the "ever-ceasing" present with everyday presenting a new task. The facts of everyday life are details on the blueprint that one is enacting. One sees the design more than the incomplete material world in which one effects changes.

The qualitative temporality of the fourth phase is that of dwelling perforce in a collective reality common to all. Every episode of experience is measured by the principles of "the right order" worked out in the previous phases of cultural systematization. Time is seen to change gradually, being measured in terms of an institutional development common to all. Material realities surround one, evidence of the tangibility of the "right order"–a seemingly immovable order–that has been established. These "meta" assumptions find their way into disciplinary expression and popular culture in the years involved with each phase. As Kuhn argues, existing conceptual terms take on new meanings, and new concepts are coined.

From a systems theory perspective, the Diltheyan intergenerational sequence that I have modified and presented can be considered an "organismic analogy." Human beings require a stable context of beliefs, assumptions, and the organizational forms that maintain these perspectives. There is a balance of mind and body in any culture. As Dilthey understood, ideation and biology are separate realms, but the nature and pace of ideation accommodate physical needs, and is best imparted in a natural rhythm of human information-processing. The four-phased introduction, modeling, development, and stabilization of a new cultural system through the arts and the sciences and the popular culture are a "self-evident" process.[24] Ludwig von Bertalanffy quotes M. Haire in this regard:

> The biological model for social organizations–and here, particularly for industrial organizations–means taking as a model the living organism and the processes and principles that regulate its growth and development. It means looking for lawful processes in organizational growth (1968, 118).

The gradual integration of new ideas into models, and then actual change of the culture through an application of those ideas requires several decades to accustom a populace to the significance of what is afoot. The work of deconstruction and reconstruction that reorganizes institutions can be traumatic, and requires consensus and accommodation. The new ideation that seems sufficiently significant to reach public effect undoubtedly resolves issues that ease the populaces that can see the value. Then, the establishment of a durative "right order" that serves as the normal life and standard of right and wrong develops that as a final phase continues for another generation (approximately 30–40 years) before the culture again engages in large-scale reexamination of its life issues.

4.   THE THREE METAPARADIGMS OF THE MODERN AGE: THE 1640S TO THE 1740S, THE 1750S TO THE 1860S, AND THE LATE 1860S TO THE 1970S

The first metaparadigm of the modern age was the Western advent of secularism after the century of religious wars. The metaparadigm of secularism was set into tension with religion through the helpmeet of "natural law." By the 1640s, every religious person who was concerned with the seminal social and natural sciences had incorporated Calvin's reintroduction of "natural law" into the theoretical structure of the disciplines that involved their interest. What characterized this metaparadigm began as the Thirty Years' War came to an end on the European continent, and the English Civil War reached its conclusion, was the separation of secular knowledge as an efficient cause and effect from the first cause of all existence, the Divine. Yet, in all arguments over the life of this metaparadigm, thinkers found it necessary to reference the Divine in conjunction with the secular.

Characteristic of this new metaparadigm was the issue of human identity separate from the biblical vision (although the new secular understandings were often used in deliberating the biblical understanding). Another major issue was that of the political "right order," where the concept of a valid secular basis of "sovereignty" enabled thinkers to distance the issue from that of God's will. The natural sciences of animate and inanimate nature, freed by the division of the secular from the divine, began to study phenomena inductively and experimentally. Great divergence in what indeed was accepted as a "natural law truth" existed among populations. Differing understandings of the Divine subtly influenced premises in the arts and the sciences.

The second metaparadigm of the modern age began in the 1750s. This metaparadigm was characterized by a focus solely upon secularism, separating itself from the necessity to include the Divine in its discussions of premises or findings in the arts and the sciences. Even "natural law" dropped away as a causal base of premises or findings. The foundation for a "right order" became human reason alone. A univocal objective world was posited in the arts and the sciences that guaranteed progressive outcomes for inquiry, and the standards to assess that progress. Political sovereignty ceased to be an argument over its natural law source, i.e., in each human or in the monarch or in the nation. The political term "sovereignty" lived on as an empirical designation for how a population chose to order its polity. Human identity was made more complex as psychology became a discipline in itself, separate from philosophy. Indeed, throughout the arts and the sciences disciplines hardened their lines with the rigor of acceptable modes of inquiry.

The third metaparadigm that began in the 1860s sought a secular, yet humanly spiritual basis for enriching personal as well as communal life. Reason alone was not sufficient as a basis for meaning in the world. In doing so, the reflective ego itself was decentered, as new dimensions of intelligence became evident in inquiry. A new secular humanism emerged in the arts as well as the social sciences. The human being ceased to be the rational being whose inquiries and ethos were to be evaluated by generally agreed upon standards set by that very reason. Indeed, the very notion of a univocal objective world with laws to be discerned that were the same for everyone was put into question. Relativity in perception and judgment as well as in the material laws of nature became the study of many disciplines of the arts and the sciences. The physical sciences decentered the traditional building blocks of physical force and chemistry with new levels of material existence.

Polities in this third modern metaparadigm took on new dimensions with international and intercultural cooperation. The new organizational modes of personal and cultural life that emerged by the end of this metaparadigm in the 1960s had a distant resemblance to the decentering of human and material organizations that marked the metaparadigm in which Columbus discovered the Americas and Copernicus saw the earth as a planet of the sun. The metaparadigm that began in the late 1860s and ended in the mid-1960s was a spiral recurrence in its themes of that first age from the late 1400s through the mid-1500s of worldwide exploration as well as in its protestant innovations the first extended inquiry into the complex expressions of mind and spirit. In that time of external and internal reorganization which the metaparadigm of the 1860s through the 1960s mirrored, world cultures came permanently into contact as the first political and economic dependencies were established. Martin Luther, Erasmus, Thomas More, and Calvin found within the person new, seminal laws of reason that were under God's natural law. This was the birth of a second humanism with more complex understanding of the human spirit than the classical under- standings. The 1870s began the third humanism (argued by one of its humanistic leaders, Thomas Mann).[25]

My reference to an earlier metaparadigm than the modern era in the West is deliberate at this point of the essay as the human issues of culture are returned to in a spiraling manner. In every metaparadigm issues of human personal identity, the human polis, physical nature, and other topoii are addressed from new angles. One sees also a return in an augmented way to distant metaparadigms– as in my relation of the late 1860s to 1970 to the metaparadigm I date from the late 1460s through the 1550s. There is a making more complex of issues from metaparadigm to metaparadigm, at least from my standpoint a sign of progress in understanding.

Before I turn to the issue of the four phases of metaparadigms with a study of that reality in one of the three metaparadigms of the modern age (all the length of this essay permits), I need to address the skeptics who wonder at my insistence on such patterns in human culture, let alone accepting my rather definite dating. I make the same broad caveat as Max Weber in considering these metaparadigms "ideal types." In every metaparadigm there will be thinkers who in portions of their thought develop seminal ideas that will come into general acceptance long after the period of their metaparadigm. Thomas Aquinas and Dante Alighieri in many aspects of their insight formed ideas that centuries later became quite significant for the spiraling development of human self- knowledge. Yet, in the main Aquinas and Dante can be seen as solidly within the emergent issues and approaches of their time. Moreover, aspects in the thought of even giants in the history of Western culture can be considered regressive, or more charitably, of earlier metaparadigms. Martin Luther has been seen by many modern scholars as a warrior for a return to late medieval faith (cf. the exchange of views of Wilhelm Dilthey who saw Luther as a pioneer of the early modern understanding with the cultural historian Yorck von Wartenburg; or more recently, Heiko A. Oberman).[26]

Moreover, I recognize that most persons in the several phases of the metaparadigm of their time in spiritual and secular issues may hold opinions that do not partake of the characteristics I have assigned to the metaparadigm–either being of an older one or perhaps one to come. In this I hold the cultural vision of Johann Gottlieb Fichte who saw five possibilities of cultural identification among members of any generation. Fichte posited five ages of culture: The first age was that of humans ruled by their own instincts. The second age was the rule by authoritarian systems which directed how these instincts were lived–it was an age of sublimation to these authorities and authoritative systems through compulsion or belief. The third age was a time when denial of all authority dominated consciousness, with a concomitant rejection of positive values or the concept of truth. The fourth age was that of the rational sciences where objective truth, the fruit of scientific inquiry, reigned. The fifth age was the time of "Vernunftkunst"–the art of shaping an individual life within the locus of the rational truths of self-discovery.[27] Each was a time span whose properties were given by the divine spirit, yet in their presence in the world they overlapped "in one and the same chronological time" (1971, 7:13), rather than following one another in a sequence that could be considered interconnectedly causal. Cause lay in the insight by the individual into his or her own spiritual options. Fichte lived at a time when the fourth age was being given its modern secular bases. Yet, he captures the levels of human understanding that can be discerned among differing individuals of any past metaparadigm.

Nonetheless, I believe that the three metaparadigms I present as the modern age in this paper had the changing characteristics I outlined. Fichte's five internested realities could be found in any of them. In my criterion of a consciously self-directed participant of a new metaparadigm, one could only be a combination of Fichte's fourth and fifth ages–that is, adhering to the rational rules of the time in a thoughtful, rather than slavish, manner; and being self-directed within those guiding ideas or even newer ones of his or her own coin. The person had to be in at least the majority of his or her thought in contact with the "truths" of the age in a creative rather than merely compliant manner. The person must be shown to adhere to the principles found in its emergent, model-building, deconstructive and reconstructive, then normalizing metaparadigmatic phases. Although a creative individual discernible in the past metaparadigms may be most renowned in a particular stage of its emergence

and development, as Thomas Paine and Samuel Adams were for the initial
political activity of the Western metaparadigm in the American colonies of
the 1750s through the early 1860s, many of the greatest contributors to the
metaparadigm lived through all four phases of cultural systematization, in each
phase changing their ideas accordingly. Goethe was such a thinker for the
same metaparadigm of Thomas Paine and Samuel Adams. Goethe's thought
contributed to the emergent complex individuality of the initial phases–the
sudden new ideation, the presentation of a model for individual emulation of
the second phase, the individually focused empirical problems that served for
deconstruction of the old and the reconstruction of the new system in the third
phase, as well as the normalization of collective truths in the final phase.

Goethe's Sturm und Drang period of *Götz von Berlichingen* (1773) and *Die
Leiden des jungen Werthers* (1774), as well as the Gretchen tragedy in the
Urfaust (1774–75), reflect the characteristics of first phase of a metaparadigm
(as Dilthey characterized it):

> In the beginning a new outlook grew primarily out of a new life-relationship
> which no longer fitted within the old categories. The new life-relationship then
> expressed itself in new concepts and in fragmentary systems in poetry and
> unsystematized thought (Kluback, 1956, 38).

The second phase of metaparadigmatic development offered "models" in
the disciplines of the times that were more thorough in working through the
elements introduced in a more fragmentary way in the initial phase. Goethe's
correspondence to this second phase was his "classicist" period after his Italian
journey. Among the works that sketch a new vision of exemplary human
character in its relationships are *Iphigenie auf Tauris* (1787), deliberated during
his trip to Rome and his reflection there on classical mythology and aesthetic
issues, and *Wilhelm Meisters Lehrjahre* (1795–96), written during the French
Revolution as an alternative, as it were, for character development and future
citizenship according to the French model. The third phase of critical deconstruction of an older system and reconstruction of the new can be seen in his
Die Wahlverwandschaften (1809), written at a time of focused reorganization
of civil administration, education, and the military in Prussia. The fourth phase
of collective normalization, where individuals cease to be the primary focus
of concern, and that which is typical of all humans becomes standardized for
the long-range duration of the new values and ideas, are reflected in Goethe's
completion of Faust. Particularly Faust, Part II, which deals with Faust and the
Holy Roman Empire, concluding with Faust's community development project,
are composed in the post-1815 years of the fourth phase.

I must remind the reader that it is within the paradigm of single disciplines
(or in the first modern metaparadigm, broader interdisciplinary areas) that the

"meta" assumptions are expressed. Only the similarity of the "meta" assumptions from discipline to discipline enables the cultural historian to speak of a metaparadigm shared among many disciplines. Why do "meta" assumptions change in the fourfold manner that characterizes the life of a metaparadigm? Systems theory corroborates these changes as rational steps in the formulation of a system. Nonetheless, the larger question that lurks is why does a metaparadigm change across all cultural disciplines in the same decade? And, why do the new ideas and values I ascribe to the modern era of Europe go through three metaparadigms between the 1650s to the late 1960s? Why the change of metaparadigms in the late 1640s, late 1750s, late 1860s, and then in the late 1960s? The question of cause is a necessary one, although I base my arguments that metaparadigms exist on the "meta" assumptions of concrete disciplines in differing time periods, rather than mere speculation. One can abstract from the empirical changes in the theoretical assumptions, methods, content studied, and explicatory and explanative rhetoric of each discpline the "meta" assumptions. Then, looking for "family relationships" among the disciplines in any decade, one begins to posit a certain "phase" of a common "metaparadigm" or when a fourth phase changes to the initial phase of a new "metaparadigm," attending especially to the radical changes in assumptions of each discipline in that time.

Cause for this complex of changes is of several kinds, all interrelated–the political experience of the national and regional culture, the problems and findings within the history of the discipline, the generational issue of teachers and their students. The foundational "meta" premises of a culture emerge from the political events, and consequent understandings of the age. The political reality of a time affects all persons in the fundamental manner suggested by Aristotle, Hegel, and Johann Caspar Bluntschli, the latter a republican in the Germanies of the 1840s. Bluntschli said there was a Wahlverwandschaft "elective affinity" between political and nonpolitical engagements by a thinker that foundationally were to be ascribed to the human as a zoon politikon.[28] This chemical relationship asserted by Bluntschli is commented upon by Friedrich Wilhelm Graf, a contemporary political scientist and historian:

> In a Volk as dynamic as the Germans in the first half of the nineteenth century (Johann Caspar Bluntschli wrote), if the impulse to form political parties is suppressed through punishments and prohibitions, this impulse flees into the realm of religious or confessional policies or sharpens conflicts in the realm of scholarship, art or society. Between these political and unpolitical parties a certain affinity develops, so that for a time one can be the surrogate for the other.[29]

I contend that this affinity and "family resemblance" in expression occurs in times of peace and cooperation as well. I have developed this argument in my first essay in this journal on the Austrian and German historical narrative. While a nation may develop a national style of narrative in presenting findings, within that narrative one can also discern characteristics shared by the broader regional culture, i.e., the West, in that time.

For example, the end of the Thirty Years' War, marked by the Peace of Westphalia, had ripples that affected England as well as the Continent. Secularism began as public policy in the nations sick of religious strife. The metaparadigm where secular science was set in tension with the formal and final cause of God's will had its beginnings in its "meta" influences on all thought in the arts and the sciences. Joseph R. Strayer and Hans W. Gatzke assert that Mazarin's influence upon the Peace of Westphalia substituted "civilization" for "christendom."[30] Louis XIV's stress on a secular public culture, evidenced in his establishment of the royal academy of the arts and the sciences, was echoed by Charles II in England in the next decades. Indeed, the term "civilizing" in the sense of the creation of a secular public world and civil culture enters Western thought in 1649 with John Milton's reflections on the Articles of Peace concluded with the Irish rebels by Charles I's Lord Lieutenant of Ireland, Lord Ormond in 1648. Milton, objecting to the Articles in his adherence to Oliver Cromwell, writes that the Irish rebels contesting of the English dominance in Ireland were rejecting "a civilizing Conquest."[31] Milton's wedge of civil culture was widened with his attack on the "state-religion" in 1659, as he argued for a separation between personal religious issues and civil authority.[32] Milton's thought was encouraged by Cromwell's initial policy of toleration of all religious thought during the Civil War. James Harrington developed in the same period his vision of a "secularized providentialism" that argued for the civil development of the public realm through encouragement of rational improvement.[33] According to Christopher Hill, Harrington's writings set the agenda for English domestic and imperial public policy for the next century.

History became a new perspective, rather than the focus upon the immediacy of consciousness, perception, and judgment which had been the indirect "meta" emphases in the age of strife over conscience and praxis (cf. Descartes *Meditations* and Pascal's *Pensees*). Moreover, the Italian Renaissance experience was insufficient for the new horizon of the major nations. Each of the major nations focused upon eras of historical secular experience in past cultures, generating a new humanistic classicism. The French Academy of Painting in France stipulated that the content of classic Greek and Roman themes, heroic or tragic moments in actual history, was to be the measure of an artist's skills; this accommodated the new secular emphases that began with Richelieu and were carried forward with Mazarin and Louis XIV. French literature turned to history as well, broadening to European history in Corneille's *Le Cid*. Indeed, the modern discipline of history was created with Samuel Pufendorf's Constitution of the German Empire (1667), Leibniz's *Codex Juris Gentium* (1693), Giambattista Vico's *Prinzipi di una Scienza Nuova d'intorno alla comune natura delle nazioni* (1725, 1730, 1744), and Voltaire's *Lettres anglaises ou philosophiques* (1734).

The metaparadigm that followed the four-phased metaparadigm initiated by the end of the religious wars in England and the Continent in the late 1640s also was initiated by a war–the Seven Years' War of 1756–63, a war that ended an entire century of territorial wars concerned in the main with mercantilist issues of empire. I will address this second metaparadigm of the modern age in more depth in the next section.

The problems that emerge in each distinct disciplinary paradigm in the initial phases of the new metaparadigm, while affected by the new "meta" themes and assumptions, inevitably address the inherited concepts and methods from the previous age in its historical roots and developments. One must agree with Thomas Kuhn that new paradigms in disciplines emerge in a conservative manner. While new ideas are articulated, they are articulated through the older lexicon of concepts. Thus, comprehending "cause" in the disciplinary models must take into consideration what has preceded the new metaparadigm or each new phase in the metaparadigm. Problems, methods, and the rhetoric of explication and explanation are inherited and only gradually transformed.

The span of years from the premises of the master teacher through the maturity of his students–40 to 60 years–establishes the initial three phases, and the basic assumptions and initial developments in the fourth phase of a metaparadigm. The generation of a master teacher who has developed his or her theoretical approach to a discipline over perhaps 30 years, carried on by students who have had their premises shaped in many ways for their own maturity, is more than 60 years. The students of the students, less directly involved in the original vision, depart more easily from what has become normalized. The transition to new metaparadigmatic assumptions is more likely.

An actual person experiences the political-social eruptions and changes in his or her youth. The indirect influence that was suggested by Bluntschli affects the basic premises that generate the four phases of one's own discipline directly, but indirectly the basic assumptions of one's political-social culture–the foundation of the disciplinary intuitions. What is the foreground issue politically and socially of one's time? Individuality or community? If the former, one is solidly in the initial three phases of a metaparadigm. Time as a quantum discontinuity and/or changing or a durational continuity is felt as a public rhythm. If the former, one is in the initial three phases. A general public sense of open possibility or, rather, a determined world are also variations that become public assumptions. The latter is a fourth phase perspective. Then, is it ideas that matter or the concrete material causes of one's world? If the latter, one is probably in the fourth phase of any metaparadigm.

One can get the disciplinary emanation of these "meta" assumptions directly through one's teacher. If the teacher is older, the publicly political-social "meta" assumptions the teacher holds that are the indirect progenitor of the disciplinary "meta" assumptions, may differ from the political-social "meta" assumptions of one's own generation. If that is the case, then the "meta" assumptions the young professional brings to the discipline will begin to challenge one's teachers. The disciplinary "meta" assumptions one chooses can be seen indirectly in what one understands of one's milieu and generation. However, it is as a professional that one comprehends the disciplinary "meta" assumptions. They become paradigmatic as one carries them into one's maturity.

In the concluding section of this paper, I will study the four phases of a metaparadigm within the discipline of historical writing and historiographical theory. I will limit my scope to one nation, that of the Germanies in the metaparadigm of the 1750s through the 1860s. I will perforce speak of thinkers who share the "meta" characteristics in other disciplines over the life of the metaparadigm, but not in the depth of detail I give to the historians.

5.   GERMAN HISTORICAL THOUGHT DURING THE FOUR PHASES OF THE METAPARADIGM OF THE 1750S THROUGH THE LATE 1860S

5.1.   Transition toward the new metaparadigm of the 1750s in the final phase of the previous metaparadigm

The metaparadigm that had its beginnings in the 1750s was a radical shift of assumptions to those of a purely secular world. The scientific laws that founded one objective world wholly in material terms of cause and effect would be the outcome. The foundations for it had been set by the metaparadigm of the 1640s into that time in its tension of God's natural law and the human inquiry and experimentation that explored it. Yet, for any major shift in a metaparadigm, events in the world must become a trigger, and the very thought that allowed the change must begin to evidence the need for such a change. The fourth phase of collective normalization was interrupted in the 1740s with mercantilistic wars which served to jar the European national populaces into a new confrontation with accepted assumptions. The onset of mercantilistic wars among European nations with the War of Austrian Succession ended a period after the Peace of Utrecht that saw a relative harmony of interests among those nations. Joseph Strayer and Hans Gatzke called the period between 1715 and

1740 one of "peace and prosperity."[34] The middle years of the Enlightenment in its increasing mercantilistic conflict brought a heightened criticism to the past emphases on cooperation in culture. One need only read Montesquieu's 1748 *Spirit of the Laws* to see the growing inability of the "mixed government" of aristocrats and commoners to sustain its compromises; Montesquieu articulates the tensions between the separate notions of public virtue among aristocrats and commoners. The balanced harmonies of Rococo painting in the idylls of Watteau gave way to Boucher's troubled Rococo vision. Boucher's canvases gave evidence in the 1740s and 1750s, in their sharply crossing diagonals, of the conflict at hand among persons and parties. Indeed, paintings such as *The Rape of Europa* or *Venus and Vulcan* not only depicted by color contrast and figural position the at-odds state of affairs, but suggested the violence to come, latent in the poses themselves. The English culture, too, evidenced this growing political-social conflict as early as the 1740s and 1750s with its novels, dramas, and graphic arts. Samuel Richardson (1689–1761) wrote novels that castigated the moral turpitude of the upper class, depicting the middle class as the emergent moral guide for England. George Lillo (1693–1739) wrote the first middle-class dramas that showed the sharply divergent moral ideas of this class from that of the aristocracy. David Hogarth's (1697–1764) satirical narrative paintings of aristocrats, and his reformist images of the lower classes injured by their situations, were evidence of the growing schism in the traditional hierarchy.

These individuals served as a transitional source of ideas for the more purely secular notions with their more complex understandings of human individuality, politics, and scientific law that emerged as outcomes in the metaparadigm to come. One of the German thinkers who were contemporary to the French and English transitional thinkers was the historiographer Johann Martin Chladenius (1710–1759). Johann Martin Chladenius was both of his time and a visionary of a time to come. The initial phase of any metaparadigm offers a radical break with the existing in its disciplinary purview. Radical new ideas are accompanied by a notion of time that sees it as having major interruptions. This vision of time allows for the new and the disappearance of the old. In what can be considered the second phase of the metaparadigm of the 1750s through the 1860s, Immanuel Kant made this point of quantum changes in time as he criticized Leibniz's notion of a continuum in nature [*Critique of Pure Reason*, 1968, 548 (A 668, B 696)]. Leibniz was one of the thinkers who laid the groundwork for the collective norming of the earlier metaparadigm, particularly in the notion of the continuity of nature. Chladenius, writing in the early 1740s, saw quantum differences in perspective among persons who shared the same state-of-affairs. The fourth phase of any metaparadigm strives to show general principles shared by all in a culture. Chladenius through historiographical principles offered this collective commonality a major challenge. His book on historical interpretation–*Introduction to the Correct Interpretation of Reasonable Discourses and Writings*–was published in 1742, as the War of Austrian Succession ended a generally pacific generation among European nations. The War of Austrian Succession and the Seven Years' War, which followed closely, evidenced the emergence of political and social criticism that would widen the breach between the aristocratic and republican world-views, ending the attempt at the balance of powers among them sought by liberal aristocrats such as Bolingbroke and Montesquieu . Chladenius's thought was a basis for the deconstruction of that consensus; his creation of a critical understanding of historical objectivity challenged the notion of one common objective world with a single interpretation. He posited that in any experience shared by more than one person, each would have a differing vision of what transpired because of (1) the positioning of his own body in time and space; (2) differing objects of attention; and (3) differing associations that were generated by the experience. He disagreed with the "generally accepted" truism that "there can only be one correct representation for each object and that if there are some differences in description, then one must be completely right and the other completely wrong."[35]

5.2.   First phase of the new metaparadigm, late 1750s through the 1770s

As the new metaparadigm emerges, one will see thinkers emphasizing abrupt, quantum changes in the phenomena they study. Individual choice and self-direction will be stressed, rather than actions that are determined by one's place and time (one sees the determinism of place and time even in Chladenius's insistence upon individual difference). Secularity, of course, will be the domain of the new evidence, but a secularity increasingly independent of any metaphysical speculations. Gotthold Ephraim Lessing (1729–1781) brought a new vision of historical time to German thought through drama–yet, his notion of an unceasing movement in culture carried by the free, self-directed choices of individuals can be seen as the root of the German historicist emphasis on a changing history that becomes its regularized paradigm by the fourth phase. Lessing developed a notion of drama where each scene is complete with one significant action by the hero or heroine. Space and time in his dramas violated the "three unities" that had governed metaparadigmatic thought from the 1640s through the 1750s: in the "three unities" of time, space, and manner of action the first models of a secular world were erected, and measured with mathematical precision. Lessing's unity was guided solely by action, action that usually jarred any existing preconception of motivation or action. Action established the ground for depiction of a time and place, rather than conforming to it.[36] Lessing based this rule on the study of perception: the human sees details and integrates them into a highly personal unity based upon his motive and focus in that moment or episode of action.[37] Every action in its parts to be comprehended must be associated with the conceptual whole which it instantiates, thus becoming a coherent event-moment (*Laocoön*, 1962, 78). Edmund Husserl made this discrimination when he spoke of the time-stretches that in the complete sentential predication become a temporal concretum (Husserl, *Logical Investigations*, 1970, 2:487–488). For Lessing, each event-moment has a time that is singular to that person and place–a qualitative, singular temporality. Such event-moments are of short duration, the aggregate of event-moments offering the complex of a theatrical scene (*Hamburgische Dramaturgie*, 1966, 196ff.). Staging thus stresses ceaseless activity, and the meaning of the drama is located in the qualitative temporalities so generated. This complex of qualitative temporalities, each singular and as an aggregate generating the sense of a whole, is a radically different notion than personal action in the fourth phase of any metaparadigm. The fourth phase of a metaparadigm subsumes personal action with its complex time into the unities of a collective understanding of time, place, and manner. Enduring commonalities impart the salient sense of time in this collective final phase. Time is objectively neutral and a background for a communal life, rather than the complex foreground created by personal choice.

When a new metaparadigm is being created, by the combined and coexistent efforts of persons who intuitively follow the "meta" imperatives of their discipline, one cannot know its final collective shape. Thus, one stresses attention to certain kinds of praxis rooted in human cognition and competence, rather than intending the final shape of things. Disciplines offer new axiomatic guidelines for inquiry. Overviews only begin to be formed in the second phase of models. Lessing's dramas had scores of scenes establishing this ceaseless change from one qualitative time to the next, each scene depicting a differing quality of temporality based upon the kind of action. Human existence became that of constant creative activity. It was not the products of human action that counted, rather its spiritual process in the creative individual:

> Not the truth, in possession of which at any time a man is or thinks he is, but the genuine effort he has made to discover the truth, constitutes the worth of the man. For not through possession, but through the search after the truth, are his powers expanded, wherein alone consists his ever growing perfection. Possession makes [him] quiet, lazy, proud–.[38]

This emphasis upon motivation, intention, and praxis was the type of content one will find in the initial three phases of any paradigm (and its larger metaparadigmatic kinship with other disciplines in that time). Ideas and their personal cognitive/emotional/spiritual ground are the content probed in any of the humanities, fine arts, or social sciences, not the material bases of human life. The material is the stuff which is shaped by the maker; thus, the maker in the initial phases is the subject. A new kind of thought and praxis is most salient. In the natural sciences in these initial phases, one studies the dynamics of forces or evolving growth rather than static, structural aspects which have enduring spans of temporal existence.

Another way to put the difference between the initial phases of a metaparadigm and its fourth and concluding phase is that in the initial phases efficient causes are the focus–the formal cause (the shape of things sought) is allowed to emerge from the new practices. While the "models" of the second phase are important to view as the end and means, the "model" is necessarily vague as it is but a horizon to approach. The fourth phase is necessarily detailed in all its integrated parts, for it is the ends and means for maintaining a persistent reality. Material, final and formal causes pervade any scientific or humanistic presentation, rather than the empirical complexity of an array of efficient causes. In the fourth phase of the previous metaparadigm (1640s to 1750s) Montesquieu had explored the structural relationships between organic life and climate. He stressed the determined relationships thus created by soil, weather, and organic structure.[39] Montesquieu's findings will become a basis for Charles Darwin's deterministic, collective principles in the fourth phase of the next metaparadigm. Montesquieu's presentation is in short chapters that are hardly more than a paragraph. He need not be more discursive as his principles are generally understood and accepted. Charles Darwin, whose research was characteristic of this fourth phase in the late 1830s through the early 1860s, said that inquiry should move from one discovery immediately to the principles it validates. Inquiry and explanation in the initial phases of a metaparadigm are quite different: one writes at length of one's observations, as one must prove a new perspective. The explanatory narrative is detailed, lacking the pithy rhythm of "self-evident" facts. The German botanist Joseph Koelreuter (1733–1806) is an example of the emergent new metaparadigm of the 1750s. His work habits and guiding ideas are quite different than those of Montesquieu. Rather than stable truths for particular environs, Koelreuter found great variation in the relationships of organic life and climate because of inherent characteristics of the plants he studied. Koelreuter changed his focus from that of environmental determinism to that of the complex individuality of each plant species that changes its character because of its own genetic variation. Koelreuter derived quickly changing generations through hybridization, each generation differing in marked ways from its predecessor, but also returning in later generations to its earlier forms. Koelreuter thus instilled complex time into the study of the life of a species.[40] This vision of interrupted generational manifestations of plants that differ from their parents is a process later called "saltation" (Olby, 1985, 67–68). Koelreuter tracked the quantum changes in a species from generation to generation in the detailed monographs that are the norm of the initial phases of a metaparadigm.[41] Interestingly, the botanical concept of saltative change fell into disuse in the fourth phase of the metaparadigm which was dominated by Charles Darwin and Alfred Russel Wallace, not returning again until Mendel and Sir Francis Galton in the late 1860s (Olby, 1985, 67–68). Darwin and Wallace considered time as a continuum of incremental change, typical of this stress in the fourth phase of the metaparadigm on collective continuity.

Another German who was contemporaneous with Koelreuter in instilling episodic change into the vision of organic life was Caspar Friedrich Wolff (1733–1794), the seminal evolutionary biologist. Although Wolff was not a historian, nonetheless like Koelreuter his theory of epigenesis *Theoria Generationis* (1759) can be considered the introduction into the European history of ideas of quantum changes in the qualitative temporalities that order the development of an evolving state-of-affairs.[42] The Frenchman Lamarck (1744–1829) will create a model of organic change that is generationally singular and saltative, initiated in animal and human life by the most competent members of the species. Sudden changes in a species initiated by the "super" individual are capable of being inherited by progeny. This overemphasis upon self-direction that is freely willed and unbound by existing organic norms is reflected also in Erasmus Darwin (1731–1802), the grandfather of Charles Darwin and a contemporary of Lamarck, who claimed that the sex of a human offspring can be attributed to the power of the imagination of the father in coitus (Olby, 1985, 1). Erasmus Darwin may have voiced this idea in the late 1750s, for Laurence Sterne begins his famous satire of English life and thought *Tristram Shandy* (1760) with the hero remarking on the formative influence of what his mother and father were thinking as he was conceived.[43] Sterne is another example of the emphasis given by thinkers in the initial stage of a metaparadigm to ideas as well as to the efficient cause of the individual as the bases of what occurs in human activity. The epigraph of *Tristram Shandy* reads: "It is not things that disturb men, but their judgments about things" (1980, 1). Insofar as human action, the emergent metaparadigm stresses the genius, departing from the emphasis upon typicality of the final phase of the previous metaparadigm.

The 1750s introduced the notion of "genius," articulated first by the Englishman Edward Young in 1759. Germans took up the notion in the 1760s when considering how culture changed.[44] Lessing stressed individual competence in his depiction of the hero or heroine whose action creates new pathways of comprehension. Lessing develops the theme of heroic action further in his discourse on tragedy *Briefwechsel ü ber das Trauerspiel*. The hero must resist oppression within the normal functions of his or her milieu. Heroism was action, but action within the actual options of a milieu. The hero must enable the audience to identify with his or her plight, the moral idea being the possibility of such decisive action by the ordinary person.[45] Lessing's dramas were called "middle-class tragedy," because of his persona who came from the emergent middle class. The themes were of the concerns of this class. Morality in his plays was problematic: new ideas as to what was moral were raised. More situational freedom to a class of persons on the move toward a new political and social organization became the norm, rather than adherence to traditional moral concepts based upon a static vision of the societal hierarchy. In Lessing's *Sara Sampson* (1755) the heroine is at pains to forgive her seducer Mellefont and even the woman Marwood who poisoned her. Compassion for human striving with its attendant imperfections becomes a new understanding, rather than judging by a fixed moral code. Many disciplines in the new metaparadigm inquire into human passion and its pathological action, rather than merely considering the perverse as sin. Immanuel Kant is among the first to consider the "psychopathology" created in ideas because of emotional stress.[46] The new Germanic term for "empathy" "Einfühlung" was coined in this period, a term that will fall into disuse until the initial phase of the metaparadigm that begins in the late 1860s that returns in a spiral manner to deepen comprehension of complex individuality and interpersonal understanding.[47] Separating traditional views of Judeo-Christian morality from the complexities of secular human situations was a vital aspect of the new wholly secular metaparadigm. The new metaparadigm rejected the previous metaparadigm's balance of the divine and the human. The tension of God's providential plan with human behavior was dissolved, leaving human behavior as a new subject of study with no standard other than what was humane and just in human terms. Disciplines such as psychology, the fine arts, and the emergent social sciences of economics considered behavior as a new object of study in order to comprehend how what had been immoral now was either merely problematic or necessary within the societal intentions of progress. The separation of morality from God's plan is seen in the new attention to theories of morality from David Hume through the Utilitarians in England, and in Immanuel Kant and the German idealists in Germany. Not that either the English or Germans doubted the existence of God, rather a personal rational responsibility for defining what indeed was moral was emphasized.[48] Kant's "categorical imperative," articulated in his *Critique of Practical Reason* (1788), was a self-wrought insight into how human nature functioned, and upon that consideration what was moral in human action.[49] For Kant and the Germans, God could be felt dimly by the fact of one's interest,[50] i.e., "rational appetite," but one must act always within the rational precepts won through careful deliberation of one's possible action under the guidance of the rational categorical imperative. Adam Smith in his *The Theory of Moral Sentiments* (1759) made the famous Deist analogue of the separate realms of God and human when he posited humanity's realm as that of the wheels and mainspring of a watch, and God's realm as that of the watchmaker. Only through one's mindful attention (the watchspring) to the evidence imparted by one's own human nature (the wheels) can one fulfill God's plan.[51] God meant us to attend the efficient causes of the wheels, not speculate upon God's notion of the time fulfilled by our actions, i.e., the final cause of morality. For Smith, morality must be self-wrought as well since traditional mores are often self-serving for the community that establishes it (1948, 189–208). True moral precepts were fashioned by inquiry into human feelings, intentions, and interactions–the "wheels" of the watch, and limited to the principles so derived. Jeremy Bentham's "utilitarian" moral rule was derived from these kinds of considerations, although a reading of Smith's chapter "Of the Utility of This Constitution of Nature" in his *Theory of Moral Sentiments* (1948, 124–130) will show that Bentham found other invariants than Smith as he developed "utilitarianism."

The new metaparadigm's increasing separation of self-wrought human morality from the beliefthat God's hand was directly in our definition and praxis can be seen as a gradual transition which by the 1770s is largely complete. Friedrich Gottlieb Klopstock (1724–1803) is a typical transition figure who contributes to the new concepts of temporality taken on by the German historians, but nonetheless has a sense of God's action in nature that is of the older metaparadigm. His imaging of the natural world in the late 1750s can be considered a major step in the new historical temporalization initiated by quantum changes. The over sixty strophic forms Klopstock invented between 1764 and 1767 supported a sense of radical cultural innovation, disrupting the standard notions of rhythmic poetic diction.[52] Klopstock's somewhat earlier *Frühlingsfeier* (1759) had begun his experimental verse. *Frühlingsfeier* envisioned God's creation of singular times through the tension and release of dramatic action.[53] It will be a key work in Goethe's *Die Leiden des jungen Werther* (1774), which was perhaps the most radical of all calls for quantum cultural change in this initial period of German historical thought. Nonetheless, Klopstock's use of the concept of a "cataclysmic" change reflected the older metaparadigm's notion of God's direct action in history. In the metaparadigm of the 1640s through the 1750s, fossils, for example, were understood as artifacts of earlier periods of life before God's cataclysmic ending of each particular period; Buffon (1707–1788) who championed this view was of the older generation who remained attached to the Secular/Divine vision (Jacob, 1982, 131–142).

Sharing this initial stage of the new metaparadigm was the Sturm und Drang "Storm and Stress" movement in the Germanies in the early to late 1770s. A collection of essays to be a significant stimulus to Sturm und Drang thinkers appeared in 1773, entitled *Von Deutscher Art und Kunst*. Its contributors were three authors–Justus Möser (1720–1794), Johann Gottfried Herder (1744–1803), and Johann Wolfgang von Goethe (1749–1832).[54] Justus Möser's essay Deutsche Geschichte was first composed in 1768 as the introduction to his several-volume *Osnabrückische Geschichte*. The essay presented a historical conception of successive periods of German history from an indefinite time before Charlemagne through his own eighteenth century present. Möser's division of history into four "Hauptperioden" reflected historical norms that had emerged during and immediately after the Seven Years' War which stressed the quantum character of historical periods. Möser named the first period he delineated of German history "golden," playing upon Hesiod's notion of a descending succession of periods (1924, 148). Each of the four periods for Möser evidences further the alienation of the ordinary person from authority in their own affairs. Möser states the fourth and present period can be reversed by a new consciousness in the aristocratic governors and the educated commoner that leads to the granting of more authority to the latter. In the spirit of this first metaparadigmatic phase of the German historical cycle, Möser leaves the future vague but promising. The next period of German history is intimated rather than demanded–caution was in order in his statements given the situation Möser had in the service of the state. He writes in the essay's final paragraph of "The new turn which a Strube gives to the German manner of thought, in that he like Grotius links history, scholarship, and philosophy, is also notable for its attention to decisions of state" (1924, 158). David Georg Strube (1694–1777) was a Hanoverian scholar who made a special study of the original sources of Roman and German law. In 1758 he published *Entdeckte Verdrehung des Westphälischen Friedensschlusses* and in 1767–77 *Rechtliche Bedenken*. The enlightened creation and application of law could generate a Rechtsstaat "a state under just law" for all Germans. A new time span could arise, different from that of the present where public policy was too "comfortable" within existing norms that neglected the history of Germanic law and tradition (1924, 157). Enlightened judgments could move culture toward the greater participation that existed once in Germany's "golden age." Möser saw himself as the public policy leader who might initiate this new time span. Strube's thought was seminal in the new purely secular understanding of law's origins, and served Möser's own scholarship. Strube's thought is another instance of how older terms, those of Grotius's concepts of the Rechtstaat between men and nations under natural law took on new meanings under the assumptions of a new metaparadigm.

Herder's essays in *Von Deutscher Art und Kunst* were "Auszug aus einem Briefwechsel über Ossian und die Lieder alter Völker" and "Shakespeare." They present the value of a departure from existing norms, and an embrace of a new, more original relation to human experience–the quantum call of regeneration that typifies the late 1760s and most of the 1770s. Herder's Ossian essay stresses the lyrical nature of the supposed Celtic poem, attacking Denis's German translation of Macpherson's English into hexameters. Herder felt the hexameter made the vision of reality that of an epic, eclipsing the spontaneous, moment-to-moment energy of the original (1924, 13, 48). Herder praised the poem itself, holding it to be an original work, rejecting Heinrich Wilhelm von Gerstenberg's claim that it was a forgery by the contemporary Scot James Macpherson.[55] Herder saw in the poem a primitive, simple conception of reality which was worthy of emulation in the German present. Epic visions were too controlled recalling well-known realities; lyrical visions captured life in nature as a fresh orientation each moment, each moment separate from the previous or the next: "Ossian, so kurz, stark, männlich, abgebrochen in Bildern und Empfindungen" (1924, 48).

Herder's praise of Shakespeare focused upon his ability to depict a period of time as a whole, yet through a sensual complexity of contrasting individualities that made up that time (1924, 101, 108, 111). Herder's turn to Shakespeare thus deliberated not only the radical disjunctions of time, but how a new model of historical coherence might be shaped. The new model would not privilege a Divine preestablished harmony played out in natural law; rather, human events would form their integration out of the very laws found in its own accidents over time. The unintended consequences of persons following differing self-directed paths would generate a culture in common. Rational self-correction enabled commonalities of consensus, albeit reflecting distinct traits in common that differed from culture to culture. Culture thus evolved through the epigenesis of personal self-development and development of one's communal group through their interactions. Public time becomes a complex amalgam of individual epigeneses that create a common fabric. As Adam Smith posited, attention to one's distinct nature was the indirect, but efficient causal means of realizing God's intentions, even when one never knew Divine intention.

Shakespeare violated the rules of unity so precious to early Enlightenment culture, yet found a unity merely within the natural expression of human emotions expressed individually and intersubjectively. Natural unities replaced the artificial adherence to Voltaire's and Gottsched's mid-Enlightenment notion of "la belle Nature," the imposed unities of time, place, and manner of rational closure and consistency in narrative design (1924, 97, 108–109). Shakespeare's unifying art enabled him to coalesce the diversity of human expressions in a coherent flux that needed no cohering form other than the interactions of the diverse human expressions themselves. Shakespeare's "protean form" was shared time and mutual engagement. This activity was history in itself: "Im Gange seiner Begebenheit, im *ordine successivorum* und *simultaneorum* seiner Welt, da liegt sein Raum und Zeit... Jedes Stück ist History im weitesten Verstande" (1924, 118, 120)."

Herder's Sturm und Drang vision of German renewal by a return to the racial character of assertive immediacy suited the quantum demands of the time in its allowance for any new direction based upon spontaneity. However, by the 1780s, Herder, Goethe, and other leading thinkers of the culture sought a longer range plan of cultural development. Herder's universal history of nature and humankind provided this evolutionary plan, where immediacy was replaced by a telic guarantee of the fulfillment of what had been begun.[56]

5.3.   The second phase of the new metaparadigm, 1780 through the early 1790s

Herder in the 1780s began to examine world history as a series of morphological differences between cultures, each culture depicted in its phased fulfillment of the form which guided its cultural meaning. These studies would build a morphological model for a future German culture. His *Auch eine Philosophie der Geschichte zur Bildung der Menschheit* (1774) articulated the "protean form" he was to further research for the next seventeen years in the initial two sentences:

> The more one explains in the investigation of the oldest history in its population migrations, languages, mores, inventions, and traditions, the more probable it becomes with each new discovery that the origin of the species was but one source. One becomes clearer that it was a favorable climate, where a human couple developed the cultural thread, under the mildest and facilitating influences of a creative providence, that subsequently became in its effects their history: where every accident could become the occasion for a motherly care in order that the fragile double germ of the entire species might develop with choice and circumspection.[57]

Herder articulates, evidently influenced by Montesquieu, the essential form that came to be the dominant paradigm of human evolution. Both natural ·selection under the influence of climate and topos, as well as inspired intervention by humans in their own development, are offered as the facilitating mechanisms of cultural development. Herder imparts a notion of self-directed temporal change in the species that was never present in Montesquieu's ideas of the material cause of the environment in human development. This is an instance of Kuhn's point that the same concepts take on new meaning in a new paradigm. Herder's *Ideen zur Philosophie der Geschichte der Menschheit*

(1784–1791) offered a finely nuanced differentiation of the German peoples, showing differences in temperament among German tribal stems and how these temperaments in their interaction with the accidents of time and place gave rise to the cultural institutions indicative of each stem. Herder pointed out common proclivities of mind and character among the Germans as well as differences. German communality coexisted with a constant recognition of individuality. German conceptions of law in Herder's eyes were oriented to justice based upon a living law of egalitarian, communal principles, rather than the abstract letter (1953, 2: 336–337). Herder's historical model integrated Möser's sketched German history establishing a natural teleology toward constitutional and democratic governance. Progress was political. English "Whig" history, partaking of the same sense of teleological progress based upon the rule of law, was created in these same years, modeled by thinkers such as Edmund Burke (1729–1797).

Immanuel Kant's (1724–1804) historiographical viewpoint was a major contribution to the second phase of the metaparadigm in question. His 1784 essay *Idee zu einer allgemeinen Geschichte in Weltbürgerlicher Absicht (Idea for a Universal History from a Cosmopolitan Point of View)* was similar to Herder's vision of the accidents of secular occurrence when critically monitored by human intention and will cohering through their cause and effect an interconnected secular history that evidenced progress in humankind. Kant sketched an intergenerational progress through written laws that secured as institutional guides human self-realization within society. The future beckoned as a world government transcending national differences in the common, objective understanding of human nature and its best forms of self-governance. Kant offered a truly Germanic vision, nonetheless, expressing his insight within the the German narrative characteristics detailed in the first essay in this collection. Only in the encounter of ceaseless intersubjective conflicts where the products of an individual mind meet the frustrations of interpersonal understanding can consensus lead to the written constitutions which mark the zigzag, often regressive path of political-social development.[58] Can the ontological "social antagonism" he speaks of in this fourth thesis, indicative of the human species who as individuals are made of "crooked wood" (1963, 17), ever be overcome sufficiently to enable one or more leaders to administer the perfect civic constitution? "Only the race" may humankind attain the destiny of a perfect constitution (1963, 18, fn 2). No one person can generate the maxims, hypothetical imperatives, or categorical imperatives that can construct a more perfect civic constitution for a time, as "art is long, life is short." Kant cites this aphorism of Hippocrates in a 1786 essay, *Conjectural Beginnings of Human History*.[59]

5.4. The third phase of the new metaparadigm, the late 1790s through 1815

The third phase of the new metaparadigm was one of pragmatic new developments in the disciplines of the arts and the sciences. New methodologies were needed to realize the models developed by thinkers in the previous decades. German culture and society shared the European activity that was quickened by the spirit of the French Revolution with its actual changes in society and culture. Friedrich Carl von Savigny (1779–1861) was among those historians, who included Wilhelm von Humboldt (1767–1835) and Barthold Georg Niebuhr (1776–1831), whose historiographical principles and methodologies provided the mainspring and wheels for what would become German historicism. German historicism is the genre that emerged from the initial conceptions of changing qualitative temporalities generated by Klopstock, Lessing, Möser, and Herder. The third phase made this vision of truths relative to a time, always changing through the action and interaction of identifiable individuals, operative through new methodological procedures that included source criticism, philology, and a more studied address of human motivation. German historicism removed God's plan from any causal discussion, even when it remained as a personal belief in the historian. The individual was the efficient cause that mattered in history. The life and thought and decision of leading individuals gave a distinct character to the public world so affected. As individuals were so prominent, the character of a society changed as his or her will lessened or changed in its intentions. The public world was the product of its governing individuals. In Leopold von Ranke, in the fourth phase of the new metaparadigm, German historicism as a formalized approach to historical knowledge will be realized in its normative paradigm.[60] Savigny's historical thought was within legal history, but its influence was a major one in the development of German historicism in general. Savigny's historical logic, and the conscious historical philosophy which grew from its implicit premises, enabled German historical thought to escape the universals of natural law whose categorical apodicity hampered a complete freedom to criticize existing principles of law and legally justified institutions. Natural law as it had been pursued in the previous century among jurists was a universal standard true for any age. Savigny felt this generalizing standard injured one's appreciation of the specific intentions of identifiable persons influenced by the changing conditions in which they lived.[61] Savigny historicized the expression of law in historical cultures without disputing the actuality of natural law in the Kantian sense, that is, the universal logic which is the skeleton upon which every historical culture articulates its law. Historical contingency is the warp of this logical universalism: historical contingency gives idiosyncratic form to the logical cognition of the legislator (1951, 32).

A keen legal mind can generate the rational premises which are contained in natural law or discern them in legal historical analysis (1951, 50). The legal norms of any period in a culture stem from the normative system of understanding and intention: one must comprehend those historical intentions, and through comprehension of those intentions, be able to weave into a plausible architectonic the legal thought of a time even from incomplete evidence. Natural law is found in how one has reasoned and within one's own critical analysis as a legal historian (1951, 23–25). The logic of a point of view normative in any time is undergirded by the timeless laws of the mind's modes of logical assertion. Kant's critical method served as a helpmeet for Savigny in divorcing the study of Roman and Germanic law from any metaphysic that rooted the conception and articulation of these bodies of law over generations to a teleological principle.[62]

Savigny's development of an empirical method, to be known as the historical school of legal study, was largely a product of the decade between 1806 and 1815 (Wieacker, 1956, 41). The decade's call for empirical study and caution in relation to any deductive system based upon unquestioned principles or values was exercised in Savigny's approach to the history of law. Savigny saw each generation of a culture as singular in its spirit, a spirit formed within the matrix of the cultural issues and principles of its time. The language of that cultural period, in law and in other forms of expression, generated the ideation which informed the law itself. The historical interpreter must fathom the particular spirit of the times through the time-bound, idiosyncratic wording of the law, and the direct and indirect cultural stimuli upon its author (Wyss, 1979, 69–70, 75ff.). Law itself was a kind of literature, an expression of the normative vision of that generation (Wieacker, 1956, 45).

Savigny saw time spans that passed on core concepts of Roman and Germanic law, but always expressed within a unifying vision characteristic of the particular age. Savigny's notion of time periods was qualified by his continuum logic. Time periods were not conceived as having a teleological necessity upon the thoughts of all who lived within them. While irrational thought and intention might lead to a normative basis of law among a people, it was a conscious outcome involving deliberation and choice. The only determinative influence for such a period or age will be "an inner relationship" to the age that preceded (1951, 53).

Savigny presented a methodology for discerning the intentions of past legal minds derived from his conception of what constitutes legal assertions. Every legal statement consisted for Savigny of a (1) logic which orders content; (2) a grammatical expression of this logical intent; and (3) the historical influences upon the law maker which condition the semantic intent and logical/grammatical expression of the laws in that time (1951, 14–17, 19). The methodology begins with ascertaining the authenticity of the documents and their chronological geneses, a step prior to interpretation (1951, 18). Philology is the critical instrument as the interpretation begins: what do the words used mean at that time; how do they point to the guiding idea which as formal cause informs each particular law. Philology thus furthered the logical analysis which could reconstruct the system of laws as a whole, even when content is lost; philology also allowed the historical influences to be recognized as one pondered the implications of certain terms, and how terms had changed from earlier periods.

5.5. The culminating fourth phase of the new metaparadigm, 1815 through the middle 1860s

> The organism can no longer be considered as a monolithic structure, a sort of autocracy whose powers are not shared by the individuals it governs. It becomes a 'cellular state', a collective system in which, Schwann said, "each cell is a citizen." Although constructed on the same plan, the different cells of an organism are of different types and perform different functions in different tissues; each type carries out a particular mission for the whole community. In the cellular community, there is a distribution of tasks and a division of labour.

> Francois Jacob on the German biologist Theodor Schwann's defining of the cell in 1839

> ...the Spirit in objectifying itself and thinking its own being, on the one hand, destroys this (particular) determination of its own being and, on the other hand, grasps its universality. It thus gives a new determination to its principle. The substantial determination of this national spirit is therewith changed; its principle passes into a new and higher one.

> Hegel, *Lectures on the Philosophy of History* (1830–1831)

The period of 1815 through the middle 1860s was the culminating fourth phase of the cultural systematization that had begun in the late 1750s, extending in its emergence through the Germanic Sturm und Drang. Why 1815 as a threshold to the phase of normalization? The end of the French Revolution and Napoleon's assertive presence in Europe led to the reestablishment of societal order by the Quintuple Alliance. After 25 years of war, quiescence and an account of the societal gains, losses, and the diverse interests that had emerged was a consequence of the victor's desire to return Europe to the "legitimate" hierarchical order. The secularization of society had regularized the notion of a common objective reality through the achievements in the arts and the sciences that spoke only of the natural world rather than natural law in the initial phases leading to this forced focus upon collective unity with its collective subcategories. Secularization now was standardized. The two citations above, articulated by German thinkers in this period, touch upon a significant aspect of this final phase of secular cultural systematization. Theodor Schwann's language of cellular citizenship and community expressed the several characteristics which are manifested in the fourth phase of any cultural systematization–collectivity, determinism, gradual evolution, and an emphasis upon material structure. The collective perspective is the culmination of every new systematization of a new cultural order as norms are emphasized and solidified for the general populace. The determinism of the fourth phase contrasts sharply with the value of free will in the earlier phases. Freedom had been a major slogan and value in all German thought in the initial three phases that accompanied the emergent middle class, nascent democracy, and the anthropological insight that humans were cognitively and physically equal beings. The fourth phase was deterministic because the menu of cultural options had been fixed. Cultural consensus required a determined range of choice. The time was at hand to articulate what was necessary and generally acceptable, rather than allowing the free-ranging thought and action that brought innovative change through competing ideas. The fourth phase stressed also gradual evolution of institutions that have begun, rather than the allowance of the quick or quantum changes known in the third phase. Moreover, material realities are the focus rather than the competing ideas that have led to change. Material realities emerged as important in the third phase, but within the competition of individual voices who each sought to initiate the pragmatic directions these culturally material changes must take. One thinks of David's sketch of the Tennis Court Oath with its anarchy of voices, none listening to the other. The fourth phase is one in which a range of consensus has emerged: augmentation and modification of the extant is the rule, rather than new beginnings. Schwann's vision of cellular development in the post-1815 era is but one example of how these characteristics of collectivity, determinism, gradual evolution, and materialism entered into the theories and explanations of the sciences.

The opposite general assumptions dominate in the initial three phases of any cultural renewal and systematization–individuality, free will, quantum or quick change, and the guiding format of ideas (more significant than material determinants). In the three phases of cultural renewal that extended from the late 1750s until 1815 even the natural sciences emphasized the individually unique–whether the diversity of the chemical elements or that of the anomalies and individual differences among organic and inorganic species. In this time of individual emphases, the natural sciences focused as well upon the freedom of change–in chemistry upon interelemental dynamics. The sciences of chemistry and zoology (natural history) drew attention to the tempo of change as quantum or quick–chemistry in its exploration of interelemental dynamics, zoology in the rapidity of morphological variation. Free will in the face of natural forces, guided by innovative idea supported the invasive human manipulation of nature.

What was called "directed variation" found its expression in the burgeoning of hybrid experiments and animal husbandry from the 1760s. Evolutionary theory moved away from attention to sudden changes in species development after 1815, Charles Darwin's skepticism regarding the permanence of effect in pigeon breeding being one example of the new attitude toward change, that of a gradual, evolutionary determinism.

Eighteen fifteen through the mid-1860s was an era of collective concepts that sought to integrate into a common purpose the complex individuality and diversity of political and social visions that had emerged in the initial three phases of the metaparadigm. From Metternich through Bismarck "Vereinbarkeit" "unity" became a constitutional premise. To be sure, from Metternich through Bismarck the concept was manipulated by a constitutional interpretation that favored aristocratic privilege. The king became a constitutional force who protected the unity through an unchallengeable will.[63] Conflict persisted as always within a German frame of public affairs, but the conflict was contained within a cultural framework of acceptance and accommodation of the many to the one effective system. Although "the one" was imposed upon republicans and democrats by the aristocratic victors over France and Napoleon, everyone found an active or passive accommodation to this system. Class consciousness furthered the accommodation of the time as the disempowered found community in subgroups. Nonetheless, such imposed unity created a growing "precancerous" tissue in the culture. Conflict hardened class divisions and began to erode the confidence many educated, middle-class citizens and artisans had that a benign paternalism might increase the political-social equity among the estates. This precancerous social malaise also began to separate nonskilled from skilled wage-earners, and people of property from wage-earners, with ever-widening political-social distance. The resolution of conflict expected in the history of Germanic public practices and laws became a more tenuous hope, although trust in a solution facilitated by the aristocratic governors was still extant in the *Vormärz* era. When the 1848 revolutions occurred, suspicion became articulate difference; articulate difference then led to permanent hostility or a consensus sustained with bad faith. The realization of the *Rechtsstaat* of a united Germany in 1871 was a troubled achievement. The concepts of "the bourgeois," "the proletariat," "social alienation," and "socialism" first were coined between 1815 and 1848, as the collective *ethos* of the postrevolutionary years exercised its imperative among the populace.[64] Although collective political-social philosophies differed even among adherents to the same general principles, it was the time to formulate coherent systems and measure everyday life within their purview after the chaos of pragmatic experimentation during the upheavals of the French Revolution and the age of Napoleon. Time became an extended, enduring form of existence. Continuity thought ruled: basic themes which subsumed individual events, giving the sense of incremental continuity in all the practices of life. The Biedermeier ethos of a private life, a domestic world, and public security and stasis were among the themes which bridged the classes, and slowed the notion of progress to a glacial speed. Dialectical thought became less radical in its proposed changes, promising teleological development rather than attempting to realize it. While class divisions hardened, the public norms of apparent consensus were imparted by these long-range, privatizing Biedermeier themes.

Schwann's image of the cellular state was at once an analogue for democratic-republican aspirations and a metaphor for one's individual unimportance in a determined world. The metaphor was echoed in the Austrian concept of the "little man," conceived by their national poets Grillparzer and Stifter. As an analogue, Schwann's image did signal a covert step forward in constitutional principle. The "reasons of state" that elevated the state into what Savigny termed a "handelndes Wesen" were qualified and entailed by the interests of the citizenry. Schwann still depicts the state as an organ whose functions are more than any cell that constitutes it, but he clearly criticizes in his analogue the notion of a monolithic state whose reasons are apart from the cellular citizens that constitute it. The constitutional laws must reflect the special functions of each cell. Each cell had a somewhat differing configuration and function, thus each organ which was constituted by the diversity reflected also in its form the kinds and placements of these differentiated cells. Schwann's history of the cell in its becoming tissue, then organ contributed to the notions of gradual evolution and stasis that were the "meta" assumptions of all disciplines in this fourth phase of the metaparadigm.

Hegel's reference to the "Aufhebung," the "lifting up" or "synthesis" of the particular expressions of a person or thing in an event to the universal which was expressed, characterized the difference between the third and fourth phases of cultural systematization. Events were conceived as the activity of specific persons and things in the third phase. Dynamic interactions were seen in their processes, but never as complete in their outcomes. The fourth and culminating phase of cultural systematization was less dynamic, but seen as the activity of categorical realities, collective essences. The fourth phase was a time of synthesis which gave order and relationship to the political-social memberships and values that had sought form between 1790 and 1815. Hegel's philosophy of history was significant to a whole school of historical thinkers in the Vormärz period. Among them, of course, was Karl Marx (1818–1883). His location of historical agency within class and technology rather than the State departed from the norms of aristocratic and middle-class collective understanding, but these concepts were as collective and typifying in their own way. Indeed, Marx gave the idea of a secular historical continuum its most rigorous form. Marx inherited the Hegelian metaphysical continuum from the Left Hegelians Bruno Bauer (1809–1882), Arnold Ruge (1803–1880), and Ludwig Feuerbach (1804–1872) who further secularized Hegel by offering a wider scope of "proximate cause" in events. Feuerbach's relocation of the source of historical movement from the absolute spirit to the elements of human nature allowed Marx to conceive a dialectic in history based upon the ontological needs of the human being. Particularly the economic plane of daily survival with its attendant technologies and divisions of labor were viewed as the channels and sources of historical cause and effect. Marx's stress on the human being as a "work animal" reflected the typification of a democratizing historical thinker in this fourth phase.

Leopold von Ranke (1795–1886) was educated within the historicism of Savigny. To write history "wie es eigentlich gewesen" is to allow the events of a historical milieu to signal the character of that milieu without the introjection of the historian's cultural values. This tempered the German propensity to use the past as a helpmeet for guiding the present. Ranke did recognize an implicit, tranquil progress in history within "dominant trends" that could be identified, and, thereby a "continuity." This search for the "dominant trend" lessened complexity, and instructed those who read Ranke to think in general themes. Ranke reflected the attention given to the power of the nation-state by the other historians of his generation in his focus upon political and diplomatic records as the best source of historical reality. The influence of his "objective" thoroughness persisted well into the twentieth century in Western historical scholarship.

Ranke exhibited in his rhetorical style the same shift in point of view from the individual to the collective, from the freedom of will to the deterministic, from quantum change to gradual evolution, and from the power of idea to material determinants all European and German thinkers evidenced in the shift from the third to the fourth phase of cultural systematization. In Ranke's adolescent essay Welchen Einfluss hat die Erlernung der Geschichtes auf das Leben der Menschen? (1807–1809), written between his twelfth and fourteenth year, his topic sentence reads:

> So verschieden die Wissenschaften sind, die die Jugend lernen muss, so verschieden sind auch ihre Schwierigkeiten, und noch verschiedener ist ihr Nutzen; aber alle sind doch gleich unentbehrlich.[65]
>
> [Just as the sciences are different, which youth must learn, so different are also their difficulties, and even more different are their advantages; yet, all are equally indispensable.]

Ranke's reflection attests to the pre-1815 emphasis upon the singularity and difference, but also implies the freedom of will to choose direction in one's interests and engagements. This sense of difference is replaced by an emphasis upon the common and collective after 1815. For example, the topic sentence of his incompleted essay on Luther, written in 1817 when he was 22 years of age, reads:

> Wer Bild einer grossen Zeit erneuen will, der muss den Einzelnen zum Typus der Gattung machen.[66]

> [One who will renew the image of a great time must make the individual into a species of genus.]

6.   CONCLUSION: THE EMERGENCE OF THE FIRST PHASE OF THE NEXT METAPARADIGM, THE LATE 1860S UNTIL THE 1880S

Bismarck was reputed to have said after the unification of Germany in 1871: "What is left for us? What will seem worth experiencing after such great successes and great and mighty events?"[67] For the moiety of Germans a centuries-old dream had been realized. Moreover, the new nation was a Rechtsstaat, guaranteeing civil liberties (i.e., Article 3) in an extensive constitution, one that gave universal male suffrage.[68] Austria, too, had achieved a new constitution in 1867, with a more limited suffrage, but nonetheless was in principle a Rechtsstaat in matters of civil liberties (Law No. 142).[69] Special problems emerged from the design of these constitutions that furthered the seminal "bad faith" between the aristocracy and the commoners, and between social classes that had heightened after 1848–most notably the Notverordnungen which give each Emperor the authority to adjourn or dissolve Parliament and to govern by decree (article 12 of the 1871 constitution of Germany; article 14 of the Austrian-Hungarian constitution of 1867).[70] Nonetheless, a ground of law and unity had been formed that was indisputably a structural advance toward a democratic-republican society in governance, and a material gain in Germany's place among the Western nations. Austria did not gain materially in the events that led to the new constitution, aside from the enthusiasm of its middle classes. Its economy remained what it had been, and its territorial expanse became less secure with the example of Hungarian autonomy to be digested by its other nationalities. As a cultural-historical vision, however, these constitutional gains had an enormous import for the life-meaning of the entire population of each nation. Such a "sea-change" in culture brings forth new aspirations.

Indeed, across Europe and even in the United States the years between 1867 and 1871 saw the extension of suffrage to the general populace in major revisions of national constitutions. The United States legislated the 14th and 15th amendments that extended due process of law and equal protection under the laws to all persons. The Civil War, which paralleled Bismarck's wars, established this new horizon. In England the Second Reform Bill and in Russia Alexander II's creation of the mir and the zemstvo brought serfdom to an end and empowered the entire populace. Many civil inequalities made these changes aspirations rather than realities; nonetheless, the first phase of a new metaparadigm is but an aspiration toward new goals, and thus a new cultural systematization.

The American poet-physician William Carlos Williams stated this sense of "next goals" when he queried his culture: "after health, then what?" The German always sought what was next, what was greater or higher. While the Austrian-Germans were rooted in a historical becoming out of past perspectives that were never wholly rejected or "overcome," they did pursue new avenues that augmented tradition, if not radically new beginnings. Aside from the maintenance issues involved in articulating into public practice the rights under law of the new German nations, what long-range vision might guide Germans and Austrian-Germans to new cultural-historical horizons?

Political-social goals within the Rechtsstaat were sufficient horizons for many. The "social question" was a public issue that now augmented the maintenance and modifications of the newly developed Rechtsstaat. The salience of the new goal of social justice led to its general designation as "the Social Question" "Die soziale Frage."[71] For socialists, the Rechtsstaat was only one phase toward new forms of social equity and political organization, and thus politics remained the central concern of the coming age. The emergence of the "social question" as a public issue was not solely the work of German Social-Democrats or social reformers. It became a significant public policy issue throughout society with the reinforcement of Chancellor Bismarck. Bismarck had been counseled in the late 1850s by Ferdinand Lassalle that an alliance with the lower classes would be more productive for aristocratic authority than an alliance with property. Bismarck's manipulations hardened the notions of "class" as his public policy was premised upon these divisions. Bismarck's introduction of "the social question" was in "bad faith" insofar as its political motives, but nonetheless it became a public issue that took on life meaning for many with this public recognition. Equity among the classes also engendered the cry for gender equity after 1871. The women's movement for equal rights under law began in earnest, and offered sufficient complexities and challenges to orient a career of effort.

These augmented goals of the Rechtsstaat were not even necessary for many. The Rechtsstaat itself was enough. If the German narrative convention of "ceaseless striving" was a spur to the new, most Germans found that in simply joining the contest of Western nations for economic and technological dominance, adapting Germany to the norms of imperialist competition. Where

Bismarck was uncertain about the extent of his commitment to economic or political expansion, the middle classes had the same patriotism that fueled imperialism among all Western nations.

Even though the majority of Germans and Austrian-Germans found the next horizonal goals within the materialist enhancement of the productive capacities of the nations, expanding markets, and in consumption of the higher quality of goods and services that were forthcoming, a few creative minds that saw beyond this amplification of the existent generated cultural goals that subjectively had an import equivalent to the objective gains embodied in the Rechtsstaat. Another cycle of cultural systematization was to begin that can be comprehended under the aegis of ideas offered by minds that ranged from Nietzsche and Wilhelm Dilthey through Ferdinand Tönnies, Otto von Gierke, Max Weber, and Max Scheler in Germany, and from Franz Brentano and Sigmund Freud through Christian von Ehrenfels, Edmund Husserl, Carl Menger, Hans Kelsen, and Max Adler in Austria.

NOTES

1. Ortega y Gasset, Die Aufgabe unserer Zeit "The Task of our Time" "El tema de nuestro tiempo" (1923) in *Gesammelte Werke*, trans. Helene Weyl and Ulrich Weber, 4 vols. (Stuttgart: Deutsche Verlags-Anstalt, 1950), 2: 84. Further reference to this essay in this text and edition.

2. See Ortega y Gasset on his correspondence to the historical thought of Max Scheler in his *Gesammelte Werke*, trans. Gustav Kilpper, Ulrich Weber, Gerhard Lepiorz, Helene Weyl, Curt Meyer-Clason, Karl August Horst, Else Görner, 4 vols. (Stuttgart: Deutsche Verlags-Anstalt, 1950), 1: 395; 2: 351, 465; 3:214; 4: 14f., 119, 306, 352. Further references to Ortega y Gasset in these texts and edition.

3. Friedrich Nietzsche, "Der unveränderliche Charakter," *Menschliches, Allzumenschliches*, Vol. 1 (Leipzig: C.G. Naumann, 1903), 66 (par. 41).

4. Nietzsche's notion of a new transcendence in being human–the Übermensch–is well-known, present in all his works. Max Scheler speaks of the challenge in the generation of the 1920s for transcending what history has meant by showing God a new way through a deepened knowledge of being human. Scheler writes, for example:

"History" is the time and its content, in which a still undefined and undefinable living being (objectively understood–not subjectively posited)–until now called "a human being"–decided, what it "is"–in essence–and thereby will become. When it has decided, everything that has until then been called "history" will cease completely.–For history is a process of overcoming–itself–objectively, insofar as the "tensions" which drive it steadily are decreased–as they are capable of being known, in that the synthesis of their powers are in us and are in the present in their sensuousness; Scheler, *Grundlagen der Geschichtswissenschaft* in *Schriften aus dem Nachlass*, Vol. 4, *Philosophie und Geschichte* (Bonn: Bouvier Verlag, 1990), 158.

Scheler sees human praxis as a guide for God, human inquiry as a function of God's knowing:

Even God doesn't know, what he wills or becomes. Everything–even God's "destiny"–as far as he can see–depends upon your decision (1990, 158).

Ortega y Gasset speaks of the challenge to human transcendence as the "task of our time" in his essay of that name in this same Schelerian view; Gesammelte Werke, 1950, 2: 79–141 (especially 141).

5. Ortega y Gasset, *Man and People*, trans. Willard R. Trask (New York: W.W. Norton, 1957), 27–29.

6. Dilthey's theory of staged cultural systematization is encapsulated "Der Entwicklungs-geschichtliche Pantheismus nach seinem geschichtlichen Zusammenhang mit den älteren Pantheistischen Systemen," in Wilhelm Dilthey, *Gesammelte Schriften*, Vol. II (Stuttgart: B. G. Teubner, 1957), 312–314. The entire second volume *Weltanschauung und Analyse des Menschen Seit Renaissance und Reformation*, however, is the cultural history of the genesis of the modern age.

7. William Kluback, *Wilhelm Dilthey's Philosophy of History* (New York: Columbia University, 1956), 38. Kluback refers to Dilthey's essay "Der Entwicklungs-geschichtliche Pantheismus nach seinem geschichtlichen Zusammenhang mit den älteren Pantheistischen Systemen," in Wilhelm Dilthey, *Gesammelte Schriften*, Vol. II (Stuttgart: B. G. Teubner, 1957), 312–314. Further references to Dilthey's own writings are to this edition of his *Gesammelte Schriften* in multiple volumes (each volume with its own publication date).

8. Margaret Masterman, "The Nature of a Paradigm," Criticism and the Growth of Knowledge, *Proceedings of the International Colloquium in the Philosophy of Science*, London, 1964, Vol. 4, ed. Imre Lakatos and Alan Musgrave (Cambridge: Cambridge University Press, 1970), 65. Further reference to this text and edition.

9. Thomas Kuhn, *The Structure of Scientific Revolutions* (Chicago: University of Chicago Press, 1962). Further reference to this text and edition. The second and third editions kept the same wording for the most part, their paginations the same, but differing from the first edition by only several paragraphs.

10. Ernst Mach, *Principles of the Theory of Heat, Historically and Critically Elucidated*, trans. P.E.B. Jourdain and A.E. Heath (Dordrecht: D. Reidel, 1986), 5.

11. See Ernst Mach on the continuing fecundness of the concept of "attraction" and its alternative "acceleration," in *Popular Scientific Lectures*, trans. Thomas J. McCormack, Fifth Edition (LaSalle, Ill.: The Open Court Publishing Company, 1943), 226, 253–254. Mach dwells upon the new vistas opened by use of the concept "acceleration" instead of "attraction" on pp. 299–308. Mach's cleaving to "acceleration" as a new conceptual viewpoint enables him to devise ways to demonstrate variations in physical energy and speed through the use of photography; he writes of this in an essay in this text "On Some Phenomena Attending the Flight of Projectiles," pp. 309–337. Further reference on Mach's physical concepts in differing paradigms in this same text and edition will be noted. Mach does not credit Oresme with the use of "acceleration," but this fact was perhaps too self-evident for attribution. As Mach speaks of the eternal fecundness of ideas, albeit with innovative reconfiguration for a specific practice, in pp. 226–228 in

his essay on "Mental Adaptation," I surmise he was familiar with the history of the concept which became his major vehicle in new physics research.

12. Ludwig Wittgenstein, *Philosophical Investigations*, 3rd ed., trans. G.E.M. Anscombe (New York: Macmillan, 1958), 48e (Prop. 115). Further reference to this text and edition.

13. There is a nonverbal grammar in the conventions whereby a subject is rendered in any given period of painting. The second part of this article on metaparadigm change in nineteenth century Europe will address nonverbal grammar, and then analyze it in the paintings of 1815 through the late 1860s, and then in the paintings from the late 1860s into World War I.

14. Max Scheler, *Die Wissensformen und die Gesellschaft* (Munich: Francke Verlag, 1960), 58.

15. Thomas Mann, *Reflections of a Nonpolitical Man*, trans. Walter D. Morris (New York: Ungar, 1983), 202. Further reference to this text and edition.

16. G.R. Elton, *The Practice of History* (New York: Crowell, 1967), 10–11.

17. Immanuel Kant, *Critique of Pure Reason*, trans. Norman Kemp Smith (New York: Macmillan, 1968), 131 (A 99). Further reference to this text and edition.

18. Husserl states that one experiences the flux of time itself in formulating a sentential judgment; *Experience and Judgment*, trans. James S. Churchill and Karl Ameriks (Evanston: Northwestern University Press, 1973), 258 (Par. 64c). The sentential judgment is a grammatical conveyance of the Kantian extensive magnitudes, called by Husserl "time-stretches," in the expressed judgment (Husserl, *Logical Investigations*, trans. J.N. Findlay, 2 vols. (London: Routledge and Kegan Paul, 1970), 2: 487–488.

Husserl does not use the term "extensive magnitude" for the flux of spatialities, but in his *Philosophy of Arithmetic* he makes clear his indebtedness to Kant's view of the generation temporal orders in cognition. He speaks of F.A. Lange's "augmentation" of Kant which stresses that temporality is not created by abstract number, rather by the spatialities that underlie number. Edmund Husserl, Philosophie der Arithmetik, ed. Lothar Eley (The Hague: Martinus Nijhoff, 1970), 34–35. As I pointed out above, Kant articulates this same appreciation in his concept of extensive magnitudes, e.g., "The schema of magnitude (quantity) is the generation of time itself in the successive apprehension of an object" (1968, A 145, B 184). Lange merely expands upon it. Kant's "number" is a representation resulting from the originary spatial division that generates temporal succession: "Number is therefore simply the unity of the synthesis of the manifold of a homogeneous intuition in general, a unity due (my emphasis) to my generating time itself in the apprehension of the intuition" (A 143, B 182). Kant calls "number" "a concept of the understanding...a representation "Vorstellung" which comprises the successive addition of homogeneous units" (A 143, B 182). "Number" as a concept of the understanding is the abstraction of the "pure schema of magnitude," which is the spatial division. Kant writes in the German: "Das reine Schema der Grösse aber (quantitatis), als eines Begriffs des Verstandes, ist die Zahl, welche eine Vorstellung ist, die die sukzessive Addition von Einem zu Einem (Gleichartigen) zusammenbefasst" [*Kritik der reinen Vernunft*, Akademie Ausgabe, 2. Auflage (Berlin: Walter de Gruyter, 1968), 137].

19. See F.E. Peters for a definition of the Greek term diairesis in *Greek Philosophical Terms, A Historical Lexicon* (New York: New York University Press, 1967), 34–36. I use the term diairesis to emphasize the problem which is at the center of my inquiry and method: the term was used by the ancient Greek to refer to dividing a thing or event "according to its natural joints." I will present a theory and demonstration of styles of division that are a lifelong time ordering in persons, which differentiate one person's history from another's. What is the natural joint for one is not the natural joint for another.

20. See Mark E. Blum, "Paracelsus, Goethe, and C.G. Jung: The Logic of Individuation and its Implications for Health Care," *International Review of Comparative Public Policy*, Vol. 6 (1995): 245–274, for studies of the historical judgment of Paracelsus, Goethe, and Jung. See Mark E. Blum, "Breaks or Continuity in Sombart's Work: A Linguistic Analysis," *Werner Sombart (1863–1941) Social Scientist*, ed. Jürgen G. Backhaus, 3 vols. (Marburg: Metropolis, 1996), 3: 1–109, for analyses of Werner Sombart and Max Weber, as well as the difference in historical logic of Immanuel Kant and Gottfried Wilhelm Leibniz (p. 47). Further references to these texts and editions.

21. See Walter J. Ong, *The Technologizing of the Word* (London: Metheun, 1982), 115. Ong believes that one's being schooled in the rhetoric of antithesis contributed to attitudes and behavior that fueled conflict; Ong, *Rhetoric, Romance, and Technology* (Ithaca: Cornell University Press, 1971), 66.

22. Francis Bacon, *The New Organon* (Cambridge: Cambridge University Press, 2000).

23. See *Critique of Pure Reason*, 1968, 114 (A 81, B 107) for Kant's chiding of Aristotle's categorical list for its lack of cognitive foundation.

24. See Ludwig von Bertalanffy, *General System Theory*, revised edition (New York: George Braziller, 1968), 112. Further reference to this text and edition.

25. Thomas Mann writes in *I Believe*:

    I believe in the coming of a new, a third humanism, distinct, in complexion and fundamental temper, from its predecessors. It will not flatter mankind, looking at it through rose-colored glasses, for it will have had experiences of which the others knew not. It will have stouthearted knowledge of man's dark, daemonic, radically "natural" side; united with reverence for his superbiological, spiritual worth. The new humanity will be universal–and it will have the artist's attitude: that is, it will recognize that the immense value and beauty of the human being lie precisely in that he belongs to the two kingdoms, of nature and spirit. It will realize that no romantic conflict or tragic dualism is inherent in the fact; but rather a fruitful and engaging combination of destiny and free choice. Upon that it will base a love for humanity in which its pessimism and its optimism will cancel each other out.

    Clifton Fadiman, ed. *I Believe: The Personal Philosophies of Certain Eminent Men and Women of Our Time* (New York: Simon and Schuster, 1939), 193.

26. See Wilhelm Dilthey, *Briefwechsel zwischen Wilhelm Dilthey und dem grafen Paul Yorck von Wartenburg* [Halle (Saale): M. Niemeyer, 1923]. Also, Heiko A. Oberman, *Luther, Man between God and the Devil*, trans. Eileen Walliser-Schwarzbart (New York: Doubleday, 1992).

27. Johann Gottlob Fichte, *Die Grundzüge des gegenwärtigen Zeitalters in Fichte's Werke*, ed. Immanuel Hermann Fichte, 11 vols. (Berlin, Veit & Comp., 1845/1846; Reissued in Berlin: Walter de Gruyter, 1971), 7: 13. Further reference to this text and edition.

28. See James J. Sheehan, *German History, 1770–1866* (Oxford: Clarendon Press, 1989), 621.

29. Friedrich Wilhelm Graf, *Die Politisierung des religiösen Bewusstseins: Die bürgerlichen Religionsparteien im deutschen Vormärz: Das Beispiel des Deutschkatholizismus* (Stuttgart, Frommann-Holzboog, 1978), 23.

30. Joseph R. Strayer and Hans W. Gatzke, *The Mainstream of Civilization*, 3 vols. (New York: Harcourt, Brace, and Jovanovich, 1979), 2: 432.

31. John Milton, "A necessary representation of the present evills, and eminent dangers to Religion, Laws, and Liberties, arising from the late, and present practises of the Sectarian party in England (February 15th 1649)," in *The Works of John Milton*, vol. 6 (New York: Columbia University Press, 1932), 245.

32. John Milton, "A Treatise of Civil Power in Ecclesiastical causes (1659)," in *The Works of John Milton*, vol. 6 (New York: Columbia University Press, 1932), esp. p. 23.

33. Christopher Hill, *The Experience of Defeat, Milton and Some Contemporaries* (New York: Viking, 1984), 199.

34. Stanley Chodorow, Macgregor Knox, Conrad Schirokauer, Joseph R. Strayer, and Hans W. Gatzke, *The Mainstream of Civilization Since 1500*, 6th ed. (San Diego: Harcourt, Brace, and Janovich, 1994), 561–562. The initial four editions were solely the work of Strayer and Gatzke, where this appellation of "peace and prosperity" originated.

35. See *The Hermeneutics Reader, Texts of the German Tradition from the Enlightenment to the Present*, ed. Kurt Mueller-Vollmer (New York: Continuum, 1989), 65 (Par. 308). Further reference to this text and edition.

36. Gotthold Ephraim Lessing, *Hamburgische Dramaturgie* (Munich: Wilhelm Goldmann, 1966), 187ff. Further reference to this text and edition.

37. Gotthold Ephraim Lessing, *Laocoön, An Essay on the Limits of Painting and Poetry*, trans. Edward Allen McCormick (Baltimore: Johns Hopkins University Press, 1962), 78ff. and 85ff. Further reference to this text and edition.

38. Gotthold Ephraim Lessing, *Theologiekritische Schriften III, Eine Duplik* in *Gotthold Ephraim Lessing Werke*, Vol. 8 (Munich: Carl Hanser, 1979), 32–33.

39. Montesquieu, *The Spirit of the Laws*, trans. and ed. Anne M. Cohler, Basia Carolyn Miller, and Harold Samuel Stone (Cambridge: Cambridge University Press, 1989), 231–336.

40. Robert Olby, *Origins of Mendelism*, 2nd ed. (Chicago: University of Chicago Press, 1985), 6–19. Further reference to this text and edition.

41. J. G. Koelreuter, *Vorläufige Nachricht von einegen das Geschlecht der Pflanzen betreffenden Versuchen und Beobachtungen, nebst Fortsetzungen 1, 2, und 3 (1761–1766)* Lipsae. Reprinted in Ostwald's *Klassiker der exakten Wissenschaften*, No. 41. Leipzig. 1893.

42. See Francois Jacob, *The Logic of Life, A History of Heredity*, trans. Betty E. Spillman (New York: Pantheon Books, 1982), 66, 121.

43. Laurence Sterne, *Tristram Shandy*, ed. Howard Anderson (New York: W.W. Norton, 1980), 1–2. Further reference to this text and edition.

44. See Alan C. Leidner, *The Impatient Muse: Germany and the Sturm und Drang* (Chapel Hill: University of North Carolina Press, 1994), 4–5.

45. Gotthold Ephraim Lessing, *Briefwechsel über das Trauerspiel*, ed. Jochen Schulte-Sasse (Munich: Winkler Verlag, 1972), 64. Lessing writes of the characteristics of the hero in drama: "Es muss eine gute Eigenschaft seyn, deren ich den Menschen überhaupt, und also auch mich, fähig halte." Further reference to this text and edition.

46. See Ilza Veith, *Hysteria: The History of a Disease* (Chicago:University of Chicago Press, 1965), 188 and fn 62. Kant's monograph on this issue is *Von der Macht des Gemüths durch den blossen Vorsatz Seiner krankhaften Gefühle Meister zu sein "On the Power of the Mind to master One's Pathological Feelings [Sensation] Through Sheer Will-Power."* This text was published in 1929 by Philipp Reklam. Kant also refers to the pathological ideas in a footnote in the first pages of his *Critique of Judgement* (1790); *The Critique of Judgement*, trans. James Creed Meredith (Oxford: Oxford at the Clarendon Press, 1952), 16 (fn 1).

47. See Keith Spalding, *An Historical Dictionary of German Figurative Usage* (Oxford: Blackwell, 1966), 19: 872.

48. An interesting transformation of meaning from a maxim proposed by the Congregation-alist Presbyterian Oliver Cromwell (1599–1658) to its later life as a cynical comment upon the accidents of nature in the philosophy of Adam Ferguson (1723–1816) allows us to see Thomas Kuhn's paradigmatic principle that older terms are conserved, but given new meanings. Cromwell said, according to his contemporary Cardinal de Retz, "that man never mounts higher, than when he knows not whither he is going," the meaning within the Presbyterian faith being that predestination can never be completely understood, only lived if one lives by faith and just judgment. Adam Ferguson, however, imputes pure accident to the maxim: "Every step and every movement of the multitude, even in what are termed enlightened ages, are made with equal blindness to the future; and nations stumble upon establishments, which are indeed the result of human action, but not the execution of any human design. If Cromwell said, That a man never mounts higher, than when he knows whither he is going; it may with more reason be affirmed of communities, that they admit of the greatest revolutions where no change is intended, and that the most refined politicians do not always know whither they are leading the state by their projects"; Adam Ferguson, *An Essay on the History of Civil Society* (Edinburgh: A. Kincaid & J. Bell, 1767; reprinted by Garland Publishing, New York, 1971), 187. For a short history of the life of this maxim, see F.A. Hayek, *The Constitution of Liberty* (Chicago: University of Chicago Press), 39, 428–429.

49. See *Critique of Practical Reason*, trans. Lewis White Beck (Indianapolis: Bobbs-Merrill, 1956).

50. Kant allows for the subjective impulse of the Divine that will be so vital to the German idealists in the aforementioned footnote that begins the Critique of Judgement. He writes: "But why our nature should be furnished with a propensity to consciously vain desires is a teleological problem of anthropology. It would seem that were we not to be determined to the exertion of our powers before we had assured ourselves of the efficiency of our faculty for producing an Object, our power would remain to a large extent unused. For as a rule we only first learn to know our powers by making a trial of

them. This deceit of vain desires is therefore only the results of a beneficent disposition in our nature" (*Critique of Judgement*, 1952, 16). Hegel's "der List der Vernunft" "the deceit of reason" is his ascription of our guiding interest to the Divine. However, as I will elucidate, the German decentered God's presence and Providence by using other names for the Divine. Hegel will use the term "spirit"; Kant, too, in the above citation is indirect in ascribing God as the author of the deceit.

51. Adam Smith, *The Theory of Moral Sentiments* in Adam Smith's *Moral and Political Philosophy*, ed. Herbert W. Schneider (New York: Hafner, 1948), 126. Further reference to this text and edition.

52. See Robert M. Browning, *German Poetry in the Age of the Enlightenment: rom Brockes to Klopstock* (University Park: Pennsylvania State University, 1978), 249.

53. Friedrich Gottlieb Klopstock, *Der Messias, Oden und Elegien, Epigramme, Abhandlungen* (Leck/Schleswig: Rowohlt, 1968).

54. *Von Deutscher Art und Kunst*, ed. Edna Purdie (London: Oxford University Press, 1924), 7. Further reference to this text and edition.

55. Heinrich Wilhelm von Gerstenberg, *Briefe über Merkwürdigkeiten der Litteratur* (1766) (Stuttgart: G.J. Göschen'sche Verlagshandlung, 1890), 56ff.

56. The period of "classicism" is debated in contemporary German letters. Wilhelm Vosskamp, most recently, had used the same dates as I infer; see "Klassik als Epoche. Zur Typologie der Weimarer Klassik," in *Literarische Klassik*, ed. H.-J. Simm (Frankfurt am Main: Suhrkamp, 1980), 259–266. However, my attribution differs from Vosskamp's in that he saw classicism as a reaction against the chaos of the French Revolution. I see it as the positive phase of vision building for long-range development that followed necessarily from the insights into a greater individual freedom and new, dynamic culture formulated in the previous decade. Classicism's articulation of personal "Bildung"– an aesthetic education where man and nature find harmony through the individual's creative autonomy–gave delineation and depth to the earlier, originating vision. The creative genius of Goethe and Schiller in construction of "classicism" can be considered as the culmination of the classical project sketched earlier by Winckelmann, Nicolai, Gerstenberg, Lessing, and others who debated the aesthetics of integrating Greek and Roman art, literature, and ideas into contemporary thought.

57. Johann Gottfried Herder, *Werke in Zwei Bänden* (Munich: Carl Hanser Verlag, 1953), 2; 9. Further reference to this volume.

58. Immanuel Kant, *Idea for a Universal History from a Cosmopolitan Point of View* in *On History, Immanuel Kant*, trans. Lewis White Beck (Indianapolis: Bobbs-Merrill, 1963), 15.

59. Immanuel Kant, Conjectural Beginnings of Human History in *On History, Immanuel Kant*, trans. Emil L. Fackenheim (Indianapolis: Bobbs-Merrill, 1963), 62.

60. One of the most thorough reviews of the historicism is offered by Georg Iggers, *The German Conception of History, The National Tradition of Historical Thought From Herder to the Present*, revised edition (Middletown, Conn.: Wesleyan University Press, 1968). Friedrich Meinecke has written the most definitively exhaustive study of German historicism, although he coined the term "historism" to encompass the movement as it developed from Leibniz through Ranke. See Friedrich Meinecke, *Historism, The Rise of a New Historical Outlook*, trans. J. E. Anderson (New York: Herder and Herder, 1972).

61. Friedrich Karl von Savigny, *Juristische Methodenlehre, nach der Ausarbeitung des Jakob Grimm*, ed. Gerhard Wesenberg (Stuttgart: K.F. Koehler, 1951), 42, 48–50. Further reference to this text and edition.

62. See Ulrich Wyass, *Die wilde Philologie, Jacob Grimm und der Historismus* (Munich: C.H. Beck, 1979), 75–80, and Franz Wieacker, "Friedrich Carl von Savigny," in *Die Grossen Deutschen, Deutsche Biographie*, ed. Hermann Heimpel, Theodor Heuss, and Benno Reifenberg (Berlin: Propyläen Verlag bei Ullstein Berlin, 1958), 3: 41. Further reference to these texts and editions.

63. See Ernst Rudolf Huber on the pervasiveness of the concept of "unity" in the state from Metternich through Bismarck, and its subtle constitutional manifestation as a state of affairs protected by the office of the king (or even in the Weimar years by the President); *Deutsche Verfassungsgeschichte seit 1789*, 4 vols. (Stuttgart: W. Kohlhammer, 1957–1963), 3: 12–20. Further reference to these texts and edition.

64. See a discussion on the varied interpretations of social "facts" that led to the coining of terms like the proletariat in James J. Sheehan, *German History, 1770–1866* (Oxford: Clarendon Press, 1989), 646–647, 651–653.

65. Leopold von Ranke, *Welchen Einfluss hat die Erlernung der Geschichtes auf das Leben der Menschen?* in Leopold von Ranke, *Frühe Schriften*, ed. Gunter Berg and Volker Dotterweich (Munich: R. Oldenbourg, 1973), 50. Further reference to this text and edition.

66. Leopold von Ranke, *Das Luther-Fragment von 1817*, ed. Elisabeth Schweitzer, in *Deutsche Geschichte im Zeitalter der Reformation*, Vol. 6 (Munich: Drei Masken Verlag, 1926), 315. Further reference to this text and edition.

67. Hans-Ulrich Wehler, *The German Empire, 1871–1918*, trans. Kim Traynor (Oxford: Berg, 1985), 90. Wehler cies a letter from the historian Sybel written in 1871, included in J. Hederhoff and P. Wentzke (eds.), *Deutscher Liberalismus im Zeitalter Bismarcks*, Vol. 1 (Osnabrück, 2nd imp., 1967), 494.

68. See *The Democratic Tradition, Four German Constitutions*, ed. Elmar M. Hucko (New York: Berg, 1987), 122.

69. See Robert A. Kann, *The Multinational Empire*, Vol. 2 (New York: Columbia University Press, 1950), 131.

70. See a discussion of this issue in Ernst Rudolf Huber, *Deutsche Verfassungsgeschichte seit 1789*, Vol. 3 (Stuttgart: W. Kohlhammer Verlag, 1963), 6–9, 11–13, 29–30, and 60–61 for Germany. See Hucko, *The Democratic Tradition, Four German Constitutions*, 126. See Robert A. Kann, *The Multinational Empire*, Vol. 2, 130–131 and 341, fn. 115 in his discussion of art. 14 of the Austrian 1867 constitution.

71. See, for example, Gustav von Schmoller, "Die soziale Frage und der preussische Staat," in *Zur Sozial- und Gewerbepolitik der Gegenwart, Reden und Aufsätze von Gustav Schmoller* (Leipzig: Duncker &ss Humblot, 1890), 55ff.

7. The European Metahistorical Narrative and its Changing "Metaparadigms" in the Modern Age (Part II): Western Painting 1815–1914

Abstract   In the second part of my article "The European Metahistorical Narrative and Its Changing 'Metaparadigms' in the Modern Age," I focus upon painting in the West in order to demonstrate both the shift from one metaparadigm to another, and at the same time, the nonverbal characteristics of the fourth phase and initial phases of a metaparadigm as found in the nonverbal historical logic of the composition of paintings.

The nonverbal or visual historical logic of artistic communication is founded upon the same part-whole *diareses* of experience as the historical logic of verbal communication in a culture. I derive this claim from the epistemology of Immanuel Kant and Edmund Husserl. Every judgment is a temporal claim as well as a spatial one. A nonverbal spatial communication is also a temporal claim. I enlist the mid-twentieth century aesthetic and rhetorical theory of Stephen C. Pepper to augment my Kantian and Husserlian epistemology. Based on these ideas I detail the temporal-spatial historical logic of paintings that correspond to the four phases of verbal historical logic that constitute a cultural systematization of ideas and values over time. In Part I, I demonstrated the four-phased development and dissolution of the metaparadigmatic assumptions that guide the arts and the sciences in the several generations of its existence. Wilhelm Dilthey's theory of the four-phase development of guiding humanistic and scientific beliefs that inform the arts and the sciences in an era was the basis of my own historiographical theory.

In Part II, in order to demonstrate the correspondence of nonverbal and verbal historical logic, I show how the second major modern metaparadigm in the West that began in the 1750s was completed in its fourth phase within the paradigm of painting which extended from the post-Napoleonic period until the late 1860s. Then, I demonstrate how the paradigm of painting introduced the third modern metaparadigm within its domain beginning in the late 1860s. Although I use only French painters, the characteristics I demonstrate in their temporal-spatial historical logic are those of the regional reality, not

Correspondence to: Mark E. Blum, Department of History, University of Louisville, Louisville, Kentucky 40292 the national, nor the personal of the painters themselves. I spoke in Part I of this article of the difference between the regional, national, and personal in regard to verbal historical logic.

To demonstrate the fourth-phase characteristics of the metaparadigm that began in the 1750 and culminated in the 1860s, I use the landscape painting of Camille Corot (1796–1875) and the realism of Gustave Courbet (1819–1877). To demonstrate the initial phases of the metaparadigm that began in the late 1860s and culminated in the 1960s, I use the landscape painting of Corot's student Camille Pissarro (1830–1903) whose Impressionism carried this new historical logic, and the "Second Realism" of "Edouard Manet (1832–1883).

The second metaparadigm of the modern age began in the 1750s. This metaparadigm was characterized by a focus solely on secularism, separating itself from the necessity to include the Divine in its discussions of premises or findings in the arts and the sciences. Even "natural law" dropped away as a causal base of premises or findings. The foundation for a "right order" became human reason alone. A univocal objective world was posited in the arts and the sciences that guaranteed progressive outcomes for inquiry, and the standards to assess that progress. The fourth phase, as seen in painting, was a collectivization of the ideas of univocal objectivity: the painterly image stressed the "typical" in the organic, inorganic, and societal existence; an "objective" time was depicted as an enduring reality all shared; a sense of determined, material conditions that constrained everyone and everything was imparted, thus securing the enduring existence "in common."

The third metaparadigm that began in the 1860s sought a secular, yet humanly spiritual basis for enriching personal as well as communal life. Thomas Mann has called the inception of this period the "third humanism." Reason alone was not sufficient as a basis for meaning in the world. In doing so, the reflective ego itself was decentered, as new dimensions of intelligence became evident in inquiry. A new secular humanism emerged in the arts as well as the social sciences. The human being ceased to be the rational being whose inquiries and ethos were to be evaluated by generally agreed upon standards set by that very reason. Indeed, the very notion of a univocal objective world with laws to be discerned that were the same for everyone was put into question. Relativity in perception and judgment as well as in the material laws of nature became the study of many disciplines in the arts and the sciences. The physical sciences decentered the traditional building blocks of physical force and chemistry with new levels of material existence. In painting, this "decentered" reality was imparted by the myriad light sources contained in a perceptive judgment; Impressionism introduced this complex myriad of integrities that constituted any synthetic moment. The "relativity" of perception was imparted by painters instructing the viewer in how a perceptive image was constructed: each painter brought to the viewer's attention the tension between the two-dimensional canvas and the three-dimensional image. The painter made clear by several techniques that reality was imposed upon the flat canvas through choices in perspective. His or her momentary or more extended vision of a state-of-affairs became the assertion. The painter recognized the subjective values in this impression or more conceptual expression. Painting became a lesson in the responsibility of becoming aware of how each person constructs a judgment, the corollary being that no state-of-affairs has a univocal objectivity apart from the human judgment. The historical logic of time was depicted as rapidly changing; the extreme "freedom" in choice and life movement was emphasized; material reality was made evident as a product of interest and intentional point-of-view (as the venue of what existed as it comes to consciousness).

Keywords: Metaparadigm, paradigm, landscape painting, Impressionism, Realism, Stephen C. Pepper, Camille Corot, Gustave Courbet, Camille Pissarro, Edouard Manet, historiography

We now come to the subject of organizing patterns [in art]...There are two main kinds of organizing patterns, which we shall call the embracing and the skeletal. An embracing pattern is one that embraces a number of other patterns within it....The embracing principle can be carried up through many levels making a system as complicated as necessary to take in all the material requiring to be organized....A skeletal pattern is one that brings order out of complexity on the principle of a tree formation or of an animal skeleton. A tree has a simple trunk from which grow a number of branches, from which grow a number of twigs, from which grow a number of leaves. If the number of branches falls within the limits of attention, and the number of twigs on each branch, and the number of leaves on each twig, then the whole system will fit comfortably in the attention, and appear clear and well-ordered.

Stephen C. Pepper, *Principles of Art Appreciation*[1]

Structural corroboration consists in the convergence of qualitatively different items of evidence in support of [a state-of-affairs]....Structural corroboration requires a theory or hypothesis for the connection of the various items of evidence, and what is said to be corroborated here by the convergence of evidence is not so much the evidence itself as the theory which connects it together....When the structure is conceived of as wholly abstracted from the evidence, we call it the theory or hypothesis; and when the various items organized by the structure are considered in abstraction from their structure, they are called evidences for the hypothesis.

Stephen C. Pepper, *World Hypotheses*[2]

Stephen C. Pepper had an acute visual as well as abstract intelligence. His insights into verbal and visual "arguments," i.e., structural alignments that cohere the empirical facts of a state-of-affairs, are in the spirit of my work, indeed parallel my work in a profound manner in their discernment of narrative organization. Pepper sought the part-whole alignments which were "invariant" in the verbal and visual arguments generated by a communication (*World Hypotheses*, 1970, 52). He discerned part-whole structures of verbal and visual argument that were both a guide to the several moments of data that formed one's cognitive production part by part, and the totality of organization, i.e., the cumulative product cohered by the several moments that were the part-whole alignment. Pepper's findings can be translated into Edmund Husserl's notions of part-whole dependencies and independencies in the formulation of how states-of-affairs are conceived. My own theoretical exposition relies more explicitly upon Husserl as I consider the temporality generated by the part-whole alignments of facts as they form "event-structures," i.e., the coherent, yet dynamic episodes of persons, place, and things in time that are referred to in their culmination as a "state-of-affairs." Nonetheless, Pepper's discernment of differing types of "invariant" part-whole alignments in human cognition undergirds theoretically my own findings that cultural communications, be they verbal or nonverbal (imagistic), reflect "invariant" manners of discerning and communicating states-of-affairs by individuals over a career of thought. Moreover, my contention that there are regional (i.e. ,Western, East Asian, Near Eastern, etc.) modes of invariance in the construction of events, and national modes of invariant "event-structures" within those regional styles, can be understood within Pepper's conceptions.

Pepper's "world hypotheses"–he identified four of them in Western rhetoric–was a generic manner of ascribing cause-and-effect sequences explaining any state-of-affairs. Cause and its effects were delineated in each respective "hypothesis" by invariant orders of dependent and independent relationships. As in my schemata of temporal concretums, this invariance was applied as a diairesis for comprehending how an event came to be in its link with prior or coexistent states-of-affairs. The invariant schemata did not turn the argument into a fictive tour de force, rather the invariant schemata enabled one to see a certain justifiable order of cause and effect that another schemata could not delineate as clearly. Pepper argued that each of the four "world hypotheses" was valid within its own purview. Pepper restricted the term "world hypothesis" to verbal arguments, but an interpolative reading of his aesthetics allows that a "world hypothesis" as an "argument," i.e., point of view, could be either verbal or visual (see his definition of aesthetics in *Principles of Art Appreciation*, 1949, 104 fn, where he speaks of an aesthetic judgment as the internal organization of an artist's production). "World hypotheses" are generic "arguments" whose alignment of the part-whole members generates a sense of continuity, discontinuity, change, or duration in how cause and effect operate in the world. Pepper did not develop fully the correspondence of the part-whole alignments of verbal argument to the visual skeletal or embracing organization of nonverbal arguments. However, his last work *Aesthetic Quality, A Contextualistic Theory of Beauty* was a beginning in that direction.[3] In this work, he related one of his verbal "world hypotheses," the "contextualist" part-whole argument, to the nonverbal alignments of the contextualist perspective in the act of painting and its corresponding aesthetic judgments. Pepper was aware that he was a "contextualist" thinker, and argued within that frame of discernment.

Immanuel Kant helps us understand why a visual statement is also an argument when he points out that every coherent articulation of the mind is a cognitive judgment, whether it be verbal or visual.[4] Indeed, according to Kant, a schematic visual argument–a configuration of parts and wholes–coheres a state-of-affairs as a temporal episode that carries a distinct meaning. All verbal judgments arise from that nonverbal alignment, the meaning articulated in concepts.[5] Kant holds that all concepts arise upon the part-whole schema of how one comprehends a state-of-affairs [*Critique of Pure Reason*, 1968, 134 (A 104); 183 (A 142 B 181)]. Kant is among the first Enlightenment thinkers to see that an artistic judgment, i.e., a figurative cognition, is an intuition, i.e., image of a state-of-affairs, that can be more adequate in its grasp of evidence than any other cognition ("Critique of Aesthetic Judgement," *Critique of Judgement*, 1952, 168, 175–180).

Leonard Shlain in his *Art and Physics* (1991) has demonstrated the parallel structures of argument between the fine arts and physics in Western cultural history.[6] For example, he shows the shift in art and science as three-dimensional space is discerned in both art and science in the fourteenth century (1991, 47ff.), and later how the univocal, objective world created in these respective disciplines were relativized by the same disciplines in the last decades of the nineteenth and initial decades of the twentieth centuries (1991, Chapters Nine and Ten). Shlain lacks an epistemological ground for his parallels of art and sceince over time, thus his demonstrations while conceptually sound (in my estimation) are speculative. I have discerned many of the same characteristics as Shlain in the similarity of the arts and the sciences in the closing decades of the nineteenth century. My verbal findings are located in my discussion in Part I of this essay. I address the nonverbal parallel in this section of the essay. My findings are not solely analogical, however, but have a firmer etiology for why and how these changes occur. My analyses are based upon a Kantian/Husserlian ontology and epistemology of cognition. I examine the part-whole successions of verbal and nonverbal language that create the temporal organizations of a generation in the meanings they convey. The patterns of part-whole alignment in their temporal rhythms and conceptual implications provide evidence of the several phases of development in the systematization of cultural values and ideas that I argue are the presence of a coherent metaparadigm in the culture.

To track as Shlain does the continuities and changes in Western thought since the reemergence of representational painting in the early fourteenth century in the West in its parallel with a science of representation time and space, and to show the major shift toward a relativity of temporal-spatiality in late nineteenth and early twentieth century physics in the corollary discipline of painting, one must augment analogy with a grounding of these kinds of judgment in a theory of judgment, especially historical judgment. Kant and Husserl are foundational sources in this endeavor, as well as Stephen C. Pepper who helps us to see how forms of argument that rely on the perception of temporal episodes are at play even in the profound changes of scientific and artistic schemas from generation to generation. Hayden White uses the thought of Stephen C. Pepper, his four "world-hypotheses" in particular, as an analytical tool for discerning kinds of "historical arguments" made in the West that are formed out of a lexicon of syntactical/semantic constructs. White's demonstrations are linguistic and semiological, finding temporality and the "event arguments"'that typify a perception of time and space in a generation in the forms of narrative structure and enabling grammar.[7] My findings have many parallels with his. Yet, White does not offer a genetic epistemology that allows a comprehension of the origin of the part-whole arguments or their grammatical/rhetorical venues. Lacking this epistemological grounding, White cannot explore in his narrative findings that define a generation's historical logic the nonverbal expressions of that "deep generational temporality" which I explore as a metaparadigmatic generational imperative.[8]

My work as demonstrated in the several essays in this publication provide the epistemological foundation of judgment which enables one to discern the genetic development in language, concept, and historical argument of what White and his own mentor Pepper have discerned. I have linked Pepper's four "world hypotheses" in their event-structure to the four kinds of personal historical logic I have discerned.[9] Pepper sees how certain part-whole dependencies and/or independencies as aligned temporal moments in a judgment generate continuities, discontinuities, durations, and changes in a state-of-affairs. The manner of alignment of these parts and wholes configures the historical presence and its relationships. While Pepper does not use the terminology of part-whole diaireses as temporal-generating moments fundamental to my phenomenological historical methods, his discussion of how each of the four schemata links evidential moments into a coherent cause-consequence event is essentially a part-whole diairetic discussion. Pepper grasps the temporal geneses of part-whole designs upon a forming judgment at one point in his discussion (see *World Hypotheses*, 1942, 237–238), but he is neither a Kantian nor a Husserlian, and thus fails to pursue the notion. Pepper's analyses of verbal arguments, however, do provide the diairetical outcomes that show inherent kinds of historical logic. Consider him a mereologist of verbal and visual rhetoric who need only enliven the formation of the part-whole discernments to realize its temporal reality. His visual analyses of painting, while not dwelling on the temporal implications, are nonetheless the bases for temporal understandings.

My discussion in this essay considers the aesthetics of Western painting between 1815 and 1914 from the perspective of how norms of temporal understanding can be discerned in the embracing pattern (pace Pepper) that persists through distinct phases of the Western metaparadigm in its four-phase cycle. What is embraced is a national cultural historical-logical norm by the larger regional norm, as those distinctive norms are expressed in the visual syntax of part-whole diaireses. The skeletal pattern will not be an issue in this essay: the skeletal pattern is the personal historical logic of the artist which gives the painting an intrinsic temporal style that is the Kantian transcendental schema that underlies visual production and its verbal equivalents. In contradistinction to the skeletal, the embracing regional generational norms, with their nested national generational norms are what Kant called regulative habits-of-mind instilled by the culture (*Critique of Pure Reason*, 1968, 547ff). The four temporal phases of the metaparadigm, as evidenced by the patterns of temporal-spatial organization, are implied by the internested embracing design of part-whole alignments. It must be borne in mind, however, that these patterns are a cultural rather than an individual time. While the historical-logical conventions of region and nation are assimilated into the cognitive palette of self-expression by the artist, they are not originary temporal constitutions arising from highly individual diaireses, rather mediate impositions assimilated by the person of a general cultural understanding. The historian who uses aesthetic products of temporal judgment as evidence of the person, the nation, or the region must dissect each of these aspects of temporal judgment in any complete statement, i.e., artistic artifact. In this essay, I will only discuss the embracing structure as a regional organization of temporal-spatial events. I will refer to these in Husserl's terminology as "temporal concretums," that is, a state-of-affairs formed out of the "time-stretch" moments that cohere the episode as a whole (*Logical Investigations*, 1970, 2: 486–488). I will discuss four characteristics that constituted the fourth and final phase from 1815 through the late 1860s of the Western metaparadigm that had been introduced in the late 1760s, and four characteristics that can be discerned in the paintings of artists from the late 1860s until World War I as visual initial phase of a new metaparadigmatic presence.

1.   THE VISUAL CHARACTERISTICS OF THE CULTURAL LOGIC OF THE FOUR PHASES OF A METAPARADIGM

I have described four categorical assumptions in Part I of this extended essay which underlie the development and implementation of cultural activity in the first three phases of a regional, e.g., Western, metaparadigm that precede the fourth phase of normalization:

(1) the complex individual differences of all integrities (person, place, or thing) that participate in an assumed common totality;
(2) the freedom of intelligent beings or accident/chance for things without mind or will;
(3) quantum change in states-of-affairs;
(4) visual or conceptual perspective more salient than its material content.

These four characteristics that birth and mature the new metaparadigm can be simply stated, respectively, as complex individuality, freedom and chance, quantum (or rapid) change, and conceptual relativity in discernment (rather than an assertion of sameness in what is materially shared). The decades which express the emergence of the new metaparadigm are fraught with conflicts in judging what might be a new "right order." As Laurence Sterne said in the 1759 epigraph to his radical, culture-changing satire *Tristram Shandy*, quoting Epictetus "It is not things that disturb men, but their judgments about things."[10]

The fourth phase presents the converse of these concepts: one sees:

(1) the collective expression of persons, places, and things–that is, having the totality formed by them in common by dint of shared characteristics;
(2) determinism in the laws of function in intelligent beings and in things without mind or will;
(3) a conception of duration of states-of-affairs;
(4) the material content of the judgment rather than its perspectival mediation as the chief focus.

These four characteristics lend to the typification and norming of the new cultural systematization. The four characteristics can be simply phrased as complex interdependence, determinism, duration (or in the modern era, gradual evolution), and materialism. The diversity of ideational positions in such an era finds a common basis within the material and institutional structures shared by all persons, placing the radical disjunction of ideas between persons in the background–arguing rather within the modifying implications of ideas to commonly understood structures.

The visual counterparts of the four categorical characteristics of the initial three phases and the fourth phase seek to impart as imagistic configuration the same meanings as their verbal equivalents. Just as the verbal statements are genetic products of distinct part-whole diaireses of experience, so the nonverbal. Representations of space/time in painting conform the objects and acts to the potentialities of the same part-whole event arguments that underlie all judgments of verbally communicated spatial/temporal acts. The initial three phases of a metaparadigm are chiefly concerned in showing a new possible order of states-of-affairs beyond what has become the typifying norm. These three phases seek also to gradually deconstruct the prior "fourth phase" typification, replacing the traditional meanings with new ones. Graphically, images will be used that challenge the traditional conceptions in a radical manner, and show the new in every place where the old was customary–always with an implicit or explicit challenge to the old.

The figural equivalents of (1) complex individuality, (2) freedom/chance/ accident, (3) quantum change, and (4) conceptual relativity are, respectively:

1) **Complex individuality: delineations that clearly separate spatial areas within the canvas, be they of persons or other animate figures, or areas of nature or artifact.**

The seeing of distinct persons, places, and things enhances contrast and difference, rather than typification, sameness, and things in-common. Complex interdependence is always achieved by pairing, complements, and integrative unities of one kind or another. Kant would refer to such a demarcation between "extensive magnitudes," or parts and wholes, as imparting separateness and distinctiveness by giving "an ever-ceasing synthesis" of the thing that is objectified (*Critique of Pure Reason*, 1968, A 171, B 213). The boundary of each thing is clear and final. Kant will offer in this passage the converse manner of creating boundaries when he speaks of the complex interdependence manifested by a quantum order:

A quantum is a unity of particulars in which discontinuities are obliterated in favor of cohesive continuity: a mark of fine silver (in which the thirteen thalers that lie on the table are subsumed into a unity by a productive synthesis). (as contrasted with...)

An aggregate is the thirteen thalers, seen separately that make up the mark of fine silver (in which each thaler is separated from another by the repetition of "an ever-ceasing synthesis").

2) **Freedom/chance/accident**
   2a) **Asymmetry forms the figural judgment as an entire composition (judgment) as well as in those part-whole moments that constitute the entirety. Imbalance, rather than balance, is the rule for composition as a whole.**

Although I will focus upon the shift from the fourth phase of the metaparadigm that began in the late 1750s and culminates in the 1860s to the initial phases of the new metaparadigm that begins in the late 1860s in comparing painting, I find it helpful to initially speak of an aesthetic contrast between the early and late Enlightenment. Eighteenth-century aesthetics, that is, the very beginnings of the discipline, made a distinction between the regularities of a unified schema of time, place, and manner through continuities of representation and the violations of the "three unities" of time, place, and manner by asymmetrical forms of figural judgment. Aesthetic theories of the middle Enlightenment–1715–1755–stress the "three unities." These were the years that include what I have termed the fourth phase of the transition from the age of religion to the first secular age. It began in the late 1640s in the wake of the era of religious wars and extended to the 1750s. The fourth phase of this metaparadigm was that of the balance of powers politically and economically in the interdependent world postulated by Bolingbroke, and a bit more skeptically by Montesquieu [whose *The Spirit of the Laws* (1748) was published in the dawning of the metaparadigm to be], and Voltaire. Complex interdependence between all the social classes was preferred to any conflict in political-social values. An art that represented the integrative interdependence of all persons in a common time, place, and manner was the rule. Voltaire argues for the "three unities" of a common time, place, and manner for the narrative of events as a standard of taste and beauty in the first section of the article "On Taste" in Diderot's *Encyclopedia*.[11] The "Essay on Taste" had three authors, Voltaire, Montesquieu, and D'Alembert, who respectively articulated the notion of "taste" from an Early Enlightenment, Transitional, and Late Enlightenment perspective. Voltaire (1694–1778) calls the complex interdependence of persons in time, place, and manner of expression "la belle natur," or that which is truly beautiful in its harmonious blending. Asymmetry in this vision is but anomaly, the "ugliness" of disharmony.

Montesquieu (1689–1755), who actually began the essay, dying two years before its publication, in his later years after *The Spirit of the Laws* was increasingly skeptical of the interdependent possibility. His aesthetic vision was that of the value of both interdependence through the three unities and the emergent complex individuality which violated the unities with asymmetries. Moreover, Montesquieu considers aesthetics as a science that studies the "rational appetite" of an inquiring mind, rooting the beautiful more inherently in the operations of judgment than in its outcomes, as did Voltaire. Emphasis upon process over the balanced outcome sought in a states-of-affairs is the modus vivendi of the new that disrupts the old. An age of individualism in its conceptual relativity will stress alternative modes of judging and their underlying operations, as in Kant. The late Enlightenment will increasingly focus upon how one judges and the perspectival issues, rather than what is judged. Montesquieu wrote in this essay:

> Concerning curiosity. Our soul is meant to think, which is to perceive. Now such a being must be endowed with curiosity: since all object are in a chain where each idea both precedes and follows another, it is impossible to wish to see one object without desiring to see another one, and if we did not feel desire for the latter, we would not take pleasure in the former. Thus when we are shown part of picture our desire to see the part that is hidden is in proportion to the

pleasure we have taken in the part we have already seen. The pleasure given us by one object inclines us toward another. This is why the soul always seeks new objects and is never at rest. Therefore one sure means of always pleasing the soul is to present it with many objects or with a greater number than it had expected to see. This explains why we take pleasure in seeing a symmetrically ordered garden, and yet also in seeing a wild and rustic spot. Both these effects are produced by the same cause. Since we like to see a large number of objects, we would like to expand our vision to be in several places and to cover greater distances. Our soul abhors limits (1967, 344–345).

Montesquieu's aesthetic theory articulates a transitional time, i.e., a time where "change" is evident, and is reinforced as a creative state-of-mind. This transitional time in the Germanies produces the beginnings of historicism: Klopstock writes of God's creation of tension and its release that brings into being new solutions to existence in his *Frühlingsfeyer* (1759), and the young Lessing of *Sara Sampson* (1755) examines the ceaseless change of circumstances, personalities, and history.

The man who finished the essay "On Taste" was D'Alembert (1717–1783). D'Alembert, an editor of the *Encyclopedia*, was younger than the previous authors, and had an aesthetic perspective that differed radically from Voltaire's emphasis upon the unities. D'Alembert urged a "bold" and "spontaneous" creativity in aesthetics that paid no attention to existing rules (1967, 365–367). He commended the late seventeenth century critic and dramatist Houdar de la Motte (1672–1731) for de la Motte's attack on the three unities (1967, 368 fn 27). De la Motte's early maturity was shaped by the third, deconstructive phase of the metaparadigm of the 1640s to the 1750s. D'Alembert was to enhance this perspective as he introduced the new metaparadigm that emerged in the late 1750s. Challenging Voltaire's stress on rational balance, D'Alembert refers to the primacy of emotion in the truth of the moment (1967, 370). D'Alembert foresees Lessing's criticism of Winckelmann's understanding of the *Laökoon* in 1766, where Lessing made the same case of spontaneous emotion over rational restraint as the crux of truth–the emotive disrupting symmetrical behavior:

> The philosopher knows that genius wishes to be left free of all constraint at the moment of creation. He knows that it prefers to forge ahead without bridle or rule, to create the monstrous next to the sublime, and to carry both mud and gold irresistibly along with it (1967, 371).

Genius becomes the new standard, that which is not typifying or regular in its movement or expression, as the quantum appearance of the new metaparadigm emerges that will be regularized in its tenets from 1815 through the 1860s in the final fourth phase of that cultural system of ideation.

The new content introduced with the violation of the unities was that of human psychology and the further secularization of all understandings, where natural law becomes divorced from its divine origins and values. Content issues will be taken up in my discussions that compare the fourth phase of the new metaparadigm with the metaparadigm that follows.

Another graphic characteristic that enables one to see "freedom/chance/ accident" in the emergent phases of a new metapardigm is an asymmetry introduced by the erasure or transgressing of the boundaries that frame the temporal-spatial event:

2b) The borders or boundaries of picture are violated by figuration. Partial persons, places, and things extend into implied space beyond the canvas or frame. Actual figuration may extend beyond a pictorial faux boundary.

The convention of using the external frame or a painted frame border within a painting in a manner that creates the illusion of the person, place, or thing extended beyond or through the frame can be discerned in Western cultural-historical periods where a new metaparadigm emerges, usually in the initial two phases where the ideas are a prominent challenge to existing realities. Sixten Ringbom studies this boundary violation in Giovanni Bellini (1430–1516) and Andrea Mantegna (1431–1506) and their contemporaries in northern Europe who are among the creative minds ushering in a new metaparadigm in the late 1460s.[12] The 1460s began an era which in Italy and Northern Renaissance produced a more complex humanism in its attention to the complex individuality of the person and his/her experience.[13].The notion of "freedom" as attention to one's own willed acts and control of personal states-of-mind can be dated earlier to Aquinas and Dante, but in this particular period insights into this human complexity abounded. Ringbom's book *Icon to Narrative, The Rise of the Dramatic Close-up in Fifteenth Century Devotional Painting* explores the graphic characteristics of painterly temporal-spatial representation that generate a vision of the conative freedom inherent in the narrative event (1965, 12–13). The boundary violations are a spatial-temporal depiction of this conative urge which visibly suggests a free choice of movement across a boundary that customarily in a fourth-phase metaparadigmatic thought frames all action. Kant, in the initial phases of the metaparadigm that began in the 1750s, pointedly defined this conative freedom with an example of the will defying deterministic boundaries in his discussion of the determined aspects of human motility as well as its freedom. Kant describes the ability to rise from a chair according to an intentional conation, despite the determination of gravity, musculature limitation, etc. (*Critique of Pure Reason*, 1968, 414 [A 450, B 478]). Painterly violations of frame boundaries are to be found in this same late Enlightenment period. A particular dramatic example of this is Peale's *Man Climbing a Staircase* (Philadelphia Art Museum) where the prominent figure walking up a staircase beckons the onlooker to follow him, the frame having two wooden steps extending into the exhibit space.

3) Quantum change

Painting of the human figure in action in the initial three phases of a metaparadigm offers thematic moments undergirded by spatial-temporal ploys that show an exact moment of action. This specifying of the moment is in contradistinction to the fourth-phase painting that stipulates no exact moment, rather a general condition that may extend minutes or hours. The specification of the exact moment underscores the idea of ceaseless change that in itself encourages change in the cultural-ideational norms of the society.

David's *Oath of the Horatii* (1784) and *Socrates Taking the Hemlock* (1788) are two of the more well-known neoclassicist examples of this characteristic. Even Fragonard's late Rococo style incorporates this theme in *The Swing* (1766), where a shoe in midair suggests the exact moment. My discussion of the initial phases of the metaparadigm that begins in the late 1860s will show this emphasis with the school of Impressionism whose very premise is such exact temporal delineation, as well as this creation of the exact moment in Manet's realism.

The entry or exit or extension into the boundary enhances this illusion of a willed movement whose egress, ingress, or progress is the tòde ti potè "the moment of the singular."

4) Conceptual relativity

Conceptual relativity is communicated visually by suggesting cognitive dissonance between competing ideas within a nonetheless unified perspective. The exactitude of the whole has a mathematic precision, within which there are contrasting moments realized by Kant's "ever-ceasing syntheses" of separate parts. One of the clearest instances I have seen of this conceptual relativity in late Enlightenment painting is David's *Socrates Taking the Hemlock* (1788), where Socrates's gestures create a parallelogram of those assembled around him. Without those precise gestures which are the act of taking the cup, his followers would be grouped in two separate triangles–thus the summative 360 degrees of the parallelogram. The *Phaedo* is rife with these ideational and physical differences among his friends.

The conceptual exactitude complements the temporal-spatial specificity of an act or natural moment in time, while augmenting with ideational perspective the complex differences among all persons, contained spaces, and other things. In human conation one must ask "what is it exactly that is transpiring in this moment, and for whom?" In a natural setting, one must ask "what is the time being shown exactly, and does it have differing affects upon how one experiences that time?" or "what exact state in the many phases of nature am I viewing?" In the collective reality of typification, there are no nuanced issues, rather a clear statement of what transpires generally (the exact moment not offered gesturally or in other material ways).

The figural equivalents of complex interdependence, determinism, duration (or in the modern era, gradual evolution), and materialism are discussed in contradistinction to those of their converse above. Nonetheless, more criteria of painting in this fourth metaparadigmatic phase will be helpful in supporting my thesis.

5) Complex interdependence
5a) Interconnection through visual means of conjoining diverse elements

Through color, texture, line, and volume an effort is made to blend and interconnect figures, objects, and other represented spatialities into a state-of-affairs in-common. Individuality is never an isolate phenomenon in the painting. The paradigm of painting from the close of the Napoleonic Wars until the late 1860s, the fourth phase of the metaparadigm that began in the late 1750s, evidences structural rules that emphasize this interdependent blending. Delacroix (1798–1863) created a color theory for blending shapes through color by gradations. Delacroix observed that "It is advisable not to fuse brushstrokes as they will [appear to)]fuse naturally at [a]...distance."[14] Delacroix derived his color perspective from a somewhat older, though contemporary landscape painter, John Constable (1776–1837). Delacroix writes:

> Constable said that the superiority of the green he uses for his landscapes derives from the fact that it is composed of a multitude of different greens. What causes the lack of intensity and of life in verdure as it is painted by the common run of landscapists is that they ordinarily do it with a uniform tint. What he said about the green of meadows can be applied to all other tones (*Art Through the Ages*, 1986, 824).

Delacroix used this diversity of tint in doing flesh tones, and was able thereby to create human contact between persons that broke new ground in the intimacy of human contact of flesh on flesh. Interdependence was made more thoroughly real in its human interactions.

Jean Baptiste Camille Corot (1796–1875), who will be more closely studied as one of the two artists who represent the fourth phase of the metaparadigm that ends in the late 1860s, also contributed to the differentiated values that move from light to dark in colors in order to achieve the effect of an integrated landscape. Corot sought a complete tonal spread in offering the diverse, yet interconnected unity of an environ. He wrote:

> In preparing a study or a picture, it seems to me very important to begin by
> an indication of the darkest values...and continue in order to the lightest value.
> From the darkest to the lightest I would establish twenty shades ... (*Art Through*
> *the Ages*, 1986, 836).

5b) Unification through typification

There are three methods by which a painter in the fourth phase of
metaparadigmatic development achieves a unity of the diverse elements of a
state-of-affairs–typifying by the mutual participation in a theme [the major
idea(s) of the time], typifying by genre renderings (the customary presentation
of person, place, or thing), and the incisive advances in depicting what is shared
(a typifying advance in grasping the characteristics of the subject). Each of
these methods enables the painter as thinker to demonstrate the shared character
of an age, the interdependence of all inorganic and organic life. Corot will offer
a major advance in the third of these methods in his depiction of the essential
planes of face and body in his portraits, as well as the recognition of what
Louis Agassiz and Charles Lyell saw in geology in his landscapes–the essential
planes of rock and soil strata.

6) Determinism

The above spatial characteristics work together to show internal boundaries
and constraints that preserve the links between each person, place, and thing.
Coupled with these internal aspects, the figuration will be contained within the
boundaries of the tableau presented. There will not be the illusion of ingress,
egress, or progress across the boundaries of the tableau or the frame itself.
Moreover, the figuration, even when in movement, will have a "posed" quality–
offering thereby the "typical" in movement, rather than the idiosyncratic and
momentary. Indeed, what is presented is a "tableau."

In figuration and general disposition of the planes of the compositions,
painting also emphasized horizontality in every fourth metaparadigmatic phase–
that is, the material stability and rootedness of states-of-affairs. The horizontality
contributed to determinism in its material structures which gravity implicitly
constrained.

7) Duration (or gradual evolution)

Duration is offered by the stillness or emblematic character of the
presentation. The posed quality of event depicted in all its aspects emphasizes the enduring. Thus, typicality engenders duration in the conception of
time.

Internally, the painterly method of light source in the fourth phase of a
metaparadigm will stress a more uniform light, where gradations of light and

dark blend to form what Voltaire understood as the three unities of :time, place, and manner." In this sameness, one visualizes that which is common to the time and correspondingly how the time itself is this qualitative sameness.

8) Materialism

Materialism is a common leaven of reality that belies the significance of volitional action in its imparting of change. Landscapes are more common in the fourth phase of any metaparadigm as they naturally offer the ecological interdependence that curtails the significance of volitional change in any person or thing depicted. In other genres such as portraits or scenes of human interaction or other themes than that of nature the "materiality" that links all persons, places, and things is offered by the horizontal emphasis of the renderings with the implicit gravity that constrains action. Kant states this material constraint best as he counterposes organic and inorganic nature to the "freedom" of volition:

> Even if a transcendental power of freedom be allowed, as supplying a beginning of happenings in the world, this power would in any case have to be outside the world (though any such assumption that over and above the sum of all possible intuitions there exists an object which cannot be given in any possible perception, is still a very bold one). But to ascribe to substances in the world itself such a power, can never be permissible; for, should this be done, that connection of appearances determining one another with necessity according to universal laws, which we entitle nature, and with it the criterion of empirical truth, whereby experience is distinguished from dreaming, would almost entirely disappear. Side by side with such a lawless faculty of freedom, nature (as an ordered system) is hardly thinkable; the influences of the former would so unceasingly alter the laws of the latter that the appearances which in their natural course are regular and uniform would be reduced to disorder and incoherence [Critique of Pure Reason, 1968, 413–414 (A 451, B 479)].

2.   THE METAPARADIGM BEGUN IN THE LATE
1750s COMPLETES ITS DEVELOPMENT
IN THE COLLECTIVE FOURTH PHASE
OF TYPIFYING INTERDEPENDENCE–FRENCH
PAINTING 1815 THROUGH THE LATE 1860s

The metaparadigm in ideation that influenced the arts and the sciences from the late 1750s until the late 1860s was that of a secularism and science separated from God as a formal causal argument. In evolutionary theory, "preformation" as a formal causal pattern was replaced with "epigenesis," the interaction of factors that led to a species maturation [Kant, "Critique of Teleological

Judgement," *Critique of Judgement*, 1952, 82–86 (Par. 20)]. Morphology was open to human intervention and natural accident. Perfection was no longer sought in nature, rather a more accurate description of its appearance, and the efficient causations of phenomena were sought with increasing rigor. Nonetheless, the metaparadigm of the late 1750s through the late 1860s was that of one objective truth composed of the univocal laws of every realm that contributed to the natural and human world. One can call this the secular alternative to God's univocal natural law. In the Aristotelian sense, God as formal cause was simply replaced by the formal cause of Organic and Inorganic Nature.

In the social sciences which began in the metaparadigm of the late 1750s more accurate understanding of human psychology and political practices left the divine out of the discussion (moving away from the kind of arguments made by Hobbes and Locke in the previous metaparadigm). Republicanism became a political and economic argument which was set in polar contrast to the renewed cameralist/mercantilist political-economic positions among German political theoreticians. Democratic, socialist, even communist secular political thought also emerged in the initial phases of the new metapradigm–particularly in France. The defeat of Napoleon, and the reestablishment of the aristocratic control in governance throughout Continental Europe led to a quiescent active conflict of these differing polarities. In fact, even in the aristocratic nation-states the constitutionalism demanded by republicans and democrats became a basis of the restoration rule after 1815–thus a form of interdependent consensus. Even the German Confederation had a constitution, and countenanced constitutions in its members. In the Germanies neither the natural sciences nor the social sciences or humanities ever moved pointedly away from the Divine– although Hegel and the Right Hegelians used the sublimation "Geist," rather than divine of natural law. The heritage of Luther and Leibniz was markedly different than that of Hobbes or Descartes insofar as the role of subjective "inner spirit" or objective spirit in nature was concerned. England and France were more explicitly disconnected since the 1750s. Nonetheless, the German natural and social scientists, and humanists were as rigorously empirical in their methodologies as the other European nations in their practice of the arts and the sciences.

In landscape painting, the German Caspar David Friedrich infused spiritual mood into his renderings, although the general characteristics of the fourth phase of the metaparadigm from 1815 through the 1860s was evident in his canvases. In this essay, I will examine only French painting in the genre of landscape and in the genre of human activities to demonstrate the contrasting characteristics I have introduced.

THE LANDSCAPE PAINTING OF CAMILLE COROT (1796–1875)

Camille Corot inherited the secular impetus in landscape painting that looked more carefully at air, land, vegetation, and its human habitation from artists of the initial phases of the metaparadigm that began in the late 1750s. The fourth phase of a metaparadigm establishes typicalities and interdependent relations out of the same new principles, themes, and content treated with a stress on individuality in the initial phases. Landscape artists between the late 1750s and the end of the Napoleonic Wars were concerned with discerning and depicting the "objective" presence of nature. With the same pretensions as natural scientists, Corot and his forebears sought to arrive at the one objective model of what transpired in a nature. The act of perception was studied in tandem with color theory; the palette was conceived as the material representation of natural appearance.

COMPLEX INTERDEPENDENCE

Corot took on this task for the landscape, informed chiefly by the color theory of Henri de Valenciennes (1750–1819).[15] Valenciennes used a range of hues and tones to show the difference and separateness between objects that shared the same environ in a landscape[16] (Figure 1, *Valenciennes's View of the Colosseum from the Farnese Gardens*, c. 1777). Corot used the same theory to emphasize the harmony of interdependent objects (Corot, 1966, 31–32) (Figure 2, Corot's *The Colosseum Seen from the Farnese Gardens*, 1826). Corot's contemporary, Eugene Delacroix (1798–1863), also derived his color theory with the aid of Henri de Valenciennes, and just as Corot, employed it to show interdependent harmony rather than difference. Delacroix writes:

> ...we notice a kind of linkage between the objects we perceive that is produced by the atmosphere enveloping them and reflections of all kinds which cause, in some way, every object to participate in a kind of general harmony (Dorra, *Valenciennes's Theories*, 1994, 188).

Heightening the harmony for Corot and Delacroix is a use of directional line that pulls the eye from one object or assemblage of objects to the next object or assemblage. The eye is guided by the induced movement so as to take in the whole as an interconnected set of linkages. Joseph Vernet (1714–1789), the fourth-phase landscapist of the metaparadigm of the early to mid-1700s, also employed this visual interconnection of all entities depicted (see Figure 3). This form of interdependent unity was called in that time "la belle natur," that is, the Divine's presence in the "sublimity" of light and airy space that shone through the whole.

Figure 1. Pierre-Henri de Valenciennes (1750–1819). *View of the Colosseum.* Photo: C. Jean. Photo Credit: Réunion des Musées Nationaux/Art Resource, N.Y., Louvre, Paris, France

Figure 2. Jean-Baptiste Camille Corot (1796–1875). *The Colosseum, seen from the Farnese Gardens.* Photo: D. Arnaudet. Photo Credit: Réunion des Musées Nationaux/Art Resource, N.Y., Louvre, Paris, France

Figure 3. Claude-Joseph Vernet (1714–1789). *A River with Fishermen* (ca. 1750). The National Gallery, National Gallery Picture Library, London, England

DURATION (OR GRADUAL EVOLUTION)

Corot has a quiescent canvas where a view will offer a particular hour of the day–the entire canvas reflecting that pervading light, especially preferring the forenoon (Corot, 1966, 30). In this he emulated the fourth-phase landscape painter Vernet (Corot, 1966, 24). Vernet was the first landscape painter to offer a full scale of differentiated hues and tones to harmonize the diverse flora, fauna, and terra of landscapes. However, his idea was not that of pure secularity. In the wont of his metaparadigm where natural law was the Divine, he preferred imaginative transpositions of a perceived landscape to accomplish la belle natur or the divine balance of the three unities of time, place, and manner. A sketch from nature had to be finished in the studio where it was given an artificial balance.[17] Typical of Vernet's treatment of time was his series *The Four Times of Day: Morning, Midday, Evening, and Night.*[18] A similar temporal picture of this period is his *A River with Fishermen,* ca. 1750 (Figure 3). This typification of times is carried forward in the next metaparadigmatic fourth phase by Corot.

Given the light of the typified hour, Corot blends its hues into an interdependent landscape. As Jean Leymarie explains:

> By simplifying the motif and by a bold pictorial architecture based on contrasting planes of light and shade, Corot avoids any dispersal of the overall effect and everywhere we sense a perfect balance; the aerial blue of the sky, the pink and lilac of the stones, the blue haze of the distant prospect, the brown and green of the leafage dappled with soft touches of yellow, the range of tones–all are held together by the iridescence of the atmosphere and a subtle handling of values (Corot, 1966, 31).

In contradistinction, landscape painting in the initial phases of a metaparadigm stresses constant change and difference. Valenciennes painted the same landscape at differing hours of the day "so as," in his words, "to record the changes that light produces in forms" (Corot, 1966, 26). In this, he is credited with foreseeing Monet, who practiced the same method in his search for differentiation in the initial phases of the next metaparadigm (Corot, 1966, 26). By the time of Monet, the landscape artist will attempt to show momentary changes in the complex light and shadow that constitute the diversity of a landscape.

DETERMINISM

Besides the interdependent weight of an ecology of landscape which locks all movement into its gravity, Corot's landscape emphasized the horizontal planes of states-of-affairs (Figures 4 and 5, Corot's *Quarry of La Chaise a Marie*, 1831 and *View of Rouen from the Cote Sainte-Catherine*, 1830). This contrasts with Valenciennes in the earlier phases where verticality predominated in terra and flora (Figures 1 and 6, A *Capriccio of Rome with the Finish of a Marathon*, c. 1788). Reality in the landscape imparted an upward thrust. Valenciennes called his landscape "the heroic landscape," taking the sketch from nature and turning it into a more dramatic depiction in his studio (Corot, 1966, 25). The "heroic landscape" was consonant in other arts and sciences of the initial metaparadigmatic phases with an emphasis upon the willed performance of animate creatures to alter evolutionary direction, and the selective intervention to produce the more perfect species in hybridism and husbandry. In the arts, Valenciennes's "heroic landscape" was consonant with the late Enlightenment cult of genius–that which is unique and stirring, a grasp, as it were, of the potential dynamism within any moment of a human life. Jean Leymarie, recognizing the heroic interlude between the stirrings of European revolution in the 1760s and the defeat of Napoleon, remarks that Corot and his time reintroduced landscape painting as a major form after "the Davidian interlude," i.e., the heroic historical paintings of David (Corot, 1966, 19).

Figure 4.   Jean-Baptiste Camille Corot (1796–1875). *Stone Quarry at Fontainebleau.*
Photo Credit: Scala/Art Resource, N.Y., Museum voor Schone Kunsten, Ghent, Belgium

Figure 5.   Jean-Baptiste Camille Corot (1796–1875). *Rouen from the Hill of St. Catherine*
(1833). Wadsworth Atheneum Museum of Art, Hartford, Conn. The Ella Gallup Sumner
and Mary Catlin Sumner Collection Fund

Figure 6. Pierre-Henri de Valenciennes (1750–1819). *A Capriccio of Rome with the Finish of a Marathon* (1788). Oil on canvas. Fine Arts Museums of San Francisco, De Young Museum, Museum purchase, Roscoe and Margaret Oakes Income Fund and Art Trust Fund, 1983.28

MATERIALISM

Corot's materialism paralleled in its constitution of landscapes the discoveries in geology by Louis Agassiz and Charles Lyell, in the period of the fourth metaparadigmatic phase, of long strata of sedimentary, igneous, and metamorphic layering that bespoke gradual change over ages of hundreds of thousands of years. In the landscape, Corot shows through squares, rectangles, and diverse quadrilaterals, triangles, and other platonic solids the massive regularities of the land (Figures 4 and 5). Even the composition of the human being was of simple solids that downplayed human difference in favor of showing material samenesses in the physiognomy of everyone (Figure 7, Corot, *The Fair Maid of Gascony*, c. 1850).

THE HUMAN PRACTICES OF EVERYDAY LIFE IN THE PAINTING OF GUSTAVE COURBET (1819–1877)

Courbet matured in the midst of the collective emphases of the fourth phase of the metaparadigm of absolute secularism, divorced from the Divine formal

Figure 7. Jean-Baptiste Camille Corot (1796–1875). *The Fair Maid of Gascony* (ca. 1850).
Smith College Museum of Art, Northampton, Mass

cause of natural law. His painting career coincided with Ludwig Feuerbach's
stress on religion as a diversion of the human from his/her own competency.
This assertive stress on the human as maker of a personal fate was also

Gustave Courbet's perspective. Courbet acquired a Feuerbachian perspective from Pierre-Joseph Proudhon, who was known as the French Feuerbach.[19] An account of a conversation between Courbet and Proudhon in the early 1850s reflects Proudhon's influence upon Courbet:

> "Tell me now, Citizen Master Painter, what brought you to do your Stonebreakers?"

> "But, answered the Citizen Master Painter, "I found the motif picturesque and suitable for me."

> "What? Nothing more?...I cannot accept that such a subject be treated without a preconceived idea. Perhaps you thought of the sufferings of the people in representing two members of the great family of manual laborers exercising a profession so difficult and so poorly remunerated?"

> "You are right, Citizen Philosopher, I must have thought of that."

> From that time on it was not unusual to hear Courbet say: "One would think I paint for the pleasure of it, and without ever having meditated my subject...Wrong, my friends! There is always in my painting a humanistic philosophical idea more or less hidden....It is up to you to find it (Rubin, 1980, xv)."

COLLECTIVITY

Just as Feuerbach's and Proudhon's social philosophies treated the individual as typical of all humankind, so did Courbet's treatment of the individual as in *The Stonebreakers* (Figure 8, Courbet,1851) offer a typification of a manner of work that is not the best venue for human praxis. The depiction of each "stonebreaker" calls to mind the social realism of the American art of the 1930s in its dignifying of work. Courbet, however, differentiated among those kinds of work that furthered human self-development and those that did not (Rubin, 1980, 6–10, 30–31, 49–50). Proudhon's putting the individual as an emblem of the collective in his remark that "the sufferings of the people (are represented by) two members of the great family of manual laborers exercising a profession so difficult and so poorly remunerated" was Courbet's understanding as well. This was the age when Charles Darwin reminded "natural historians" that every finding based upon empirical studies of individual cases must immediately be raised to a principle affecting the species studied.

While Proudhon and Courbet were predecessors of an anarchistic vision of life in society, the anarchism itself was that of a recognition of the "mutuality"

Figure 8. Gustave Courbet (1819–1877). *The Stone Breakers* (1849). Destroyed during
World War II. Foto Marburg/Art Resource, N.Y., Gemaeldegalerie, Staatliche
Kunstsammlungen, Dresden, Germany

required in every human praxis(Rubin, 1980, 13, 18–19). One sought to realize
a personal choice of work as a venue for the full development of human
capacities, but this could only be done by recognizing the actual or potential
dignity of all others. This "mutuality" is rendered even more markedly by the
shared task in *The Stonebreakers*, where the lower bodies of the two men are
made to look as one body in the similar figuration with its flexed tensions
(Figure 8). The geometry of the bodies forms a quadrilateral in their collective
spatial posture. Moreover, the hues and tones of color of the seemingly separate
objects of the canvas create a reciprocal harmony in the manner of which
Delacroix speaks in this time "...we notice a kind of linkage between the objects
we perceive that is produced by the atmosphere enveloping them and reflections
of all kinds which cause, in some way, every object to participate in a kind
of general harmony" (Dorra, 1994, 188) (Figure 9, Delacroix, *The Ocean Seen
from a Height near Dieppe*, c. 1852–54; Figure 10, Courbet, *Burial at Ornans*,
1849).

Burial at Ornans has its "mutuality" created geometrically, the long
serpentine line linking all who participate. One is reminded of Watteau's use
of the serpentine line to link into a collective body the personages of his
Rococo tableaus in a similar fourth-phase systematization of the values of
his metaparadigm–the decades following the Peace of Utrecht. Thematically,

Figure 9. Eugene Delacroix (1798–1863). *The Sea at Dieppe* (1851). Photo: Hervé Lewandowski. Photo Credit: Réunion des Musées Nationaux/Art Resource, N.Y., Louvre, Paris, France

Courbet's *Burial at Ornans* is a typical ceremony of burial that all share, each member of the ceremony participating emblematically in this meaning in common.

Figure 10. Gustave Courbet (1819–1877). *Burial at Ornans* (1849–1850). Photo: Hervé Lewandowski. Photo Credit: Réunion des Musées Nationaux/Art Resource, N.Y., Musee d'Orsay, Paris, France

DETERMINISM

Nature in its rules and constraints is seen as the ground of true freedom. Freedom for Courbet and others of his age was in the development of a system of human relations, in work and other forms social "mutuality," that enabled the potential of every human to be individuated. Thus, freedom is in the accommodation of how we are determined by our very nature. Courbet's *The Studio* (1855) (Figure 11) is emblematic of the purest freedom found in mastering one's craft. In *The Studio* Courbet paints a landscape while surrounded by those of all levels of society, vocations, and religions with whom one wishes to communicate the correspondence between nature in its laws, and a human nature that artificially orders itself, most often departing from that which all have in common. James Henry Rubin writes of this aesthetic and philosophy of freedom in Courbet where what is determined is pervasive, pure freedom to be sought in coming closer to the natural determinism:

> ...if the artist's creation was traditionally a microcosmic window on the world, then Courbet's landscape looked onto a world in which figures no longer held a privileged place...Courbet appears to have accepted that the humanity inhabiting the world was no more or less important pictorially or thematically–hence ontologically–than other elements of the texture of natural phenomenality of which it formed a part. Pure landscape painting thus became the most telling

Figure 11. Gustave Courbet (1819–1877). *The Painter's Studio: An Allegory* (1854–1855). Photo: Hervé Lewandowski. Photo Credit: Réunion des Musées Nationaux/Art Resource, N.Y., Musee d'Orsay, Paris, France

metaphor for Courbet's entire Realist enterprise: with his artistic ritual epito-
mizing all of human activity and its product symbolized as a pure landscape, he
clearly suggested that the key to liberation was a vision of reality that eliminated
all external presuppositions in favor of a material truth (Rubin, 1980, 74–75).

Pictorially, this determinism stresses the "horizontal," where gravity is an
explicit governor of human limitation, as in *The Stonebreakers*, or a leveling
force of nature that includes the return to earth as in *Burial at Ornans*.
Courbet depicts humans always in a fulfillment of ritual and ceremony, even
the ceremonies of leisure time. But, first and last the human being is a "work-
animal' for Courbet, much as he/she is for Karl Marx in this same generation
(Rubin, 1980, 30–32), a vision which stresses the limits as well as heights of
the species "ontological" determinism.

DURATION (OR GRADUAL EVOLUTION)

Time in Courbet's canvases is still, that is, movement is depicted in an
atemporal manner: One is shown at work or in a ceremony as in a pose that
does not stress a momentary action–rather, an emblematic act. Meyer Schapiro
writes of Courbet's *Burial at Ornans*:

> Courbet assembles the community about the grave. He was to say that "the
> only possible history is contemporary history," but here the history of man is
> like natural history and assumes a timeless and anonymous character, except in
> the costumes which show the historical succession of generations. The funeral
> custom replaces the occasion, the cause and effect of an individual death. The
> community at the grave absorbs the individual. The anti-romantic conception
> implies too the tranquil resigned spirit of reconciliation...(Rubin, 1980, xvii).

Just as Marx saw individual action as futile if not absorbed by the population
of the working class, Courbet asserts that only through a vocation shared
by many others can a society gradually evolve toward the kind of civilizing
foundation that then produces exceptional people (Rubin, 1980, 48–55).

MATERIALISM

Courbet shared with his times a stress on the common sensuous reality which
must be the guide for effective human laws and social institutions. Thus, in the
body-mind issues in this generation, Gustav Fechner said that the body creates
the necessity of ideas according to its physiological needs, a position to be
reversed by Sigmund Freud in the next metaparadigm, who said the mind can
affect the body with its own ends, both its fruitful conceptions and endemic
misconceptions.[20] Rubin writes of Proudhon's philosophy (which he contends
Courbet assimilated completely) in regard to materialism:

For Feuerbach, neither Hegel nor theology properly recognized the essentially sensuous-corporeal nature of man. Naturally, Proudhon, as a reader of Comte, shared this notion of man as a positive and final reality, grounded in phenomena, and would have regarded man's existence as essentially terminated rather than liberated by death–the latter a decidedly spiritual belief. To recognize work as man's means to survival was to recognize his mortality as well (as in Courbet's *Burial*) (Rubin, 1980, 33). Courbet directly voices this sentiment in his description of his painting *The Peasants of Flagey* (1850) (Figure 12):

> Here is rural France, with its indecisive mood and its positive spirit, its simple language, its gentle passions, its unemphatic style, its thoughts more down to earth than in the clouds, its mores as far removed from democracy as from demagoguery, its decided preference for the common ways, far distant from all idealist exaltation, happy when it can preserve its honest mediocrity under a temperate authority....That which characterizes our people, what you will find in all classes of French society regardless of distinctions of wealth, age, or sex...is a moderate temperament, a unified character, evenness of habits, no ambition

Figure 12. Gustave Courbet (1819–1877). *The Peasants of Flagey Returning from the Fair* (1855). Erich Lessing/Art Resource, N.Y., Musee des Beaux-Arts, Besancon, France

to rule and even less to rebellion, and the most profound antipathy for all that departs from the common, every direction (Rubin, 1980, 70).

The lauding of dispassionate custom and ceremony as the leaven of progress was in the spirit of any fourth phase of a metaparadigm, where reality is best through a consensus that regularizes the ideas and values introduced in the earlier phases of the metaparadigm.

THE NEW METAPARDIGM BEGUN IN THE LATE 1860s IN ITS INITIAL PHASES: IN THE ARTS, IN PARTICULAR IN PAINTING, A 'THIRD HUMANISM'

The new metaparadigm begun in the late 1860s in its initial phases: in the arts, in particular in painting, a 'third humanism"

Thomas Mann's proclamation of a "third humanism" as he looked back on his own contemporaries can be seen in Western painting as a whole. In this essay, I will continue to focus on French examples. I will take the changes in landscape painting from Corot to Camille Pissarro (1830–1903), one of Corot's students, and in the realism of Courbet, show how Edouard Manet (1832–1883) expressed the "third humanism."

The fundamental idea of this new metaparadigm, which inherited the purely secular and notion of one objective reality, was to generate evidence of a new depth of human spirit formulated in purely secular terms, in a manner that challenged whether one could ever speak again of an evidential basis for one objective set of facts for everyone. Leonard Shlain, who has written a book tracking some of the major shifts in metaparadigmatic ideas in Western culture, particularly in the paradigms of physics and painting from the Renaissance into the twentieth century, characterizes the emergent metaparadigm of the fin-de-siecle in both physics and painting in the light of the "theory of relativity" of physics. Some of the characteristics of relativity theory are applicable to painting, as I will demonstrate (Shlain, 1991, 137):

- There is no such thing as a favored point of view. For objects of substance, there is no inertial frame of reference at absolute rest...
- Color is not only an inherent property of matter but depends also upon the relative speed of the observer...
- A universal present moment does not exist.
- Observations about reality are observer-dependent, which implies a certain degree of subjectivity.

The characteristics Shlain articulates do not, however, stem only from physics, rather reflect a return to a notion of compossible realities to be found in the earlier religious age. Relativity theory as a metaparadigmatic metaphor emphasizes that each event-structure is relative to the mind-body state of the person who formulates the event-structure as such. Each person's Weltanschauung–in the Diltheyan sense–is in its epistemological ground of a personal Weltbild the essential basis of any possible evidential judgment.[21] Thus, there can be no evidential objectivity in-common in an absolute sense. Many thinkers of this new metaparadigm contributed diverse perspectives to this radical construction of a singular individual reality: Nietzsche saw ultimately each individual responsible for his or her own meaningful path in life; Freud compounded the diversity among individuals by decentering and relativizing the identity of the ego; Carl Gustav Jung, in his depth psychology, reformulated the individuation principle of Aquinas and Leibniz enabling each person to conform solely to his or her own "rational appetite." This is a "third humanism" because it gives a new basis for the integrity of each individual as a premise that secures the value and validity of that individual's claim to autonomy and point-of-view (Mann, 1939, 193–194). The fourth phase of this metaparadigm, beginning in the years after World War I and continuing until the early 1960s, will preserve this complex relativity of heterogeneous individuals, norming it within competing systems of political-social reality, that of social democracy and democratic-republicanism. The competing systems gave differing weight to individual autonomy, but all systems were concerned with the "third humanism" of complex individual psychology and judgment. The fascist and communist alternatives were pathological attempts to preserve the in-common objectivity of the earlier metaparadigm: perhaps such a pathology is the price for the resistance to the new ideation.

Art is always the prophet of new conduct. Aesthetics is the new guide for discernment. I make this contention in the spirit of German aesthetic criticism from Kant through Hegel into the generation of Friedrich Nietzsche, Franz Brentano (the father of modern phenomenology), his student Sigmund Freud, and Franz Kafka–though many other contributors from the Enlightenment through the early twentieth century could be cited.[22] The Germans more than other European cultures connoted aesthetic knowing with a more accurate knowing. Nonetheless, the employ of aesthetic knowing by other cultures, like the French was as rigorous, even when not as theoretical in its justification. The painters Camille Pissarro and Edouard Manet discerned new truths of being human, their changes in the inherited paradigm of painting ushering in the new metaparadigmatic ideas and values in their field.

The landscape painting of Camille Pissarro (1830–1903) as the quantum emergence of the "third humanism"

COMPLEX INDIVIDUALITY

Pissarro was the first impressionist painter, wholly transforming his teacher Corot's principles of the generalized state-of-affairs of an early morning, midmorning, midday, early or late afternoon, or evening to that of the momentary state-of-affairs of the environ from minute to minute in its complex sources of light and shadow, a differentiated complexity never before so realized in painting. Impressionism theoretically meant that one held the immediate sensation of seeing as the truest encounter with reality; the aesthetic challenge was to preserve this moment in paint.[23] Pissarro inherited through Corot the nuanced palette of hues and tones which Corot had inherited from Valenciennes. Pissarro would follow the path of Valenciennes in differentiating the objects and conditions of a landscape environ into its separate realities, while offering a complex integration that was a step forward in art. Previous individualist phases, like that of the late Enlightenment, sacrificed harmony for differentiation. The new metaparadigm of complex individuality would show difference while combining that complexity into an integrated pattern–much as the new Gestalt psychology of Christian von Ehrenfels in this time held that one sees all complexity as a form of accordant particulars without losing the multi-faceted individuality of its contents.[24] This manner of integration does not stress interdependent accord as in the fourth-phase characteristics of each metaparadigm, rather the unity is a co-ordinated diversity, "the one as the many." The unity is a cognitive unity, reflecting the synthesis of particulars created by a mind from a momentary perspective. Nature is the judgment, not something in itself as postulated by the imitative intention of a fourth-phase artist. The fourth phase is materialist in its claims. The initial phases of a metaparadigm stress new conceptualizations as organizers of evidence. Thus, Pissarro's landscapes offered a unity that comes from a cognitive synthesis, an imago which while preserving a nuanced distinctiveness of its singular parts, imparted a complex, yet coherent image. The fourth-phase method of cohering differences was and remains always that of typification and attention to commonalities. The initial stages of the new, third humanism preserved singularities while offering a coexistence among them.

Pissarro articulated this manner of accord in these words:

> *Je ne vois que des taches. Lorsque je commence un tableau la première chose que je cherche á fixer, c'est l'accord. Entre ce ciel et ce terrain et cette eau il y a nècessairement une relation. Ce ne peut être que'une relation d'accords, et c'est là la grande difficulté de la peinture. Ce que m'interésse de moins en moins dans mon art, c'est le côté matériel de la peinture (les lignes). Le grand problème à resoudre, c'est de ramener tout, même les plus petits détails du tableau, à l'harmonie de l'ensemble, c'est-à-dire à l'accord (House, 1986, 26).*

[I can only see problems. When I begin a picture, the first thing that I try to set is agreement. Between this sky and this earth and this water, there is necessarily a relationship. It can only be a relationship of agreements, and this is the great difficulty of painting. What interests me less and less in my art is the material side of painting (the lines). The great problem to resolve is bringing together everything, even the smallest details of the picture, in the harmony of the whole (l'ensemble), that is to say in agreement.]

Perhaps the key term in connoting the differentiation as unity is the French word "l'ensemble" taken over even in English as "ensemble" a coordinated assemblage that produces the effect of a unity.

The differentiation that maintains singular entities or small aggregates of entities is realized by several means. One is the circumscribing of objects with static boundary lines or polarizing colors that in contradistinction to the movement of the eye generated in a fourth phase by lines or graded hues and tones that signal interconnection to the next objects or assemblages isolate such entities (Figure 13, Pissarro, *The Coach at Louveciennes*, 1870; Figure 14, Pissarro, *Peasants' House at Eragny*, 1887). Although Pissarro in the later painting, as he stated above, does not rely on separating lines, he separates by hue and tone in the juxtaposition of objects and small assemblages. Nonetheless, the colors are sufficiently complementary to create an atmosphere that pulls all contents into an accordant mien.

A second method for preserving differentiation is that for which Impressionism is most known: every entity and parts of entities within the canvas are filled with differing moments of light; the theory of sensations as the mediate link between nature and the mind is illustrated by the manner in which the sun's light is indirectly reflected by the multiplicity of spatial hyle (see Figures 13 and 14).

FREE WILL

The landscape as a coherent state-of-affairs suggests a chance or accidental perspective by the artist (or viewer) in several ways. Incomplete or transgressed boundaries are a means to show the asymmetry of incomplete knowing, awaiting an opportunity to know more fully and completely. Objects and their aggregates show ingress and egress into or through the picture across these boundary conditions. The unfulfilled sense of seeing all, and its concomitant pregnancy (which quickens time in that one always seeks fulfillment of meaning in a cognition) is called by the phenomenologist Edmund Husserl an "imperfectly fulfilled intention."[25] One can see the visual means of achieving this with the incomplete ingress or egress of contents at the borders of the painting, and spatial transgressions of otherwise static boundaries within the painting itself. In

Figure 13. Camille Pissarro (1830–1903). *Stagecoach at Louveciennes* (Yvelines) (1870). Photo: R. G. Ojéda. Photo Credit: Réunion des Musées Nationaux/Art Resource, N.Y., Musee d'Orsay, Paris, France

Figure 13, there is a movement toward the viewer by the coach occasioned by the coach's shadow which creates a convergent triangular plane which crosses many of the separated hyle (a classic illusion that pulls the eye either to the rear if the triangular point is so directed, or toward the front if that is the location of the triangular point). In Figure 14, the same illusion of movement is created by the woman's triangular shadow which seems to move toward the garden portal which she will cross in moments.

Moreover, lines and solid forms move obtusely in relation to each other, suggesting a moving away or an accidental perspective in its juxtaposition in this moment in time (Figure 15, Pissarro, *The Lock at Pontoise*, 1872; see also Figures 13 and 14).

Free will as an intentional choice is also imparted by the dominance of "verticality" in the composition. There is the sense of energy, of rising, which is in contradistinction to the meaning imparted by horizontality in the fourth-phase renderings (see Figures 13, 14, and 15). In the initial phases of a metaparadigm, the visual vertical is always stressed. Gothic architecture in its beginnings emphasized the vertical mass and line, its structural history corresponding the

Figure 14.   Camille Pissarro (1830–1903). *Peasants House at Eragny* (1887). Art Gallery
of New South Wales, The Domain NSW 2000, Australia

political-social emergences of new constellations of power and idea. There were
several metaparadigmatic changes within the history of Gothic architecture. An
example of the movement from the initial phases of a metaparadigm that began
in the late 1100s to its fourth-phase normalization of idea is the movement from
the stress on vertical infinity with the building of the cathedrals of Chartres and
Reims to the Rayonnant style of the mid-1200s.[26] The political aggressiveness
of Philip Augustus of France (1165–1223) may be seen as one of the impetuses
of what has been termed the Second Gothic System. Philip's victorious spread
of Capetian power in France and over other nations (defeating England and
the Holy Roman Imperial army at the Battle of Bouvines in 1214) established
French dominance in military and European cultural life. His successor Louis
IX (1214–1270) was king during the Rayonnant or Third Gothic System. The
Rayonnant Gothic, most noted for its Roseate Windows which were framed by
rectangular or elliptic masses, deemphasized the vertical (Branner, 1965, 23). St.
Louis consolidated the French cultural dominance he inherited by regularizing

Figure 15.   Camille Pissarro (1830–1903). *The Lock at Pontoise* (1872). The Cleveland
Museum of Art, Leonard C. Hanna, Jr. Fund 1990.7

codes of law and establishing other forms of religious and secular unity in his kingdom. As is the case in most fourth-phase periods, his reign was for the most part peaceful and integrating.

The verticality of Pissarro's compositions parallels a new assertiveness in Western culture as the new metaparadigm emerged. The Third Humanism demanded of individuals a more active self-assessment and control of personal behavior–either through self-disciplines or with the new therapies. Rather than a consolidation of what was inherited from earlier generations, the new metaparadigm required quantum changes in how life was lived and inter-preted. In biology eugenics came to the fore, and in the animal and vegetable kingdoms, a renewed inquiry into husbandry and hybridization. Two new forms of technology–chemistry and electricity–led to major new innovations in controlling and shaping the environment and everyday life.

QUANTUM (OR QUICK) CHANGE

Quantum perspective is created as pictorial meaning by Pissarro with the obtuse angles that appear to be moving away from each other, as well as by the crisscrossing lines of vision created by those angles whose mutual violations suggested differing directionalities that could suddenly be followed (see Figures 13, 14, and 15). Another method is the constant flux of hue and tone, which when shadow or reflection is especially suggestive of the next place movement will create another shadow or angle of reflection. The viewer expects change in direction at any moment: his imaginative inclination is poised by the semiotic intent to move the spectating eye in differing angles of viewing, rather than to dwell on the scene as given.

CONCEPTUAL RELATIVITY

The stress upon "concept" is both the experience of artist and of the manipulation by him/her of the viewers' manner of observing. The emergent phases of a metaparadigm require volition and intentional change in every area of cultural norm: painting furthers this perspective by its emphasis of "differing integrities that must be recognized in their nuanced meanings, rather than by shared conventions of meaning" "free will," "quantum change," and "conceptual perspective." There are several ways Pissarro's Impressionism accomplishes this attitude in the artist and the viewer of the finished painting.

The creation of a landscape that in every part has its own variations of light (which the Impressionist insists is facilitated by the observer's sensation/mind), and where simultaneously its asymmetric organization suggests that moving imaginatively one's eye or whole stance to another place in that environ will completely change the experience of light and shadow, underscore the "point'd'appui," the "point-of-view" which is a singular percept, even if not yet a precept. Thus, given the same landscape, it will differ in its aspect from moment to moment for anyone who sees it, as each person will have a somewhat different angle of seeing. One is brought in time back to the historiography of Johann Martin Chladenius (1710–1759) who was one of the last generation in European thought to imagine a world that could not evidentially be proven to be "in-common" experientially for everyone. Chladenius preceded the "modernism'"that sought one objective world in-common. He was still of the metaparadigm that saw natural law in the Leibnizian manner—each person had a differing "rational appetite" and knew the world from his or her singular spiritual perspective. Chladenius wrote in 1742:

> Different people perceive that which happens in the world differently, so that if many people describe an event, each would attend to something in particular–if all were to perceive the situation properly. The cause of the difference is due partly to the place and positioning of our body, which differs with everyone; partly to various associations with the subject, and partly to individual differences in selecting objects to attend to. It is generally accepted that there can only be one correct representation for each object and that if there are some differences in description, then one must be completely right and the other completely wrong. This principle is not in accordance with other general truths or with the more exact perceptions of our souls.[27]

The concept is thus "relative" to he or she who experiences the so-called same state-of-affairs, turning that presumed "sameness" into the singular relation established by the knower's position in time and space, a percept undergirded cognitively by his or her singular values, ideas or other mental associations brought to the experience. The self-conscious Impressionist (or later neo-Impressionist) artist seeks to create a "decentered" canvas: what is "decentered" is the notion of an in-common objective world of the picture. The Impressionist artist eschews the visual contention of an unchanging, thus stable material environment. The Impressionist artist undermines attention to an objective material reality by reminding the viewer that it his or her percept that organizes light and dark, directionality, and mood, guided by highly personal sensations. The artist thereby teaches while presenting the landscape by offering visual cues that allow the viewer to experience the "relative" truth of this moment.

Pissarro and his new Impressionism was to change the application of the painted surface in a way that later schools of late nineteenth and twentieth century painting would emulate. Pissarro layered thicker levels of paint to enhance the texture of the canvas surface, stimulating attention toward the act of rendering (or immediate perceiving) and away from the illusion of a natural, objective depth of field that is passively experienced (House, 1986, 18). The semiotic meaning of this change that removed the illusion of three-dimensional representational imagery by World War I lay in an enhanced understanding that the world as we know it is the outcome of the mediating cognitions of human perception and intelligence, and imposed systems of idea. A calling of attention to the medium and disposition of paint itself had the intent of teaching the viewer that percepts guided how one created what was seen. What was seen must be accompanied by appreciation of how that visual meaning was articulated. John House writes of this radical stress on the two-dimensional presence of the canvas realized by thick applications of paint:

> ...the emphasis on surface planes, often very even in colour and density, estab-
> lishes a dialogue or a tension between the two-dimensional and the three dimen-
> sional. As we move towards the painting, space dissolves into surface, and we
> sense the process of transformation which the painter himself has gone through
> in translating his sensations into paint (House, 1996, 18).

The viewer was reminded that this experience of seeing was facilitated by a painting surface of two dimensions: through the line, masses, and shading angles were created, a certain depth of field, all these trompe d'oeils generated the perspective chosen and constructed by the artist. Two-dimensionality decon-structed the illusion of one three-dimensional perspective that could be shared by everyone. The human was freed thereby to insist upon a personal vision and understanding. The artist offered an invitation to the viewer, as it were, to appre-ciate how one composes one's own singular envisioning of a state-of-affairs.

Through the pliable medium of a two-dimensional or even a three-dimensional material medium, from the stone of sculpture or from the iron, steel, and cement of architecture, a highly personal three-dimensional model of a percept one wished to communicate might be rendered by an artist in tune with this new aesthetic. In sculpture, Rodin deliberately offered finished sculptures that showed stages of a process that began in raw stone.[28] In architecture, Otto Wagner exposed the steel beams which were the frames of buildings so as to expose the raw materials which undergirded modern construction.[29] Just as Pissarro, Rodin and Wagner taught the observer how to build from the stuff of life as they offered a finished statement. The "Third Humanism" was to be not only an appreciation of varying integrities, but also a challenge that one become competent to communicate one's own integrity out of the root soil of one's own mind, experience, and the materials which might serve as a venue of communication.

The second "realism" of the nineteenth century–the momentary reality of the individual in the painting of Edouard Manet (1832–1883)

Michael Fried has written books on both Gustave Courbet and Edouard Manet–*Courbet's Realism*[30] and *Manet's Modernism, or, The Face of Painting in the 1860s*.[31] I derive my heading "the second realism" from Fried's distinction between the first nineteenth century realism of Courbet and the second of Manet. Indeed, Fried employs many of the criteria I use to contrast Courbet and Manet. Although he does not consider the larger cultural implications of the paradigm of painting to the guiding ideas of an age, his keen analyses confirm my own findings.

COMPLEX INDIVIDUALITY

In color and line, Manet sought sharp contrasts that divided figures and objects from each other in a painting in order to enable the viewer to dwell separately on each figure. Fried points out that this heightened isolation of the figures from each other and the surrounding ground is aided by Manet's use of photographs of the persona in the paintings before reproducing the images with the brush "...above all...the contemporary photograph's emphasis on abrupt contrasts between areas of light and shadow with a consequent suppression of half-tones and interior modeling" (Fried, 1996, 325).

There is no linking movement that is inclusive from object to object, person to person. Oblique angles pull the eye away–toward the left and the right into different assemblages (see Figure 16, Manet, *Le Déjeuner sur l'herbe*, 1863; Figure 17, Manet, *Bar at the Folies-Bergère*, 1882). The integrative accord once differentiation was made sought by Pissarro is established, but with a subtlety that does not depend upon line or color.

Figure 16. Edouard Manet (1832–1883). *Le Dejeuner sur l'herbe* (*Luncheon on the Grass*) (1863). Photo: Hervé Lewandowski. Photo Credit: Réunion des Musées Nationaux/Art Resource, N.Y., Musee d'Orsay, Paris, France

The complex integration is accomplished in several ways–first, by the very oblique pull in diverse directions that demand, consequently, our grasping a whole or Gestalt as a viewer, even as the initial glances are inclined toward separated areas of the canvas, and second, by the cues and clues of the scene which ask us to dwell longer on the strange juxtapositions and odd contents in order to comprehend why these might coalesce. Manet's paintings are not so much puzzles, as slices of life that can be met everyday and anywhere that have coherence, yet in passing are usually ignored. Manet wants to dignify every moment of human traffic as worth attending.

FREE WILL

Manet employs the devices of border or boundary violation of the universe of the canvas found in all initial phases of a metaparadigm. In *Le Déjeuner sur l'herbe* (Figure 16) small bluish gray objects cross the lower center boundary creating the illusion that we as viewers are standing upon the same ground. As in the late eighteenth century canvas of Peale, the viewer is invited into the milieu as if suddenly glancing at a passing scene. In *Bar at the Folies-Bergère*

Figure 17. Edouard Manet (1832–1883). *Bar at the Folies-Bergere.* Foto Marburg/Art
Resource. N.Y., Courtauld Institute Galleries, London, Great Britain

the mirror serves to project behind us as viewers the people of the café, and
most importantly the man who has the attention of the barmaid who faces us.
Michael Fried emphasizes that Manet created every perspective in his paintings
from the vision of the imaginary beholder of the scene who is each of us who
visits his paintings (*Manet's Modernism*, 1996, 344). Indeed, he suggests in the
Bar at the Folies-Bergère that the reflection of the man who the barmaid is
attending is us (*Manet's Modernism*, 1996, 345).

As one looks at Manet's scenes, one may choose the initial directions as
the painting does not seek to direct our vision, only demanding that finally a
coherence that sums the aggregate glances be realized. The conflicting angles
of vision generated by the oblique angles and sharp contrasting figures make
this final summation a difficult act of intelligent visioning, but as necessary as
leaving an encounter in real life with an understanding of what has transpired.
Here the Third Humanism appears as an encoded imperative: Manet offers a
challenge to form a Gestalt out of diversity by dignifying the human situation
sufficiently as an intentional field of the viewer. He says through his composi-
tional "slice of life," "your attention has been caught, can you then appreciate
its human integrities?" Nonetheless, Manet respects your right to dwell or not to

dwell on the moment. As in everyday reality, Manet knows that the contingent, accidental aspects of reality might cause you to eschew deliberation of this particular integrity. You may move on having grasped only the surface images in passing.

FREEDOM

Freedom as a perspective is also expressed by the emphasis upon the vertical in each canvas (Figures 16 and 17). *Le Déjeuner sur l'herbe* is an observation from the standing person (you or I) in the foreground of the picture. And, although the four figures sit or bend, their lively activity is a visual resistance to the forest floor. In the *Bar at the the Folies-Bergère* the verticals are the dominant volumes.

QUANTUM (OR QUICK) CHANGE

Michael Fried in his several works that examine Courbet and Manet juxtaposes the "duration" created by Courbet of a scene in its unchanging stillness (*Courbet's Realism*,1990, 179) with the "frozen stillness" of a Manet, where an "instantaneous" glance by the viewer stops motion (*Manet's Modernism*, 1986, 318–320). Of Courbet's notion of temporality as depicted in the canvas, Fried adds that the viewer is meant to see the scene as having been before his/her arrival and enduring even after (*Courbet's Realism*, 1990, 178). Fried sees what I call the "typicality" of the figures' actions in the Courbet canvases; he refers to the figures' actions as "slow or repetitive or continuous actions, the very perception of which is felt by the viewer to take place over time" (1990, 179).

In Manet, on the other hand:

> a 'moment' (of infinite duration) of cognitive dissonance (is produced) that Manet's critics found disorienting and that is by no means simple to conceptualize. May we say provisionally that the effect is of a kind of freezing (*Manet's Modernism*, 1996, 319).

Fried's insight underscores my reference to Manet's challenge to the viewer to identify each contrasting integrity, then integrate the disparate integrities into a summative comprehension. What Fried and I point out is the imagistic equivalent of the paradox of Zeno's arrow: each moment it is at rest, which enables one to mark imaginatively the directional traverse in every point. Fried examines the rapidity of the brushwork, which he characterizes as "calligraphic" to demonstrate that Manet's subjects are caught in motion, frozen in midgesture (*Manet's Modernism*, 1996, 320).

The gestures in *Le Déjeuner sur l'herbe* (Figure 16) evidence a precise moment. In *Bar at the Folies-Bergère* (Figure 17), the hand of the man in the mirror, as well as poses of some of the patrons reflected in the mirror captured as if in motion, offer us this illusion of the moment.

CONCEPTUAL RELATIVITY

Manet uses a tension between the illusion of three-dimensional scene and the two-dimensional canvas as did Pissarro to cause the viewer to reflect upon how what is seen is an accident of perspective in a particular moment–generated by the artist but also the viewer who takes on that position in space and time. The text of the widely disseminated *Gardner's Art Through the Ages*, Eighth Edition states in this regard:

Manet's painting made a radical break with tradition by redefining the function of the picture surface. Ever since the Renaissance, the picture had been conceived as a "window" and the viewer as looking through the painting's surface at an illusory space developed behind it. Manet, by minimizing the effects of modeling and perspective, forces the viewer to look at the surface to recognize it once more as a flat plane covered with patches of paint. This "revolution of the color patch," combined with Manet's cool, objective approach, points painting in the direction of abstraction, with its indifference to subject matter and its emphasis on optical sensations and the problem of organizing them into form. In the twentieth century, not only the subject matter, but even its supposed visual manifestation in the external world will disappear (Croix and Tansey, 1986, 844).

THE FOURTH PHASE OF THE METAPARADIGM FROM THE 1920S THROUGH THE LATE 1960S

The fourth phase of this metaparadigm which begins in the 1920s and continues into the late 1960s was the "abstraction" which moved beyond specific representations to make more clear the rules of this tension between surface and image in abstract expressionism and other quasi-imagistic genres of painting, thus instructing the vision of the observer. How paint, other materials applied to the canvas, and the canvas itself condition representation became in the paradigm of painting central to the metaparadigmatic meaning that began in the late 1860s–that is, the existential freedom of the individual to choose in a world that in neither in the human sciences nor in the physical sciences offered the security of an objectivity separate from the human act of cognition. The singularity of each intelligence and character, as the discovery of the individual fingerprint in this time, made even more complex any common standard for humanistic or social scientific objectivity, and its practical forms of measure and consequent construction. The disappearance of the French Academy as a standard for painting was a casualty of this new metaparadigmatic relativism.

The initial phases of this metaparadigm as seen in the painterly paradigm erected by Pissarro's Impressionism and Manet's Realism offered exercises to the viewer in the moment-by-moment freedom of seeing, differentiating, and integrating with a personal synthesis of meaning. The fourth phase offered the viewer curricula in how line, color, and form create perspective and meaning. Artists like Wassily Kandinsky (1866–1944) and Johannes Itten (1888–1967) taught the eye with rigorous cognitive calculuses for comprehending the effects of color, line, and form. Both Kandinsky and Itten wrote texts that were primers for the aesthetic eye of the viewer, thus typifying the lessons that empowered the public to put into effect their own point d'appui.[32] A new canon of the human spirit was realized that some have called the mature fruit of modernism, as well as its culmination. Modernism is the apt term as the Enlightenment gains in the epistemology of the mind informed even the "decentering" of the ego as the role of emotion, intention, and will were augmented. Whether a metaparadigm that challenges modernist epistemologies has begun is open to debate. I choose to see our present as in the intial phases of a metaparadigm that preserves epistemological modernism, focuses instead upon the political-social integration of non-Western cultures, and the emergence of international business, thus in a decentering of the national polis. Our current time has an analogue to Europe from the Great Schism until the founding of strong, unified political realms in France, Spain, and England. The metaparadigm that began in the wake of the Great Schism of the 1370s preserved the epistemological gains of the metaparadigm begun by Aquinas and Dante, its new currents of idea in the political-social and economic realms providing a new foundation for the emerging nation-states.

NOTES

1. Stephen C. Pepper, *Principles of Art Appreciation* (New York: Harcourt, Brace and Company, 1949), 75–76. Further reference to this text and edition.

2. Stephen C. Pepper, *World Hypotheses, A Study in Evidence* (Berkeley: University of California Press, 1942), 321, 323. Further reference to this text and edition.

3. Stephen C. Pepper, *Aesthetic Quality, A Contextualist Theory of Beauty* (Westport, Conn.: Greenwood Press, 1965).

4. Immanuel Kant, "Critique of Aesthetic Judgement," *Critique of Judgement*, trans. James Creed Meredith (Oxford: Oxford at the Clarendon Press, 1952), 178–179. Further reference to this text and edition.

5. Immanuel Kant, *Critique of Pure Reason*, trans. Norman Kemp Smith (New York: Macmillan, 1968), 185 (A 145, B 185). Further reference to this text and edition.

6. Leonard Shlain, *Art and Physics, Parallel Visions in Space, Time, and Light* (New York: William Morrow, 1991). Further reference to this text and edition.

7. Hayden White, *Metahistory: The Historical Imagination in Nineteenth-Century Europe* (Baltimore: Johns Hopkins University Press, 1973), 13–21.

8. See Hayden White on the "deep temporality" which informs generational conceptions of history, as conveyed in literature and historiography in *The Content of the Form, Narrative Discourse and Historical Representation* (Baltimore: Johns Hopkins University Press, 1987), 26–57. Further reference to this text and edition.

9. See Mark E. Blum, *Continuity, Quantum, Continuum, and Dialectic: The Foundational Logics of Western Historical Thinking* (Peter Lang: New York, 2006).

10. Laurence Sterne, *Tristram Shandy* (New York: W.W. Norton, 1980), 1.

11. Denis Diderot, *Denis Diderot's The Encyclopedia*, trans. Stephen J. Gendzier (New York: Harper and Row, 1967), 336–340. Further reference to this text and edition.

12. Sixten Ringbom, *Icon to Narrative, The Rise of the Dramatic Close-Up in Fifteenth-Century Devotional Painting* (Abo: Abo Akademi, 1965). Further reference to this text and edition.

13. Some might call it the "second humanism," wherein a greater complexity of mind, emotion, and will is found in being human. Perhaps this is what Thomas Mann meant when he speaks of the era that begins in the 1870s with the new depth psychology as the "third humanism." See Thomas Mann, "I Believe," in *I Believe, The Personal Philosophies of Certain Eminent Men and Women of Our Time*, ed. Clifton Fadiman (New York: Simon and Schuster, 1939), 193.

14. Horst de la Croix and Richard G. Tansey, *Gardner's Art Through the Ages*, 8th edition (New York: Harcourt Brace Janovich, 1986), 824. Further reference to this text and edition.

15. Jean Leymarie, *Corot*, trans. Stuart Gilbert (Geneva: Skira, 1966), 24–25. Further reference to this text and edition.

16. See Henri Dorra, "Valenciennes's Theories: From Newton, Buffon and Diderot to Corot, Chevreul, Delacroix, Monet and Seurat," *Gazette des Beaux-Arts*, Vol. CXXIV (Novembre, 1994). 189. Dorra quotes Valenciennes regarding this individuation through color gradation in Valenciennes:

See how the leaves detach themselves in green against a mass which appears to be black.

Dorra adds: "Such broken up reflections of the shoreline alternating with the sky, rendered in brushstrokes of different hues and values, as well as a spreading of the reflection of the sky away from the shore, can be noticed in On the Shore of Lake Nemi.

Further reference to this text and edition.

17. Michael Kitson, "Vernet at Kenwood," *The Burlington Magazine*, Vol. 18 (July 1976): 543. Further reference to this text and edition.

18. Philip Conisbee, "The Eighteenth Centuy: Watteau to Valenciennes," *Claude to Corot, The Development of Landscape Painting in France* (New York: Colnaghi, 1990), 173–178. Further reference to this text and edition.

19. James Henry Rubin, *Realism and Social Vision in Courbet & Proudhon* (Princeton: Princeton University Press, 1980), 33. Further reference to this text and edition.

20. See Franz Brentano on Fechner's psychophysical dualism; Brentano, *Psychology from an Empirical Standpoint*, trans. Antos C. Rancurello, D.B. Terrell, and Linda L. McAlister (New York: Humanities Press, 1973), 66–70, 103–104. Brentano offered Freud hints for demonstrating the fertile role of mind in affecting the corporeal reality of the body. Nonetheless, his cautious recognition that the material laws of body had their own efficient causal creativity left Freud, himself, careful to see the efficient causal roles of both mind and body–albeit introducing the mind as an agency with its own needs demanded from the body. Brentano was Freud's teacher over a three and one-half year period of elective courses in philosophy. Brentano was a transitional thinker between one metaparadigm and another. His text *Psychology from an Empirical Standpoint* (1874) was a harbinger of the next cycle of ideas. See also Frank J. Sulloway, *Freud, Biologist of the Mind* (New York: Basic Books, 1979), 48, 50–51 for Freud's approach to the dualism of mind and body.

21. See my discussion of Dilthey's concepts of Weltbild and Weltanschauung in the second essay in this volume, The European Metahistorical Narrative and Its Changing "Metaparadigms" in the Modern Age (Part I).

22. German aesthetic thought more than the aesthetic theories of other Western nations uses the concept of "aesthetic" knowing as a form of knowing closer to discerning the actual or "truthful" in the sense of "that which persists," i.e., the German verb "wahren." For instances in the above-mentioned thinkers who continued this tradition from Enlightenment metaparadigm to that of the twentieth-century metaparadigm, I recommend these references: Immanuel Kant, "Critique of Aesthetic Judgement," in *Critique of Judgement*, trans. James Creed Meredith (Oxford: Oxford at the Clarendon Press, 1952), 196. Hegel's *Introduction to Aesthetics, being the Introduction to the Berlin Aesthetic Lectures of the 1820s*, trans. T.M. Knox (Oxford: Oxford at the Clarendon Press, 1979), 31.

Friedrich Nietzsche, *The Birth of Tragedy* and *The Genealogy of Morals*, trans. Francis Golffing (New York: Doubleday Anchor, 1956), 9ff. (Section V). Franz Brentano, *Grundzüge der Ästhetik* (Bern: Francke Verlag, 1959), 17. Sigmund Freud, *Jokes and their Relation to the Unconscious*, in *The Standard Edition of the Complete Psychological Works of Sigmund Freud*, Vol. 8, trans. James Strachey, Anna Freud, Alix Strachey, and Alan Tyson (London: The Hogarth Press and the Institute of Psychoanalysis, 1960), 10, 94ff. For Franz Kafka's contributions to the new aesthetic of the "third humanism," see Mark E. Blum, "Die ästhetische Idee der Ikone in Kafkas Beschreibung eines Kampfes," *Imprimatur* 13 (1989): 257–284. This essay includes observations upon other Germanic sources that view aesthetics as a means for discerning the truth about states-of-affairs.

23. See a succinct, yet cogent discussion of impressionist theory as held by Pissarro in John House, "Camille Pissarro's idea of unity," *Studies on Camille Pissarro* (London: Routledge & Kegan Paul, 1986), especially 16–19. Further reference to this text and edition.

24. See Christian von Ehrenfels, Über Gestaltqualitäten, (1890) in *Gestalthaftes Sehen, Ergebnisse und Aufgaben der Morphologie* (Darmstadt: Wissenschaftliche Buchgesellschaft, 1967), 11–60. When Ehrenfels discusses the perception of a spatial moment or state-of-affairs (pp. 26ff.) one sees a markedly clear understanding of the difficult

concept of "diversity in unity," which differs from the fourth-phase type of knowing, which is "unity as typification" and "unity as interdependence."

25. Edmund Husserl, *Logical Investigations*, 2 vols., trans. J.N. Findlay (London: Routledge & Kegan Paul, 1970), 1: 291–293 (Investigation 1, Par. 15).

26. See Jean Bony, *French Gothic Architecture of the 12th and 13th Centuries* (Berkeley: University of California Press, 1983), 195ff., 357ff. See also Robert Branner, *St. Louis and the Court Style in Gothic Architecture* (London: A. Zwemmer, 1965). Further reference to these texts and editions.

27. See *The Hermeneutics Reader, Texts of the German Tradition from the Enlightenment to the Present*, ed. Kurt Mueller-Vollmer (New York: Continuum, 1989), 65 (Par. 308).

28. See Albert E. Elsen, *In Rodin's Studio* (Ithaca, N.Y.: Cornell University Press, 1980), 23.

29. See Otto Wagner, *Modern Architecture, A Guide for his Pupils in this Domain of Art* , 2nd ed., trans. R. Clifford Ricker (Boston: Rogers and Manson, 1898), 19:

Every composition will essentially be influenced by the material in which it is executed and by the technical skill applied to it...because composition must always adapt itself to materials and workmanship, and not conversely. The composition must...very plainly show the materials for its execution, and the mode of working them.

Wagner's attention to this rule is evident in building throughout Vienna in this period. He would often expose beams and skeletal structures of steel in order to show how the modern edifice arose; see Carl Schorske, *Fin-de-Siecle Vienna, Politics and Culture* (New York: Alfred A. Knopf, 1980), 79–80.

30. Michael Fried, *Courbet's Realism* (Chicago: University of Chicago Press, 1990). Further reference to this text and edition.

31. Michael Fried, *Manet's Modernism, or, The Face of Painting in the 1860s* (Chicago: University of Chicago Press, 1996). Further reference to this text and edition.

32. See Wassily Kandinsky, *Point and Line to Plane* (New York: Dover, 1979), and Johannes Itten, *The Elements of Color*, trans. Ernst van Hagen (New York: Von Nostrand Reinhold, 1970).

PART III

8. Toll Bridge over Troubled Waters: New Deal Agriculture Programs in the South[1]

Jim F. Couch

Department of Economics & Finance, University of North Alabama

William F. Shughart II

Department of Economics, University of Mississippi

Abstract   In this paper, we explore the political basis of the New Deal, with special reference to agricultural programs in the South. An analysis of specific New Deal programs is largely missing from the literature. To that end, we investigate federal emergency relief efforts targeting agriculture—one of the hardest hit sectors of the economy and one of the Roosevelt administration's top priorities. Our analysis suggests that the cross-state distribution of agricultural relief was guided more by President Roosevelt's electoral strategy and by the interests of the members of key congressional agriculture committees than by objective economic need.

Keywords: New Deal, agriculture, Franklin Roosevelt

JEL Codes: H11, H83, N50

Cotton on the roadside, Cotton in the ditch
We all picked the cotton, but we never got rich
Daddy was a veteran, a Southern Democrat.
They ought to get a rich man to vote like that.

Somebody told us that Wall Street fell
But we were so poor that we couldn't tell.
Cotton was short, and the weeds were tall
But Mr. Roosevelt was gonna save us all.

Correspondence to: Jim F. Couch, Florence, Alabama 35632; William F. Shughart II, University, Mississippi 38677

Momma got sick Daddy got down
The county got the farm, and we moved to town.
Papa got a job with the TVA;
We bought a washing machine, and then a Chevrolet.

"Song of the South" *Alabama*

Public choice builds bridges between economics and political science. By bringing economic reasoning to bear on the realm of politics, public choice scholars have greatly advanced our understanding of the causes and consequences of government policies and programs that, in more traditional ways of thinking, could be explained only on the basis of error or ignorance on the part of well-meaning, but fallible "public servants." The public choice insight is that, no matter how public-spirited they otherwise may be, in a representative democracy politicians and policymakers are bound by the electoral process. The Hippocratic Oath cautions physicians to "first, do no harm"; the prime directive of politics is "first, get elected."

Politicians, in other words, must build bridges to key electoral constituencies. In the public choice way of thinking, they do so, by and large, by tailoring programs and policies to benefit individuals and groups that are prepared to repay favored treatment by marshaling votes, campaign contributions, and various other expressions of political support in their benefactor's behalf. As is true of more ordinary resource allocation decisions, considerations of economic efficiency dictate that probability-of-reelection-maximizing politicians direct government largesse toward constituencies where the marginal political benefit per dollar spent is the greatest.

In this paper, we explore the political basis of the New Deal, with special reference to agricultural programs in the South. While the Great Depression is one of the most studied events in U.S. economic history, numerous misconceptions about the period persist. Beginning in 1933, the nation witnessed an explosion of legislation designed, at least in theory, to stop the human suffering and to restore confidence in the economy. The conventional wisdom regarding the activities of the federal government during this period credits the Roosevelt administration with rescuing free market capitalism by intervening quickly and effectively to mitigate the hardships visited on Main Street by Wall Street's crash. However, a literature has developed recently which casts considerable doubt on this version of events. These modern empirical studies suggest strongly that, rather than addressing economic need, states with more robust economies received disproportionate shares of the public funds appropriated to provide relief and promote recovery. Moreover, the evidence points to the conclusion that politics motivated this seemingly perverse pattern of New Deal spending.

One important question that has not been asked hitherto is whether specific New Deal spending programs followed a similar pattern. To that end, we investigate federal emergency relief efforts targeting agriculture – one of the hardest hit sectors of the economy and, if rhetoric is any guide, one of the Roosevelt administration's top priorities. Our analysis suggests that the cross-state distribution of agricultural relief was guided more by President Roosevelt's electoral strategy and by the interests of the members of key congressional agriculture committees than by objective economic "need." One implication of the analysis is that the South was shortchanged by the New Dealers because voters there were solidly in the Democratic Party's camp and, hence, the marginal vote-buying power of New Deal spending was higher elsewhere, especially in the West. Along with our reading of contemporary historical events, the results reported herein also cast doubt on alternative explanations for the South's comparative neglect, namely, that Southerners resisted New Deal programs for ideological reasons or to avoid disruption of paternalistic postbellum labor relations.

The essay is organized as follows. The next section provides an overview of the Great Depression, the New Deal, and, in greater detail, federal agricultural programs and policies during the 1930s. Section 2 summarizes the existing literature identifying the political motives underlying New Deal spending priorities. An empirical analysis of New Deal agricultural expenditures is found in Section 3. The concluding section places the results in perspective.

1.   A NEW DEAL FOR AGRICULTURE[1]

One of the clichés of Populism was the notion that, whatever the functions of the other vocations, the function of the farmer was preeminent in importance because he fed, and thus supported, all the others. Although it has been heard somewhat less frequently of late, and a counter-ideology of urban resentment has even begun to appear, our national folklore still bears the heavy imprint of that idea. "In reality something like the opposite has become true – that the rest of us support the farmer...." (Hofstadter 1955, p. 8)

While the Great Depression is indelibly linked in the minds of many observers with the October 1929 stock market crash, the economic downturn actually began months earlier. Most industries were experiencing declines in output by the middle of 1929 and by September of that year, the economy was in recession (Williams 1994, p. 133). By destroying both consumer and business confidence, events on Wall Street exacerbated, but did not precipitate, an ongoing crisis. According to Friedman and Schwartz, "partly, no doubt, the stock market crash was a symptom of the underlying forces making for a severe contraction in economic activity. But, partly also, its occurrence must have helped to deepen the contraction" (Friedman and Schwartz 1963, p. 306).

With confidence rocked, the economy continued its slide with most measures of economic activity pointing sharply downward. Comparisons of economic statistics in 1929 with these same measures in 1933 reveal the extent of the downturn: "Net national product in current prices fell by more than one-half from 1929 to 1933 and net national product in constant prices by more than one-third" (Friedman and Schwartz 1963, p. 299). Money income adjusted for prices – real income – fell 11 percent between 1929 and 1930, 9 percent the next year, 18 percent between 1931 and 1932, and 3 percent the next year. In Friedman and Schwartz's (1963, p. 301) words, "these are extraordinary declines for individual years, let alone for four years in succession. All told, money income fell 53 percent and real income 36 percent."According to Conkin (1975, p. 39), agriculture fell faster and harder than any other sector. McElvaine (1984, p. 147) explains that farm income in 1932 was less than one-third of the already depressed 1929 figure. The parity index showing the relative level of prices farmers received compared to prices for what they bought (1910–1914 = 100) fell from a bad 89 in 1929 to a disastrous 55 in 1932.

Many farmers lost their homes and their land, while others slipped closer and closer to financial ruin.

To President Roosevelt, restoring farmers' purchasing power was essential to bringing the economy back from the depths of depression. Propping up commodity prices would give the farmer a "fair" share of national income and, hence, speed recovery. These sentiments were echoed by many observers, including New York Mayor Fiorello LaGuardia:

> Bringing agriculture to a parity with industry by fixing prices according to actual cost of production will establish in this country a new era of prosperity, enjoyed not by a small class but by all the real producers of wealth.

> (Zinn 1966, p. 229)

The administration quickly pushed for a new farm program. The Agricultural Adjustment Act (AAA) of 1933 that emerged from the emergency session of Congress, called by FDR immediately upon taking office,[2] included many of the ideas pushed by those encouraging greater government intervention into the economy – subsidized loans, inflation, and production controls. The central purpose of the legislation was to reduce agricultural output and to raise farm prices.

Title I gave the Secretary of Agriculture authority to make voluntary agreements with producers to limit acreage or to curtail the production of basic agricultural commodities, and to make rental or benefit payments to the producers in an amount that seemed fair and reasonable to the Secretary (Hosen 1992, pp. 64–65). Section nine of Title I authorized a processing tax to fund the program.

Through this program, almost a third of the 1933 cotton crop was destroyed, with planters receiving in return more than 100 million dollars (Schlesinger 1958, p. 61). "As of June 30, 1939, total rental and benefit payments under this program amounted to $1,357,969,394.00" (Office of Government Reports 1939, p. 2).

The destruction of existing crops was controversial – even the mules pulling the plows seemed to balk at plowing under the cotton crop. But the public's reaction to the AAA policy on hogs, which called for the destruction of between five and six million young pigs despite the hunger that existed throughout the nation, was one of outrage. Others accused the administration of mistreating the pigs. Secretary of Agriculture Henry Wallace was unimpressed. He remarked that "people seem to contend that every little pig has the right to attain before slaughter the full pigginess of his pigness" (Schlesinger 1958, p. 63).

The processing tax which funded the payments to farmers was declared unconstitutional in 1936 (McElvaine 1984, pp. 150–51). However, "the fundamental idea of curtailing production and subsidizing the farmer was maintained in the Soil Conservation Act of 1936 and the Agricultural Adjustment Act of 1938" (Zinn 1966, p. 232).

The Commodity Credit Corporation (CCC) was another program put in place and utilized by the Roosevelt administration to aid planters. Under the CCC, the government could make loans to farmers, valuing the commodities pledged as collateral at prices above those determined by the market. By holding the commodity as security for the loan, the government would help prop up prices by keeping supplies off the market. If commodity prices increased, the grower was allowed to redeem the crop. Otherwise, the government kept the commodities in storage (Schlesinger 1958, p. 51).

In other words,

> farmers had the choice of either letting the government keep the commodity and not repaying the loan or repaying the loan and reclaiming his crop for sale on the open market. This was popularly known as a 'non-recourse loan.' The loans for products were made at a flat rate per unit for each product included under the program. Due to the fact that the farmer would only reclaim his production if he could sell it for a higher price than received on the loan, this flat rate amounted to a price support for the commodity. (Reading 1972, p. 116)

Such non-recourse loans totaled $1160 million from 1933 to 1939 (Reading 1972, p. 117).

Title II of the 1933 Agricultural Adjustment Act was known as the Emergency Farm Mortgage Act. It was designed to provide financing to farmers in danger of foreclosure. In particular, "it provided for refinancing, reduction of interest rates on land loans, extension of time obligations, and direct loans along with financing aid to farmers" (Reading 1972, pp. 28–29). These emergency measures were extended by the Farm Credit Act passed in June 1933. The act established the Farm Credit Administration (FCA) and put all existing agricultural loan agencies under its direction.

The agricultural policies adopted during the New Deal had some "unintended" consequences: they created incentives that led to the displacement of thousands of tenant farmers. Frequently, "plantation owners evicted their tenants in order to collect AAA payments for taking the land out of production" (McElvaine 1984, p. 150). Indeed, "croppers showed a decrease of 63,000 or nearly a ten percent" reduction in a survey of farms across the South from 1930 to 1935 (Holley et al. 1940, p. 49).

Whatley (1983, p. 919) suggests that the temptation to evict tenants may have been irresistible. "On an acre yielding 350 lbs. of cotton the return from displacing a sharecropper increased from $1.78 in 1934 to $16.78 by 1939." Whatley goes on to say that "a once 'fair' landlord, responding to his tenants' pleas for 'fairness' may soon have to reply 'I'm sorry, but the cost has simply become unbearable.'"

In an attempt to deal with this growing problem, in 1935 FDR established the Resettlement Administration (RA) – the forerunner of today's Farmers Home Administration (FHA) – and, two years later, the Farm Security Administration (FSA). Both of these programs sought to remove the rural poor from their

Table 1. Total AAA expenditures per farmer, by state, 1933–1939

North Dakota	$271.32	South Carolina	$71.43
Kansas	$255.47	Georgia	$68.50
Montana	$252.83	Alabama	$68.50
South Dakota	$240.05	Maryland	$63.18
Nebraska	$212.92	Ohio	$57.55
Iowa	$200.53	Nevada	$55.12
Wyoming	$157.58	North Carolina	$52.01
Texas	$156.58	Wisconsin	$50.82
Colorado	$151.37	Tennessee	$45.10
Idaho	$139.28	Kentucky	$44.45
Oklahoma	$133.89	Delaware	$44.07
Illinois	$129.01	Michigan	$43.73
Minnesota	$99.13	Florida	$35.59
Arizona	$97.83	Connecticut	$29.61
Washington	$96.75	Massachusetts	$28.33
Louisiana	$90.09	New York	$25.55
Indiana	$87.75	New Jersey	$24.86
Arkansas	$86.35	Virginia	$21.42
Oregon	$83.99	Maine	$19.53
Mississippi	$82.77	Pennsylvania	$16.99
Missouri	$81.65	Vermont	$16.99
California	$80.14	New Hampshire	$13.09
Utah	$77.98	Rhode Island	$8.83
New Mexico	$73.79	West Virginia	$8.79

infertile land, resettle them on good land, and provide them with access to tools, seed, and expert advice. These agencies primarily made loans and grants to agricultural families in need (MacMahon et al. 1941, p. 131).

The foregoing were the major programs of the New Deal which targeted the agricultural sector as well as the rural poor. Whether these specific programs brought the promised relief and reform is unclear. But what is clear is that the controversies that surrounded the New Deal at its inception are being debated once again.

The renewal of the debate followed the discovery of a unique data set that has enabled researchers to test a number of hypotheses about New Deal spending priorities empirically. These data allow us to examine specific agricultural program expenditures by state, revealing that such spending varied widely – and in ways apparently at odds with the Roosevelt administration's stated objectives.

Table 1 shows the allocation of AAA funds across the states on a per farmer basis. (The number of farmers in each state was taken from the *Statistical*

Table 2. Total FSA expenditures per farmer, by state, 1933–1939

South Dakota	$63.18	Maine	$6.85
Montana	$62.63	Utah	$6.77
Maryland	$60.95	West Virginia	$6.56
North Dakota	$59.99	Missouri	$5.96
New Jersey	$26.52	Michigan	$5.29
Wyoming	$23.26	South Carolina	$5.24
Rhode Island	$22.54	Delaware	$4.59
Arizona	$21.87	New York	$4.28
Wisconsin	$18.57	North Carolina	$4.16
Colorado	$16.91	Louisiana	$3.95
Florida	$16.31	Illinois	$3.87
New Mexico	$16.10	Tennessee	$3.82
Oregon	$16.08	Indiana	$3.71
Nebraska	$14.93	Georgia	$3.51
Ohio	$14.37	Virginia	$3.50
California	$10.85	Pennsylvania	$3.39
Nevada	$10.72	Kentucky	$3.43
Kansas	$10.32	Mississippi	$3.32
Idaho	$8.74	Texas	$3.33
Oklahoma	$8.51	Connecticut	$2.69
Alabama	$8.12	Iowa	$1.43
Washington	$7.95	New Hampshire	$0.89
Arkansas	$7.93	Vermont	$0.55
Minnesota	$7.41	Massachusetts	$0.43

Abstract of the United States 1937.) "Farmers" include all persons living on farms regardless of occupation in 1935. Fourteen of the top fifteen recipient states are located west of the Mississippi River. The most surprising finding is the relatively small amounts going to the Southern states – states with economies that were dominated by agriculture.

Tables 2 and 3 show the distribution of RA and FSA loans and expenditures on a state-by-state basis. Dividing RA and FSA funds by the states' respective 1935 farm populations again indicates that Southern states received fewer dollars from a program that was supposedly directed at the South. Table 4 breaks down RA and FSA spending by census region. Expenditures in the mountain states were significantly higher than those made in the other regions.

The next section examines this issue more systematically by reviewing prior empirical research on the cross-state allocation of total New Deal expenditures. This literature points to a political explanation for the observed pattern of federal spending.

Table 3. FSA loans per farmer, by state, 1933–1939

Wyoming	$91.01	California	$11.99
Montana	$46.83	Georgia	$11.45
Nevada	$42.46	South Carolina	$10.65
Colorado	$42.04	New Jersey	$9.95
Utah	$35.85	Minnesota	$9.91
South Dakota	$35.08	West Virginia	$9.52
Idaho	$28.72	Iowa	$9.25
Maine	$28.06	Rhode Island	$9.08
North Dakota	$24.37	Wisconsin	$8.83
Nebraska	$22.47	Illinois	$8.30
New Mexico	$18.51	Indiana	$8.05
Florida	$18.30	Vermont	$7.95
Washington	$17.65	Ohio	$7.03
Kansas	$17.61	Michigan	$6.97
Oregon	$17.23	North Carolina	$6.56
Arizona	$16.61	New York	$5.40
Oklahoma	$15.30	Tennessee	$4.22
Arkansas	$14.83	Virginia	$4.13
New Hampshire	$14.07	Massachusetts	$4.06
Alabama	$13.32	Kentucky	$3.82
Louisiana	$13.25	Connecticut	$3.64
Texas	$13.17	Pennsylvania	$3.40
Mississippi	$12.71	Maryland	$2.70
Missouri	$12.04	Delaware	$2.36

Table 4. Per farmer FSA loans and expenditures, by census region, 1933–1939

	Dollars	Z-score*
New England	$15.39	0.53
Middle Atlantic	$10.23	0.90
East North Central	$17.27	0.41
West North Central	$30.70	0.55
Pacific	$25.80	0.20
South Atlantic	$15.69	0.52
East South Central	$13.33	0.69
West South Central	$19.36	0.26
Mountain	$59.54	2.60**

* Based on difference in mean regional and national average per farmer FSA loans and expenditures.
** Denotes significance at the 1% level.
Source: Office of Government Reports (1939).

2. PRIOR EMPIRICAL LITERATURE

Empirical analysis of New Deal expenditures was made possible after Leonard Arrington's discovery in 1969 of documents prepared by the Roosevelt administration to showcase its accomplishments. "Produced late in 1939 by the Office of Government Reports for the use of Franklin Roosevelt during the presidential campaign of 1940, the fifty page reports – one for each state – give precise information on the activities and achievements of the various New Deal economic agencies" (Arrington 1969, p. 311). According to Arrington, these reports were produced so that the administration could advertize its efforts in combating the Depression to voters in each state.

On the basis of state-by-state comparisons of federal expenditures, Arrington found that the West benefited more than other regions of the nation. Despite Roosevelt's description of the South as the nation's number one economic problem, on a per capita basis, sixty percent more was spent on the Westerner than the Southerner.

Don Reading (1972) was the first economist to model the allocation of New Deal spending econometrically. Using Arrington's data set, he attempted to uncover the underlying motivation for the observed spending pattern. Including a number of explanatory variables that proxied economic need – per capita personal income in 1933, the unemployment rate in 1937, the decline in income between 1929 and 1933, and the percentage of the state's farmers who were tenant farmers, among others – he found that only the decline in income between 1929 and 1933 had the predicted sign and was statistically significant.

Observing that "the New Deal years offer a laboratory for testing the hypothesis that political behavior in a democracy can be understood as a rational effort to maximize the prospects of electoral success," Gavin Wright (1974, p. 30) presented evidence consistent with a political explanation for the distribution of federal emergency relief spending. Wright first constructed an economic need-based model that explained only 17 percent of the variation in per capita New Deal expenditures across the 48 states.

Next, he included a number of political variables which were designed to control for each state's importance to FDR's reelection strategy. These included measures of the number of electoral votes at stake and the marginal vote-buying efficiency of federal spending, determined by the closeness of the Democratic Party's historical presidential vote share to 50 percent. Wright found the political variables to be statistically significant and, in addition, their inclusion improved the overall explanatory power of his model to almost 60 percent.

John Joseph Wallis (1984) built upon the work of Reading and Wright by including a variable, STATE SPENDING, meant to test an alternative hypothesis about the seemingly perverse distribution of New Deal funds. Some of the emergency relief programs required matching state and local government expenditures, and this requirement might help explain why relatively wealthy states were able to attract proportionately more federal grants. Wallis found indirect support for the matching hypothesis in the data for only one of the programs he investigated – the Works Progress Administration – and even in this case, all of the political variables retained their statistical significance.[3]

In a later paper, Wallis (1987) identified a limitation associated with all previous empirical studies, including his own, of the allocation of New Deal dollars. Because of the level of aggregation of available economic data, researchers were forced to sum New Deal spending over the entire depression period. In an attempt to circumvent this problem, Wallis developed a time series data set of annual state-level employment statistics.

Wallis then estimated a pooled time-series, cross-sectional model with a total of 336 observations. His results were consistent with those of the previous studies, though. The political variables were significant in all cases.

More recently, Wallis (1998) reexamined the relative importance of politics and economic need associated with total New Deal spending. He concluded that "the importance of political variables, whether presidential or congressional, is critically dependent on Nevada" (Wallis 1998, p. 155). Nevada received the largest total per capita appropriations ($1,499.39), considerably more than the next highest state (Montana, $986.30) (Reading 1972). Because Nevada does not appear to be an "outlier" with respect to agricultural relief, however, our results are not sensitive to its inclusion (see Tables 1–3).

Anderson and Tollison (1991) also investigated the cross-state distribution of New Deal dollars empirically. Aggregating New Deal spending over the period 1933–1939, they note that it is Congress and not the President that appropriates funds and authorizes spending. Anderson and Tollison included a number of additional explanatory variables in the model to explore the role played by the legislative branch in New Deal spending decisions. These were the length of tenure in office (in consecutive months) of each state's congressional delegation, representation on key committees – namely, the House and Senate Appropriations Committees – and positions of leadership in the Congress.

They find somewhat mixed evidence that congressional influence helped explain the allocation of funds. Overall, however, Anderson and Tollison's results, along with the previous research surveyed, suggest that political factors were important determinants of the distribution of New Deal dollars across the states.

3.   THE NEW DEAL'S AGRICULTURAL PORK BARREL

The wealth of detail in Arrington's data set makes an analysis of individual New Deal spending programs possible. In this section an agricultural expenditure model is developed and estimated. The evidence enables us to shed light on questions concerning whether New Deal expenditures which targeted the rural poor and the agricultural sector were, like total expenditures, driven by politics rather than by economic need.

Those programs identified as agriculture-related and included in our analysis are the Agriculture Adjustment Administration; the Farm Security Administration; the Soil Conservation Service; research, extension and agriculture education expenditures; Forest Service funds; the Farm Credit Administration; the Commodity Credit Corporation; and the Rural Electrification Administration.

The variables utilized in the statistical analysis, their definitions, and their sources are listed in Table 5. Four regression equations are estimated which contain both "need" and "political" variables.

Two dependent variables are considered. These are AGFARMER, which is the ratio of total New Deal agricultural spending to total farm population, by state, and AGFARM which is the ratio of agricultural spending to the

Table 5. Variable definitions: agricultural model

Variables	Definitions
AGFARM	Ratio of total agricultural spending to the number of farms within a state, 1930
AGFARMER	Ratio of total agricultural spending to a state's farm population, 1935
FARMVALUE	Average value per farm, 1930
BLACKFARMER	Percentage of the farm population that is black, 1935
FARMLAND	Percentage of land area in farms, 1930
TENANT	Percentage of farms operated by tenants, 1930
SENAGCO	The length of consecutive tenure in office of senators serving on the Senate Agriculture and Forestry Committee, by state, for each year 1933–1939. If the state had no member, it was assigned a value of 0
HOUSEAGCO	The length of consecutive tenure in office of members of the House Agriculture Committee, by state, for each year 1933–1939. If a state had no member, it was assigned a value of 0
SPEAKER	Dummy variable equal to one if a U.S. Representative from the state was either Speaker of the House or House Majority Leader in a given year from 1933 to 1939
PROTEM	Dummy variable equal to one if one of the state's U.S. Senators was president pro tem of the Senate between 1933 and 1939
FDR32	The percentage of the state's popular vote for Roosevelt in the 1932 presidential election
ELECTORAL	The number of the state's Electoral College votes per capita

Sources: AGFARM, AFGARMER, FARMVALUE, BLACKFARMER, FARMLAND, TENANT, and ELECTORAL: *Statistical Abstract of the United States* (various years). SENAGCO, HOUSEAGCO, SPEAKER, and PROTEM: *Congressional Directory* (various years). FDR32: Robinson (1970, pp. 42–46).

number of farms. The results are presented in Table 6. A cross-sectional, time-series analysis is utilized so that observations total 336. The equations estimated explain between 33 and 39 percent of the variation in the dependent variables.

The results, like those of previous studies, are at odds with the conventional wisdom regarding the New Deal. Those states with more valuable farms on average received larger, not smaller, appropriations. The generosity of the New Dealers toward those farmers with little or no economic power is, at the very least, called into question. The results also indicate that states with larger percentages of blacks among their farm populations received fewer dollars as well. The percentage of farms operated by tenant farmers was insignificant in both models. TENANT and BLACKFARMER are highly correlated though, so

Table 6. Agricultural model

Dependent variable:	AGFARMER		AGFARM	
Independent variables	Model One	Model Two	Model Three	Model Four
CONSTANT	−45.43(−1.65)	−64.82(−2.92)***	−217.76(−1.59)	−262.19(−2.39)**
FARM VALUE	0.0036(7.49)***	0.0035(6.72)***	0.017(7.22)***	0.016(6.28)***
BLACKFARMER	−0.936(−2.66)***		−2.66(−1.52)	
FARMLAND	−0.397(−2.33)**	−0.189(−1.57)	−1.59(−1.874)**	−1.47(−2.48)**
TENANT	0.447(1.35)		0.063(0.038)	
SENAGCO	1.031(2.78)***	1.215(3.3)***	4.29(2.33)**	4.71(2.6)***
HOUSEAGCO	−0.606(−1.15)	−0.569(−1.08)	−3.33(−1.28)	−2.98(−1.15)
SPEAKER	2.806(0.227)	5.91(0.483)	26.44(0.43)	23.55(0.39)
PROTEM	26.14(1.01)	22.67(0.884)	65.55(0.51)	62.8(0.497)
FDR32	0.988(2.02)**	1.287(3.5)***	5.61(2.31)**	6.45(3.57)***
ELECTORAL	1707.2(1.72)*	1774.7(1.786)*	6168.3(1.25)	6358.8(1.3)
BLACKFARMER*TENANT		−0.012(−2.02)**		−0.059(−2.05)**
R^2	38.83	38.09	33.23	33.6
F	20.63	22.28	16.2	18.33

(t-statistic in parentheses)
* 10% level of significance
** 5% level of significance
*** 1% level of significance

that this result may suggest that, despite rhetoric to the contrary, the plight of the tenant farmer was largely ignored.

To explore the effects of race and tenancy status further, the second and fourth models contained in Table 6 include as an independent variable an interaction term which is the product of BLACKFARMER and TENANT. This term is significant and negative in both specifications, suggesting that one or both factors were important in determining where dollars were allocated. The results do not allow us to disentangle the marginal contribution of the individual variables, however. All other explanatory variables behave as before.

The political variables increase the explanatory power of the regression models. In all four specifications, representation on the Senate Agriculture and Forestry Committee is positively and significantly related to New Deal agriculture spending.[4] Other things being the same, each additional year of seniority for Senators sitting on that committee translated into about $1 more per farmer – and over $4 more per farm – than received by states without such representation. None of the other variables measuring congressional influence – representation on the House Agriculture committee or leadership positions in the House or Senate – are significant, however.

The Republicans had a bare majority of the Senate Agriculture and Forestry Committee in the 72rd Congress that met to consider the Agricultural Adjustment Act of 1933. The committee, chaired by Charles McNary (R-OR), consisted of nine Republicans, eight Democrats, and one member of the Farm-Labor Party (Henrik Shipstead of Minnesota).[5] All told, eleven of the committee members represented states located in the upper Midwest's farm belt – Nebraska, Kansas, Oklahoma, North Dakota, South Dakota, Idaho, Wyoming, and Montana. Indeed, both of the senators from South Dakota (Republican Lynn Frazier and Democrat William Bulow) and from Kansas (Republican Arthur Capper and Democrat George McGill) sat on the committee. Only three Southern states were represented (South Carolina, Alabama, and Arkansas) by members of the committee's Democratic Party minority. Although South Carolina's Ellison Smith replaced McNary as committee chairman, this lack of Southern representation continued when that party took control of both houses of Congress in June 1933. Not until the 74th Congress was seated in January 1935 was a fourth Southerner (Democrat Theodore Bilbo of Mississippi) appointed.[6] Allen Ellender (D-LA) became the committee's fifth Southern voter in 1937; Arthur Stewart (D-TN) added a sixth vote for the South in 1939.[7] Thus, despite the fact that Alabama's John Bankhead was one of the most effective champions of New Deal farm policy,[8] the Midwest's domination of the Senate Agriculture and Forestry Committee throughout the 1933–1939 period is consistent with that region's favorable treatment.[9]

Things were different in the House. Chaired by Marvin Jones (D-TX),[10] Southern states were represented by 9 of the 13 Democrats holding a majority of the seats on the House Agriculture Committee in the 72nd Congress. But when the Democratic Party increased its majority in the 73rd and subsequent congresses, new committee members were added mainly from Midwestern states, thereby diluting the South's political influence on farm policy.[11] Southerners held 8 of the 19 majority seats on the House Agriculture Committee in the 73rd Congress, 7 of the 19 majority seats in the 74th (there were 5 vacancies), 8 of the 20 majority seats in the 75th, and 7 of the 20 majority seats in the 76th (five vacancies). Other than the seats held by Democrats Santiago Inglesias of Puerto Rico and Anthony Dimond of Alaska, the remainder of the committee's majority represented states located in the Midwest.[12] These observations suggest that the House Agriculture Committee was pulled in two directions: with coalitions of nearly equal size representing differing regional interests, and therefore lacking the Senate Agriculture and Forestry Committee's far greater homogeneity, the members of the House Agriculture Committee were unable to reach a consensus on the distribution of agricultural relief.

Perhaps, as some have suggested, the South opposed the New Deal for ideological reasons and used its influence on the House Agriculture Committee to restrain agricultural spending overall. Alternatively, the Southern representatives on the House committee may have worked to redirect federal expenditures away from the states represented by their Midwestern colleagues, thereby neutralizing the committee's overall impact on agricultural spending priorities. In any case, the differing compositions of the agriculture committees of the House and Senate help explain why the latter was apparently more influential than the former.

FDR32 and ELECTORAL likewise supply evidence of presidential influence on New Deal spending. These variables are indicative of the New Dealers' self-interests at work insofar as they show that the administration attempted to enhance its chances of reelection when distributing agricultural largesse. The positive and generally significant coefficients on both of these variables support this conclusion. Other things being the same, states that returned larger vote margins for FDR in 1932 received proportionately more agriculture-related relief. In addition to rewarding past political support, electoral-vote-rich states also benefitted more from the New Deal's agriculture programs than states that were less critical to FDR's reelection strategy.

In sum, a political motivation for the pattern of agricultural expenditures across the states is supported by the results. The same "perverse" distribution of funds that has been identified in the literature with respect to total New Deal spending is present in agricultural programs as well.

4.   CONCLUDING REMARKS

Despite its tendency to err, the federal government is viewed by many as an entity designed to promote the public's interest. Those who hold this view often point to the actions taken by the federal government during the Great Depression as a model to be emulated by the public policy makers of today. The conventional wisdom regarding the New Deal is that every effort was mobilized toward improving the life of the ordinary person; that, in fact, the New Dealers were public benefactors incapable of considering their own personal interests.

But the rhetoric of the New Dealers simply does not match reality. The evidence presented here indicates, at least in the case of agricultural spending, that self-interest was perhaps the most important motivation of the administration. In the words of Senator Vandenberg of Michigan, who opposed much of the New Deal, "the human urge will be upon all states to get all they can, and the inevitable fallibility of human – and especially political – judgments will curse the net result" (*Congressional Record* 1935, p. 2019).

There are two alternative hypotheses about New Deal spending priorities. One is that the South's comparative lack of success in attracting federal dollars can be explained by anti-New Deal ideology. However, this explanation is undercut by the observation that serious opposition to the administration did not arise in the region until fairly late in the game: "The rift with southern Democrats began with Roosevelt's daring plan to pack the Supreme Court in 1937" (Biles 1994, p. 141). These strained relations deteriorated further later that year following FDR's nomination of the "highly unpopular" and ultraliberal senator from Alabama, Hugo Black, to the U.S. Supreme Court (Biles 1994, p. 144), and the president's Southern support ended for good during the 1938 congressional elections when he campaigned in the region personally in an effort to purge "three particularly bitter southern antagonists, senators Walter George of Georgia, Cotton Ed Smith of South Carolina, and Millard Tydings of Maryland" (Biles 1994, p. 146). All three incumbents ultimately were reelected, but Roosevelt's interference in state politics – going so far as to cut the flow of patronage to the three New Deal opponents and dispensing campaign funds to their challengers – left a bitter taste that sealed Southern opposition to the administration's programs until events in Europe allowed him to begin mending his political fences by replacing "Dr. New Deal" with "Dr. Win-the-War" (Biles 1994, p. 148).

The second hypothesis suggests that Southern members of Congress resisted the New Deal out of a desire to "keep agricultural labor cheap and dependent on southern landlords" (Alston and Ferrie 1985, p. 95).[13] Again, however, this opposition, which was directed primarily at old-age and unemployment insurance, did not surface until the New Deal was well underway:

> Southerners were in fact among Roosevelt's staunchest allies throughout the first part of the New Deal: they welcomed the Agricultural Adjustment Administration, were among the earliest to join the clamour for federal relief funds as the Depression drained their state reserves, and had a hand in drafting most of the administration's recovery legislation.
>
> Only when the emphasis shifted from recovery to reform, after the 1936 election, did a solid opposition begin to coalesce, and even then the disaffection was not generalized but limited to the "county-seat elites" who had the most to lose from high levels of welfare spending and strict federal oversight of programs. (Alston and Ferrie 1985, p. 96)

The implication is that Southern congressional delegations got behind FDR's early legislative agenda not in return for money for the region's farmers, but for a louder voice in the drafting of New Deal legislation. Because "Roosevelt was unable to count on the support of many midwestern Progressives," such as Nebraska's George Norris, a member of the Senate Agriculture and Forestry Committee's Republican minority, he "appears to have struck a tacit deal with southerners in Congress: support for the New Deal was exchanged for a relatively free hand in writing and rewriting legislation to fit the peculiarities of the South" (Alston and Ferrie 1985, p. 105). In the case of agriculture, these "peculiarities" seem to have worked not so much to create resistance to federal relief efforts per se but to direct the money to relatively well-off planters rather than to their poverty-stricken tenants. It is nevertheless true that South Carolina, represented by the chairman of the Senate Committee on Agriculture and Forestry, ranks no higher than 25th on any of our lists of New Deal agriculture benefits per farmer. Texas, represented by House Agriculture Committee chairman Marvin Jones, ranks 22nd on the basis of Farm Security Administration loans (Table 3) and shows up even lower on the list of states ranked by total FSA expenditures per farmer (Table 2).[14]

As we have seen, however, two other factors contributed to the New Deal's neglect of the South. First, while Southerners chaired both of the agriculture committees of Congress, their influence was far from overwhelming, and this was particularly true in the Senate. Chairman Ellison, for example, could count on the support of only three or four other Senate committee members on behalf of proposals benefitting farms in the South. Hence, while representation on the Senate Agriculture and Forestry Committee increased the amount of agricultural relief received by a state significantly, the chief beneficiaries of that political influence were located in the Midwest. Representation on the House Agriculture Committee, by contrast, where Southerners occupied somewhat less than half of the majority party's seats, was not a significant determinant of agricultural spending priorities. Second, the South's voters were solidly in the Democratic Party's camp and, hence, the marginal vote-buying power of New Deal spending was lower there. New Deal largesse tended to flow elsewhere as a result and, rhetoric to the contrary, the nation's number one economic problem seems to have been more the victim of politics than of anti-New Deal ideology.

The conclusion that New Deal agriculture policy was shaped more by politics than by economic need is supported further by evidence of the farm population's continuing decline. The farm foreclosure rate per 1000 farms was 18.7 in 1931, jumped to 38.8 in 1933, but only fell to 18.1 by 1937 (Alston 1983, p. 889). In sum, whatever else may be said about it, FDR's New Deal for agriculture not only did not fulfill its stated objectives, but "gave the most help to those who needed it least..." (Zinn 1966, p. 239).

NOTES

1. See Couch and Shughart (1998, pp. 37–65) for a more detailed summary of the New Deal's agriculture programs.

2. The members of the 73rd Congress elected in November 1932 would not take their seats until June 1933. FDR was inaugurated in March of that year.

3. The matching hypothesis is not supported by evidence on the amounts actually contributed by the states. See Couch and Shughart (1999).

4. As in other specialized legislative policy areas, the members of the agriculture committees of the Congress exercise proximate control over federal farm programs: "only the House and Senate Committees on Agriculture have the authority to submit agricultural legislation to the floor" (Alston and Ferrie 1993, p. 859).

5. Shipstead switched parties and ran as a Republican in 1940. He was reelected.

6. At the time of Bilbo's appointment, Democrats held 13 of the 19 seats on the committee.

7. Democrats controlled 14 of the Senate agriculture committee's 19 seats in the 75th Congress (1937–39) and 13 of 19 seats in the 76th Congress (1939–41).

8. Among other things, he sponsored the Bankhead Cotton Control Act of 1934 (Couch and Shughart 1998, p. 41) and trumpeted the merits of the Resettlement Administration, one of whose model projects was the Bankhead Community located near the town of Jasper, Alabama (Couch and Shughart 1998, pp. 55–60).

9. George Norris (R-NE), Charles McNary (R-OR), Arthur Capper (R-KS), Lynn Frazier (R-ND), and Henry Shipstead (F/L-MN) formed the core of the Senate Agriculture and Forestry Committee's minority over the years of the New Deal.

10. Representative Jones chaired the House Agriculture Committee throughout the New Deal period.

11. As in the Senate, the House Agriculture Committee's Republican minority was drawn entirely from states outside the solidly Democratic South.

12. Democrat Lincoln McCandless of Hawaii served one term on the House Agriculture Committee during the 73rd Congress.

13. Also see Alston and Ferrie (1993).

14. Chairman Jones was apparently much more influential in shaping AAA spending priorities, though: Texas ranks 8th on that list (Table 1).

REFERENCES

Alston, L. J. (1983). "Farm Foreclosures in the United States during the Interwar Period." *Journal of Economic History* 43 (December): 885–902.

Alston, L. J., and Ferrie, J. P. (1985). "Labor Costs, Paternalism, and Loyalty in Southern Agriculture: A Constraint on the Growth of the Welfare State." *Journal of Economic History* 45 (March): 95–117.

Alston, L. J., and Ferrie, J. P. (1993). "Paternalism in Agricultural Labor Contracts in the U.S. South: Implications for the Growth of the Welfare State." *American Economic Review* 83 (September): 852–876.

Anderson, G. M., and Tollison, R. D. (1991). "Congressional Influence and Patterns of New Deal Spending, 1933-1939." *Journal of Law and Economics* 34 (April): 161–175.

Arrington, L. J. (1969). "The New Deal in the West: A Preliminary Statistical Inquiry." *Pacific Historical Review* 38 (August): 311–316.

Biles, R. (1994). *The South and the New Deal.* Lexington: University Press of Kentucky.

Conkin, P. K. (1975). *The New Deal.* New York: Thomas Y. Crowell Company.

Couch, J.F., and Shughart, W.F. II (1998). *The Political Economy of the New Deal.* Cheltenham, UK: Edward Elgar.

Couch, J.F., and Shughart, W.F. II (1999). "New Deal Spending and the States: The Politics of Public Works." In Jac C. Heckelman, John Moorhouse, and Robert Whaples (eds.), *Applications of Public Choice Theory to Economic History.* Dordrecht: Kluwer Academic Publishers.

Friedman, M., and Schwartz, A.J. (1963). *A Monetary History of the United States, 1867–1960.* Princeton: Princeton University Press.

Hofstadter, R. (1955). *The Age of Reform: From Bryan to F.D.R.* New York: Vintage Books.

Holley, W. C., Winston, E., and Woofter, T.J., Jr. (1940). *The Plantation South.* Washington, DC: USGPO.

Hosen, F.E. (1992). *The Great Depression and the New Deal.* Jefferson, NC: McFarland and Company.

MacMahon, A., Millet, J., and Ogden, G. (1941). *The Administration of Federal Work Relief.* Chicago: Public Administration Service.

McElvaine, R. S. (1984). *The Great Depression.* New York: Times Books.

Office of Government Reports. (1939). *Activities of Selected Federal Agencies.* Report No. 7. Washington, DC: Office of Government Reports.

Reading, D. C. (1972). *A Statistical Analysis of New Deal Economic Programs in the Forty-Eight States, 1933–1939.* Unpublished Ph.D. dissertation.

Robinson, E. E. (1970). *They Voted for Roosevelt.* New York: Octagon Books.

Schlesinger, A. M. (1958). *The Coming of the New Deal.* Boston: Houghton Mifflin Company.

U.S. Department of Commerce, Bureau of the Census. 1932–1940. *Statistical Abstract of the United States.* Washington, DC: USGPO.

Wallis, J. J. (1984). "The Birth of Old Federalism: Financing the New Deal." *Journal of Economic History* 44 (March): 139–159.

Wallis, J. J. (1987). "Employment, Politics, and Economic Recovery during the Great Depression." *Review of Economics and Statistics* 49: 516–520.

Wallis, J. J. (1998). "The Political Economy of New Deal Spending Revisited, Again: With and Without Nevada." *Explorations in Economic History* 35: 140–170.

Whatley, W.C. (1983). "Labor for the Picking: The New Deal in the South." *Journal of Economic History* 43 (December): 905–929.

Williams, R. (1994). *The Politics of Boom and Bust in Twentieth-Century America.* Minneapolis-St. Paul: West Publishing Company.

Wright, G. (1974). "The Political Economy of New Deal Spending: An Econometric Analysis." *Review of Economics and Statistics* (February): 30–38.

Zinn, H. (1966). *New Deal Thought.* Indianapolis: Bobbs-Merrill Company.

9. Environmental Protection Agency Enforcement Patterns: A Case of Political Pork Barrel?

Jim F. Couch

Department of Economics and Finance

Robert J. Williams

Department of Management

William H. Wells

Department of Economics and Finance

Abstract This study examined the possible link between congressional membership on one of two powerful committees with Environmental Protection Agency (EPA) oversight power and the incidence of EPA citations being levied against those firms headquartered within the committee members' home districts. Using a sample of 109 Fortune 500 firms for the 1992–1993 time period, the results suggest a significant and negative link between committee membership on either the House Appropriations Committee or the House Veterans Affairs, Housing and Urban Development, and Independent Agencies Committee, and the number of EPA citations levied against firms headquartered in the districts of the congresspersons serving on these committees. The results suggest that politicians may exercise power in order to protect their constituents, rather than to protect the national interest.

Keywords: Environment, Environmental Protection Agency, public choice economics

JEL Codes: H11, Q50

Correspondence to: Jim F. Couch, University of North Alabama, Florence, Alabama 35632; Robert J. Williams, Valdosta State University, Valdosta, Georgia 31698; William H. Wells, Georgia Southern University, Statesboro, Georgia 30460

1.   INTRODUCTION

Government intervention has been justified whenever private market institutions fail "to sustain desirable activities or to stop undesirable activities" (Bator, 1958: 351). Government is called upon to correct perceived sources of private market failure with appropriate fiscal and regulatory tools, thereby improving society's welfare.In the case of pollution, an external cost is generated with a nonconsenting secondary party absorbing the harmful effects. Activities that generate external costs, like pollution, are frequently subjected to taxation or regulation.

The Environmental Protection Agency (EPA) was established on December 2, 1970, as an independent agency. Its stated mission is to "protect human health and to safeguard the natural environment–air, water, and land–upon which life depends." The EPA also asserts that it seeks to ensure that "Federal laws protecting human health and the environment are enforced fairly and effectively" (www.epa.gov).

The notion that government efficiently corrects market failures has come under increasing scrutiny. Public choice theorists assert that government ignores the so-called public interest and instead pursues private interests.

This paper examines the activities of the EPA. In particular, we advance a political pork-barrel hypothesis of EPA regulation. Despite the agency's claim of fair and effective enforcement, evidence is presented that indicates members of key congressional committees exercise substantial control over those firms receiving citations from the EPA.

This paper is organized as follows. The next section presents a public choice explanation for the activities of government. The model and the results are found in Section 3. Some final remarks are given in Section 4.

2.   PUBLIC CHOICE THEORY

In cases in which the market fails, government is called upon to correct these failures through taxation or regulation. The state was granted the authority to protect its citizens from unfettered markets.

> Behind all this was the conviction that markets went to excesses, that they could readily fail, that there were too many needs and services they could not deliver, that the risks and the human and social costs were too high and the potential for abuse too great. (Yergin and Stanislaw, 1998: 11)

Government expanded its role throughout much of the twentieth century and policymakers were quick to intervene into private markets in order to correct problems. "Government knowledge–the collective intelligence of decision makers at the center–was regarded as superior to market knowledge– the dispersed intelligence of private decision makers and consumers in the marketplace" (Yergin and Stanislaw, 1998: 11).

But experience with government intervention has led many to question the role of the state. Instead of discussing market failure, the focus is now on government failure. When government intervention fails to bring about the desired outcome, the failures are typically attributed to inadequate funding, to mistakes by well-intentioned public servants, or to politicians who do not see the full consequences of their actions.

George Stigler (1975: 140) observed, however, that the notion that governmental shortcomings can be explained away on the basis of error is untenable. Rather, those policies that are not in the public interest are pursued deliberately. Public choice theory asserts that politicians seek to advance their own self-interest. Thus, public policy that works against the public interest is likely.

Politicians, hoping to be reelected, are more likely to attain this goal by representing the local interests of their constituents rather than representing vague notions like the national interest or economic efficiency. Applying this analysis to the Federal Trade Commission (FTC), Richard Posner (1969) noted that members of Congress must advance the provincial interests of those residing in their districts. He goes on to say "the welfare of his constituents may depend disproportionately on a few key industries. The promotion of the industries becomes one of his most important duties as a representative of the district" (Posner, 1969: 83).

Pork-barrel politics is as old as the welfare state itself. The flow of New Deal dollars to the states was shown to be a function of political influence (Anderson and Tollison, 1991). Likewise, public utility pricing (Peltzman. 1971; Maloney, McCormick, and Tollison, 1984) to the enforcement of tax laws by the Internal Revenue Service (Couch et al., 1999) are subject to political manipulation.

Faith, Leavens, and Tollison (1982) provided an empirical confirmation of Posner's assertion. The authors found support for the notion "that congressional committee members who have important oversight and budgetary powers with respect to the FTC can deflect commission decisions in favor of firms in their jurisdictions" (Faith, Leavens, and Tollison, 1982: 201).

The activities of the EPA are examined in the next section.

3.   MODEL AND RESULTS

The EPA administers ten comprehensive environmental protection laws including the Clean Air Act, the Clean Water Act, and the Safe Drinking Water Act. The agency's budget for fiscal year 1998 totaled $7,360,946,000 (www.epa.gov).

The agency asserts that their "strong and aggressive enforcement program has been the centerpiece of efforts to ensure compliance, and has achieved real and significant improvements in public health and the environment".

(www.epa.gov). The agency goes on to say, "EPA maximizes its effectiveness by strategically targeting its civil and criminal investigations ...to address the most significant risks to human health and the environment" (www.epa.gov).

We empirically test to see if some other "strategic targeting" is taking place. Our sample includes 109 Fortune 500 firms. The dependent variable is the total number of citations levied against each firm for violations of EPA regulations between 1992 and 1993. The data were obtained from the U.S. Government under the 1974 Freedom of Information Act.

Independent variables include firm size as measured by the firm's total dollars of sales (SIZE), the firm's return on equity (ROE), and three categorical variables designed to capture the likelihood of EPA violations due to the nature of the firm's business–metals, chemicals, and petroleum. Firms engaging in these endeavors were thought to be more likely run afoul of the environmental laws.

The political variables include membership on the House Appropriations committee–a key congressional committee with the power to make expenditures–and the House Veterans Affairs, Housing and Urban Development, and Independent Agencies Committee–the congressional committee charged with EPA oversight. The variables were assigned a one if the headquarters of a firm was in the jurisdiction of a congressperson serving on either of the two committees and zero otherwise.

One weakness in the analysis is that a cited plant may not be located in the same district as its headquarters. Faith, Leavens, and Tollison address this concern:

> It is consistent with the pork-barrel hypothesis that a representative will seek to wield his influence when the profits of one of his constituents (the firm) are in jeopardy because of an FTC action against a division or plant of the firm not located in the district.

> Indeed, if all pork-barrel activity occurs in the district of the plant, such misassignment of firms to districts serves only to bias our statistical tests against the pork-barrel hypothesis. (Faith, Leavens, and Tollison, 1982: 205)

House seniority (SENIORITY) also serves as an explanatory variable and is the total years of continuous service for each representative.

Our results are found in Table 1. The findings suggest that larger firms, not surprisingly, receive more citations. More profitable firms, on the other hand, were cited less frequently. Firms engaged in the production of

Table 1. Dependent variable
Citations by the Environmental Protection Agency

Independent variable	Parameter estimate
CONSTANT	−4.94
	(2.18)**
SIZE	0.23
	(2.33)**
ROE	−2.03
	(1.99)**
METALS	1.75
	(4.37)***
CHEMICAL	0.49
	(1.68)*
PETRO	−0.28
	(0.87)
SENIORITY	0.02
	(1.41)
HAPPRO	−14.39
	(2.16)**
HIA	−5.25
	(2.09)**
INTERACT 1	73.74
	(2.09)**
INTERACT 2	0.65
	(2.21)**
R2	0.31
F	4.37
	(0.0001)

t-statistic in parentheses
*10%
**5%
***1%

chemicals and metals were the target of more EPA citations while petroleum companies were not.

According to our results, greater seniority of one's representative did not translate into fewer citations. However, both of the House committee variables were significantly related to EPA violations. The results indicate that the representatives serving on the House Appropriations Committee and the House Veterans Affairs, Housing and Urban Development, and Independent Agencies

Committee wielded power with respect to the EPA. In particular, fewer citations were issued to those firms headquartered in the districts of these influential congresspersons.[1]

Two interaction terms are included in the model. INTERACT 1 is the product of HIA and ROE, and INTERACT 2 is the product of HAPPRO and SIZE. Both variables are positive and significant, indicating that committee members are less likely or less able to defend larger, more profitable organizations.

One possible explanation for this result is that smaller, less profitable firms are more likely to have only a single site. Larger firms with numerous facilities located in several districts do not receive the same level of protection. Of course, other explanations are possible.

4.   CONCLUSION

The idea that market inefficiencies are easily corrected by government intervention into the private sector has come under increasing scrutiny. Rather than focusing on market failures, observers are now pointing toward government failure. Public choice scholars, by noting that politicians maximize their self-interest just like other participants in the market, claim that government failure is likely, and perhaps inevitable.

Examining the activities of the EPA over the time period 1992 through 1993, our results support a pork-barrel hypothesis. Evidence is presented that suggests that politicians exercise their oversight and budgetary power in such a manner to aid their constituents, regardless of the national interest.

Despite the lofty claims of the EPA, we find that they avoid citing those firms located in the districts of influential politicians.

NOTES

1. Membership on the Senate Veterans Affairs, Housing and Urban Development, and Independent Agencies and the Senate Appropriations Committee were also included but provided no explanatory power. This result is consistent with that of Faith et al. who stated, "Institutional sources stress that the Senate committees are relatively passive overseers" (Faith, Leavens, and Tollison, 1982: 207).

REFERENCES

Anderson, Gary M. and Tollison, Robert D. (1991) "Congressional Influence and Patterns of New Deal Spending, 1933–1939" *Journal of Law and Economics* 34, (April): 161–75.
Couch, J. F., Atkinson, K., Williams, P. M., and Singleton, T. (1999).
Bator, Francis M. (1958). "The Anatomy of Market Failure," *Quarterly Journal of Economics* 72, (August): 351–379.

"Political Influence and the Internal Revenue Service," *the Cato Journal* Volume 19, Number 2. pp 313–322.

Faith, Roger L., Leavens, Donald R. and Tollison, Robert D. (1982) "Antitrust Pork Barrel" *Journal of Law and Economics* (October) Volume 13, Number 2. pp 329–42.

Maloney, M. T., McCormick, R. E., and Tollison, R. D. (1984). "Economic Regulation, Competitive Governments and Specialized Resources." *Journal of Law and Economics* 27, (October): 329–338.

Peltzman, S. (1971). "Pricing in Public and Private Enterprises: Electric Utilities in the United States." *Journal of Law and Economics* 14, (April): 109–147.

Posner, R. A. (1969). "The Federal Trade Commission." *University of Chicago Law Review* 37: 48–49.

Stigler, George J. (1975) "The Citizen and the State: Essays on Regulation" Chicago: University of Chicago Press.

Yergin, D., and Stanislaw, J. (1998). *The Commanding Heights.* New York: Simon and Schuster.

10. Nation of Origin Bias and the Enforcement of Immigration Laws by the Immigration and Naturalization Service

Jim F. Couch

Department of Economics and Finance

Brett A. King

Department of Economics and Finance

William H. Wells

Department of Finance and Quantitative Analysis

Peter M. Williams

Department of Economics and Finance

Abstract   We examine the enforcement patterns of the INS and find that while the INS vows to enforce the immigration laws in an equitable manner, there is significant variability in the agency's enforcement patterns. In states where construction jobs represent a large portion of the workforce, INS activity is significantly lower. Furthermore, while the agency is very active in enforcement in states where Russian and Haitian immigrants are prevalent, they appear to relax enforcement in states where Chinese, Jamaicans, and Mexicans reside. The differences in enforcement patterns are statistically significant, and suggest actions taken by the INS may be politically motivated.

Keywords: Immigration, INS, law enforcement, illegal aliens

JEL Codes: H59, J61, K42

Correspondence to: Jim F. Couch, University of North Alabama Florence, Alabama 35632; Brett A. King, University of North Alabama Florence, Alabama 35632; William H. Wells, Georgia Southern University Statesboro, Georgia 30460; Peter M. Williams, University of North Alabama Florence, Alabama 35632

1.   INTRODUCTION

The decision to emigrate—to leave behind familiar places, family, and friends—is perhaps one of the greatest bridges that people choose to cross. A strange land with a new culture represents both an opportunity and a challenge to an individual making such a decision. The United States, a country of immense wealth and opportunities. is an attractive haven for those who decide to leave their country due to religious persecution or stagnant economic conditions. From the perspective of the immigrant, living in the United States represents an opportunity to achieve religious freedom, or perhaps personal wealth and/or happiness. However, from the perspective of the American people, immigration may well represent a burden on society in the form of taxpayer support for public health or increased competition in the workforce.

To mitigate unnecessary problems with respect to the immigration of foreigners who are criminals or terrorists, the American people rely on the Immigration and Naturalization Service (INS). The INS is charged with the task of administering citizenship requests, providing for the proper documentation of temporary foreign workers, and apprehending illegal aliens. The apprehension of illegals, the most controversial duty of the INS, has placed the agency squarely in the headlines. The raid to seize Elian Gonzalez from his Miami relatives brought opprobrium upon the agency. The action, which involved 131 INS agents – some heavily armed – resulted in calls of discrimination from Miami's Cuban community.

This is not the first time the agency has been accused of selective enforcement. IRS agents working on what was termed "Operation Vanguard" checked the records of employees against the Social Security Administration database. Those workers identified as potentially unauthorized were interviewed and INS agents arrested those who were not compliant with immigration laws. "Critics charged that the enforcement targeted Hispanics" (http://migration.ucdavis.edu/rmn-archive/apr), and raised the question of whether or not the INS enforced immigration policy in an equitable manner.

Additional criticism of the INS comes from representatives of the Transactional Records Access Clearinghouse (TRAC) housed at Syracuse University. While the INS pledges that their services "will be timely, consistent, fair, and of high quality" (*Toward INS 2000*, 1994), the data examined by those associated with the TRAC serves as evidence to support the notion that enforcement of immigration laws is far from consistent or even-handed. INS referrals for prosecution show wide variation from state-to-state. They report, "there often are variations that raise a preliminary question of basic fairness. Further exploration may turn up good explanations for the differences, but the differences on their face are worth probing" (trac.syr.edu/tracins/findings/about INS).

This paper examines the alleged inconsistent enforcement patterns of the INS and attempts to determine what factors may account for this inconsistency. We conjecture that the INS is influenced by political pressure and that this pressure may explain much of the discriminatory enforcement of the immigration laws. The next section provides a brief summary of the INS and its history. In Section 3, the model is developed and the results presented. The final section provides some concluding remarks.

2. THE IMMIGRATION AND NATURALIZATION SERVICE

The United States established no laws regulating the entry of immigrants until the later part of the nineteenth century. As the composition of immigrants changed – from English to Irish, Chinese, and German Catholics–so did attitudes about immigration. The Know Nothing Party was established and reflected the growing anti-immigrant sentiment.

In 1882, the nation passed the first piece of legislation regarding immigration. The Immigration Act prohibited the immigration of convicted felons, prostitutes, and lunatics and delegated enforcement responsibilities to the Secretary of Treasury.

The INS was moved from the Treasury Department to the Department of Labor in 1913 and finally to the Justice Department in 1940.

Subsequent acts followed, including the Act of 1917 which required English proficiency as a condition for admittance and the National Origins Act of 1929 which established a quota system for admittance based upon the ethnic composition of the United States population at the time (Weissbrodt, 1989).

The burgeoning multitude of illegal immigrants (illegals) led to the passage of the Immigration Reform and Control Act of 1986 (IRCA). IRCA required employers to complete an I-9 Form for new hires to establish the workers' eligibility. Immigration law was once again amended by the Immigration Act of 1990. The Act expanded the number of visas available for employment preference immigrants–an attempt to address labor shortages in the U.S. economy (Lawson and Grin, 1992).

During the 1990s, the INS received budget increases and its number of personnel swelled. The agency now ranks second in federal convictions, recently surpassing the Drug Enforcement Agency (DEA) and trailing only the Federal Bureau of Investigation (FBI). There are four criminal statutes which represent almost 90% of INS referrals for prosecution. These statutes include reentry of removed aliens, improper entry by aliens, bringing in/harboring aliens, and fraud/misuse of visas/permits (trac.syr.edu/tracins/findings).

"In 1998, the INS reported expelling or removing 172,312 aliens and referring 16,045 individuals for prosecution in the nation's federal courts" (trac.syr.edu/tracins/findings/about INS/insResponsibilities.html).

Despite the fact that the level of employment at the INS has grown in number from 17,368 in 1992 to 29,420 in 1998 (trac.syr.edu/tracins/findings/national), hundreds of thousands of illegal immigrants slip into the country every year and the number is growing.

Increased funding along with additional border agents, immigration inspectors, criminal investigators, and detention enforcement officers has failed to slow the flow of illegals. The INS estimated "the size of the nation's illegal immigration problem at five million residents (in the country for at least a year) as of 1996. The INS also estimated that the illegal immigrant population was rising at a net amount of 275,000 per year" (www.fairus.org).

Part of the agency's problems in controlling illegal activity may stem from the challenge of carrying out contradictory tasks.[1] The current INS Commissioner, Doris Meissner, acknowledges the challenge: "generous immigration policies can persist only if the public has confidence in the Government's ability to admit people according to rules that are fair but firm" (*Toward INS 2000*, 1994). In 2003, the INS was moved to the Department of Homeland Security and the enforcement and service functions were split.

The notion that our immigration policies should be generous is certainly not universally accepted. George Borjas (1999) argues that the net annual gains to the U.S. economy from immigration amount to roughly 0.1 percent of GDP. He also asserts that immigration may have depressed the wages received by native-born Americans by 3 percent. Thus, according to Borjas, the costs of immigration exceed the benefits. This issue has been addressed further by a number of researchers including LaLonde and Topel (1991), Altonji and Card (1991), Sorensen et al. (1992), and Blackstone (1998) with mixed results.

Borjas suggests reducing immigration by about one-third and advocates a point system so that skilled and educated immigrants are given preference. Gary Becker offers a clever, market-based solution to determine the number of immigrants instead of the cumbersome criteria now utilized. Under Becker's proposal, the government would "auction off immigrant permits to the highest bidder" (Becker, 1992). The system would most likely attract highly skilled foreigners.

> Young, ambitious, energetic and skilled immigrants–the kind any country would love to have–would tend to be successful bidders since such people would be likely to have accumulated capital before immigrating and could count on high earnings afterward, which would help them recoup even a large entry fee within a few years (Becker, 1992).

Despite the lack of empirical evidence suggesting that immigrants displace domestic workers and depress wages, a substantial number of Americans want to see the flow of immigrants slowed. Pat Buchanan, in his recent book, *The Great Betrayal* (1998:271), asserts, "By early 1995 illegal aliens were pouring across the U.S. border in record numbers to take jobs and get welfare benefits." The Federation for American Immigration Reform (FAIR) agrees with Buchanan's position stating, "Americans now realize that the costs of our present high level of immigration (legal and illegal) are enormous and growing. Illegal immigrants receive taxpayer support for their U.S. born children: immunizations, subsidized public health, and other programs."

On the other hand, many industries have grown to depend on the flow of cheap dependable labor and benefit from lax enforcement. As Hedges and Hawkins (1996) point out, "Not much attention is paid to the big American industries–construction companies, nurseries, and fruit growers–that rely on these workers." They assert:

> Illegal immigrants are flocking to the United States to take the dangerous, low-paying jobs most Americans won't. There's a system that keeps the illegals coming and the industry humming–and the plants have come to rely on it (1996:17).

This "system" sometimes involves professional smugglers, known as coyotes, who lead illegals across the border, obtain fraudulent documentation, and are paid by employers per head. The illegal workers are willing to accept more dangerous working conditions and lower wages.

While workers may view both legal and illegal immigrants as a threat and consequently desire vigorous enforcement, others, particularly construction companies and the agricultural sector, want the INS to look the other way so that a reliable labor force is in place. The INS acknowledges these conflicting demands facing their agency:

> Public attitudes toward immigration will remain mixed. There will be greater pressure from some segments of the public–in states most heavily impacted by illegal immigration–for further restrictions on entry and intensified efforts to reduce the size of the illegal alien population entering and remaining in this country. Pressure ... will increase, especially from the Congress, immigration-impacted states and employers with international business interests (*Toward INS 2000*, 1994).

Thus, the inconsistent INS enforcement patterns may have its origin, at least in part, from both the type and the degree of pressure placed upon the agency. While the INS claims to discharge its duties "with proper regard for equity and due process" (*Toward INS 2000*, 1994), it also acknowledges that it is subjected to pressure from various interest groups. Thomas Sowell explains:

> Employers of agriculture and other low-paid labor have pressed for a national
> policy of more open access to the United States ... while groups concerned with
> crime, welfare dependency, or other social problems ... have pressed for more
> restrictive policies. Shifts in political strength among the contending groups of
> Americans are reflected in changing immigration policies and changing levels
> of enforcement (Sowell, 1981:249).

The immigrants themselves can likewise become an effective lobbying
group. As Huntington (American Enterprise 2000:22) explains, "Sustained high
levels of immigration build on themselves. After the first immigrants come
from a country, it is easier for others from that country to come. Immigration
is not a self-limiting process, it is a self-enhancing one." The author continues,
"And the longer immigration continues, the more difficult politically it is to
stop. Leaders of immigrant organizations and interest groups develop a vested
interest in expanding their own constituency. Immigration develops political
support, and becomes more difficult to limit or reshape."

3.   MODEL AND RESULTS

Members of TRAC compiled records about the criminal enforcement efforts
and staffing of the INS. These records come from a number of different sources
including the Justice Department and the United States Office of Personnel
Management. When an agency such as the INS investigates suspected wrong-
doing and adequate evidence is collected, the criminal prosecutions are referred
to the Justice Department "with a recommendation that the individuals involved
be criminally prosecuted" (trac.syr.edu/tracins).

The evidence from the TRAC records indicates a wide variation in INS
criminal referrals from state to state. Representatives from TRAC asserted,
"further exploration may turn up good explanations for the differences, but the
differences on their face are worth probing" (trac.syr.edu/tracins).

In order to further explore this variation in INS enforcement, we first
calculate the number of criminal referrals as a percentage of the estimated
illegal aliens residing in each state. By dividing each state's criminal referrals in
1996 by the INS estimates of illegal aliens residing in the state in that year, we
find some interesting results. The INS is most active in North Dakota, Montana,
and Iowa and least active in Illinois, Massachusetts, and South Carolina (the
difference in some cases is over 100-fold).

To examine possible reasons associated with this variability, we conduct an
ordinary least-square (OLS) regression where the ratio of referrals to illegal
residents serves as the dependent variable. The results of the analysis are
presented in Table 1. Several different regressions were constructed to insure
consistency of the independent variables with respect to the overall model.

Table 1. Empirical
Evidence–Immigration and
Naturalization Service Enforcement

Variable	Parameter estimate
MEXICO	−11.80
	(−3.10) ***
CHINA	−84.87
	(−2.10) **
CUBA	3.74
	(0.15)
ECUADOR	124.98
	(0.78)
RUS	81.20
	(3.05) ***
HAITI	104.09
	(2.00) *
JAMAICA	−127.73
	(−2.25) **
DOMREP	−60.79
	(−2.31) **
EMP	0.004
	(3.51) ***
UNION	−0.12
	(−0.82)
CONS	−2.98
	(−3.40) ***
FARM	0.31
	(0.59)

t statistic in parentheses
*10% level of significance
**5% level of significance
***1% level of significance

The final model was chosen based on overall significance and simplicity. This model explains roughly 53% of the variability in the ratio of criminal referrals divided by estimated illegals, and is significant at the 1% level.

Among the independent or explanatory variables included is the number of INS employees assigned to each state in 1996 (EMP). The agency claims:

> INS will concentrate resources in areas where the workload, or vulnerability to the integrity of our nation's immigration policies, is greatest. This requires allocating resources on the basis of risk assessment ... (*INS Toward 2000*).

As one might expect, a greater number of INS employees (EMP) results in a greater number of referrals per illegal. This variable is significant at the 1%

level. Thus, the INS does appear to be allocating resources where the need is greatest.

Another independent variable in the model is the percentage of the workforce associated with organized labor in 1996 (UNION). Increased unionization might lead to tighter enforcement of immigration laws–less legal and illegal immigrants to push wages downward. Declining membership, however, has led unions to reconsider their position:

> Eliseo Meding, Vice President of the Service Employees Union declares, "I am ... convinced that as the labor movement is the best hope for immigrants so are immigrants the best hope of the labor movement (McElroy, 2000:31).

In addition, variables representing the percentage of the state's workforce engaged in construction (CONS) in 1996 and the number of farms in each state (FARMS) in 1996 are included in the model. These sectors typically pay low wages and/or have dangerous work environments. Thus, these employers are perhaps more likely to exert pressure on the INS to ease their enforcement of immigration laws so that a reliable, low-cost workforce can be obtained.

The results suggest that neither union membership (UNION) nor states with a greater percentage of the workforce in farming are significantly related to referrals per illegal. However, referrals per illegal are significantly lower in those states where construction represented a larger percentage of the workforce. This variable is significant at the 1% level. The implication is the INS is less active in states whose economies are more dependent on construction activities. Perhaps these employers are able to exert substantial influence on the agency, and the INS ultimately yields to this pressure.

Next, we considered what role, if any, the nation of origin of immigrants played in INS enforcement. The nation of origin of the immigrants for each of the fifty states is found in "INS Data on Immigrant Settlement" produced by FAIR at www.fairus.org/html. Because nation of origin data for illegals in each of the states do not exist, the data are admittedly a proxy for illegals. This method is closely related to INS procedures for estimating illegals in each of the states:

> The state distribution of the undocumented population was based on the U.S. residence pattern of each country's applicants for legalization under IRCA [Immigration Reform and Control Act of 1986]; the results were summed to obtain state totals. This assumed that, for each country of origin, undocumented immigrants who resided in the United States... had the same U.S. residence pattern as IRCA applicants for that country (http://www.ins.usdoj.gov/graphics/aboutins/statistics/illegalien/index.htm).

Thus, the percentage of legal immigrants from a particular country to each of the states in 1996 serves as an independent variable in the analysis.

Several of the variables are significantly related to the number of referrals per illegal. In those states where Russians (RUS) and Haitians (HAITI) are more concentrated, INS activity is significantly increased. These variables are significant at 1% and 10% levels, respectively. However, in states where larger concentrations of illegals are Chinese (CHINA), Mexican (MEXICO), and Jamaican (JAMAICA), the agency exhibits significantly less activity. The referrals per illegal are significantly lower for these variables at the 10%, 5%, and 5% levels, respectively.

4.   CONCLUSION

While the INS vows to enforce the immigration laws in an equitable manner, there is significant variability in the agency's enforcement patterns. In states where construction jobs represent a large portion of the workforce, INS activity is significantly lower. Furthermore, while the agency is very active in enforcement in states where Russian and Haitian immigrants are prevalent, they appear to relax enforcement in states where Chinese, Jamaicans, and Mexicans reside. These results raise some question about enforcement parity by the INS. Further research in this area is certainly warranted.

NOTES

1. A federal advisory panel recommended breaking the INS into three parts. Control of the borders and the removal of illegal immigrants would remain within the Justice Department, the State Department would handle citizenship requests, and the Labor Department would administer the hiring of foreign workers (Schmitt, 1997).

REFERENCES

Altonji, J.G., and Card, D. (1991). "The Effects of Immigration on the Labor Market Outcomes of Less Skilled Natives". In J. M. Abowd and R. B. Freeman (eds.), *Immigration, Trade and the Labor Market*. Chicago: University of Chicago Press.
Becker, G. (1992). "An Open Door for Immigrants–the Auction," *Wall Street Journal*, Oct. 14.
Blackstone, T. (1998). Unpublished dissertation, University of Mississippi–Lewis Smith Chair.
Borjas, G. (1999). *Heaven's Door: Immigration Policy and the American Economy*. Princeton: Princeton University Press.
Buchanan, P. (1998). *The Great Betrayal*. Boston: Little, Brown.
Couch, J. F., Atkinson, K., Singleton, T., and Williams, P. M. (1999). "Political Influence and the Internal Revenue Service," *CATO Journal*, Vol. 19, No. 2.
Faith, R. L., Leavens, D. R., and Tollison, R. D. (1982). "Antitrust Pork Barrel," Journal of Law & Economics.

Hedges, S. J., and Hawkins, D. (1996). "The New Jungle," *U.S. News and World Report.* Sept. 23.

Huntington, Samuel (2000) "The Special Case of Mexican Immigration," The American Enterprise (December) American Enterprise Institute, Washington D.C. 1150 Seventeenth Street N.W,

LaLonde, R.J., and Topel, R.H. (1991). "Labor Market Adjustments to Increased Immigration." In J. M. Abowd and R. B. Freeman (eds.), *Immigration, Trade and the Labor Market.* Chicago: University of Chicago Press.

Lawson, M., and Grin, M. (1992). "The Immigration Act of 1990," *Harvard: International Law Journal,* Vol. 33, pp. 255–276.

McElroy, W. (2000). "Sweatshops: Look for the INS Label," *Ideas on Liberty,* Vol. 31.

Morgan, K., and Morgan, S. (1998). *State Rankings 1997 and 1998: A Statistical View of the 50 United States. Lawrence, KS: Morgan Quitno Press.*

Politics in America 1996 (1996). Washington, DC: Congressional Quarterly Press.

Read, R. (2000). "US Immigration Agency Vows to Change Its Image," *The Oregonian.*

Schmitt, E. (1997). "U.S. Study Panel Recommends Plan to Break Up I.N.S.," *New York Times,* Aug. 5.

Sorenson, E., Bean, F. D., Ku, L, and Zimmermann, W. (1992). "Immigrant Categories and the U.S. Job Market. Do They Make a Difference?" Urban Institute Report 92-1.

Sowell, T. (1981). *Ethnic America.* New York: Basic Books.

Toward INS 2000, Strategic Plan, Accepting the Challenge. (1994). U.S. Immigration and Naturalization Service, Office of Policy and Planning.

Weissbrodt, D. (1989). *Immigration Law & Procedure.* West Publishing Co.

York, B. (2000). "Illegal Elian," *American Spectator,* Vol. 33, No. 5, pp. 24–27.

FURTHER REFERENCES

trac.syr.edu/tracins/findings/about INS/insResponsibilities.html
trac.syr.edu/tracins/findings/national
www.fair us.org

crossing bridges

Conference venue
901 Mabry Street
Selma, AL 36701-5523

Dear Colleague,

There are still many bridges to cross – that is the motto of a public relations campaign of the City of Selma. Selma is located somewhat southwest to the point where the Alabama and Cahawba Rivers meet. The place is first mentioned as the then Governor of Louisiana (Ecor de Bienville) met the Indian tribes to negotiate trade arrangements involving the rivers. Little could be gotten here because the trading base, the agrarian Alabama valley, had already been destroyed by DeSoto 200 years before. Apparently, this was not known to the French authorities, or at least not communicated to the Governor at New Orleans. When DeSoto arrived, Chief Tuscaloosa offered arable land, fertile cattle, and women to the white arrivals. They took him hostage in order to extract gold, which either the Indians didn't have or didn't think of highly enough so as to free the chief.

Today, Tuscaloosa is the seat of the renowned University of Alabama, and next to it is the small place of Vance, where Daimler-Chrysler is trying to bridge the gap between European and American concepts of producing cars. Little Selma, once the world center of cannon production, later the stage of the Reverend King's rebellion, is now a place of no significance. Yet, the bridge is still there, and it is to be crossed.

From the point of view of the social sciences, our main problem is that with the increasing diversification of interests and pursuits of ideas and research programs, ever more subdisciplines have developed which can no longer be integrated through a singular paradigm. This is why the concept of trying to create bridges between different disciplines is now more appealing. We are talking about bridges that may span times, methods, approaches, and, of course, the ideological spectrum. If in a cooperative spirit you want to present your work with a view to a conceivable publication, **crossing bridges** may be your venue.

Questions?
Kindly contact us in Erfurt by phone (+49-361-737 45 50), fax (+49-361-737 45 59), or email (juergen.backhaus@uni-erfurt.de) or in Selma: phone and fax: (334) 8723774.

Printed in the United States
146411LV00001B/88/A

9 780387 733715